HOW TO PROGRAM
Computer Science Concepts and Python Exercises

[John Keyser, Ph.D.]

THE
GREAT
COURSES®

PUBLISHED BY:

THE GREAT COURSES
Corporate Headquarters
4840 Westfields Boulevard, Suite 500
Chantilly, Virginia 20151-2299
Phone: 1-800-832-2412
Fax: 703-378-3819
www.thegreatcourses.com

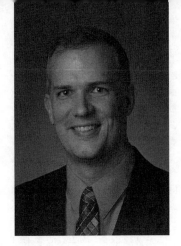

John Keyser, Ph.D.

Professor and Associate
Department Head for Academics
in the Department of Computer
Science and Engineering
Texas A&M University

Dr. John Keyser is a Professor and the Associate Department Head for Academics in the Department of Computer Science and Engineering at Texas A&M University. He has been at Texas A&M since earning his Ph.D. in Computer Science from the University of North Carolina in 2000. As an undergraduate, he earned three bachelor's degrees—in Computer Science, Engineering Physics, and Applied Math—from Abilene Christian University.

Dr. Keyser's interests in physics, math, and computing led him to a career in computer graphics, in which he has been able to combine all three disciplines. He has published several articles in geometric modeling, particularly looking at ways of quantifying and eliminating uncertainty in geometric calculations. He has been a long-standing member of the solid and physical modeling community, including previously serving on the Solid Modeling Association executive committee. He has also published several articles in physically based simulation for graphics, including developing ways to simulate waves, fire, and large groups of rigid objects. As a member of the Brain Networks Laboratory collaboration at Texas A&M, he has worked on developing a new technique for rapidly scanning vast amounts of biological data, reconstructing the geometric structures in that data, and helping visualize the results in effective ways. In addition, he has published papers on a variety of other graphics topics, including rendering and modeling.

Dr. Keyser's teaching has spanned a range of courses, from introductory undergraduate courses in computing and programming to graduate courses in modeling and simulation. Among these, he created a new Programming Studio course that has become required for all Computer Science and Computer Engineering majors at Texas A&M. He has won several teaching awards at Texas A&M, including the Distinguished Achievement Award in Teaching, which he received once at the university level and twice from the Dwight Look College of Engineering. As an Assistant Professor, he was named a Montague Scholar by the Center for Teaching Excellence, and he has received other awards, including the Tenneco Meritorious Teaching Award and the Theta Tau Most Informative Lecturer Award.

Since writing his first computer program more than 35 years ago, Dr. Keyser has loved computer programming. He has particularly enjoyed programming competitions, both as a student competitor and now as a team coach. Of the many computer science classes he took, the most important class turned out to be the one in which he met his wife. In his free time, he enjoys traveling with her and their two daughters. ■

Table of Contents

[SUPPLEMENTAL MATERIAL]

[HOW TO PROGRAM]
Computer Science Concepts
and Python Exercises

As computers are becoming more ingrained in our everyday lives and affecting every field of study, from science to the humanities, more and more people are wanting to learn how computers work. This course will teach you about the fundamental ways that computers operate by teaching you how to program computers.

Using the language Python, you will learn programming, from the most basic commands to the techniques used to develop larger pieces of software. Starting with the first lecture, you will learn about how computers operate and how to write programs to instruct them.

The course begins with a discussion of the most basic programming commands that correspond to the most basic operations in a computer. In the first two lectures, you will learn about variables, basic operations like arithmetic, and text-based input and output.

Throughout the first half of the course, the course covers all of the most common programming operations.

› With conditionals and Boolean expressions, you will learn how to make the computer respond differently to different situations.

› Loops will teach you how to get the computer to repeat the same task for you again and again.

› One of the common things you will want to do is process information that might be stored somewhere else, so you next learn about how to work with files.

> The data you read in from files is often organized in long lists, so the course discusses how to handle lists in Python. This is an area where Python particularly excels, and you will be introduced to some of the features that Python includes for handling lists.

> The course will introduce one of the most powerful ideas in all of computer science—abstraction—and show how functions help you put abstraction into action. Functions let you separate different concepts into different parts of a computer program, and the way these different parts communicate is through parameter passing, so you will learn about this process in detail.

One of the particular benefits of using Python is the ease with which we can write powerful Python programs by making use of large collections of code that other people have written. The way to do this is through Python modules, and you will learn about modules as you reach the halfway point in the course. You will learn how to write powerful Python programs, sometimes with just a line or two of code, by calling functions from these modules.

Throughout the course, you will learn how to put basic programming tools together to form more complete programs. In Lecture 4, you will learn how testing and iterative development help create and improve programs. In Lecture 8, you will learn about the idea of top-down design by building a basic data analysis program—for weather, in this case. Lecture 11 focuses on the debugging process and how to identify and deal with the various errors that people encounter when programming. Lectures 13 and 14 show you how abstraction is important when developing these larger programs. First, top-down design is used, but this time with functions, to show how to create a game. Then, the concept of bottom-up design is introduced, and you learn how it can be used in graphics and robotics applications.

In the second half of the course, you will discover some more advanced development skills. You will learn about event-driven programming and how to can create graphical user interfaces. In addition, you will learn how to use loops and modules to generate random numbers and use plots and graphs to create simulations, such as a retirement portfolio. Next, you will learn about the core ideas of object-oriented programming, including encapsulation, inheritance, and polymorphism. You will learn how to use object-oriented design to group your data together and construct larger programs.

The last portion of the course turns to some slightly more advanced topics. You will learn about how to organize data through data structures and then how algorithms allow us to describe fundamental operations on data. After learning about recursive algorithms, you will look in more detail about a particularly useful data structure, graphs, and some of the algorithms that can run on it.

After the course concludes with a look at a current trend in computing, parallel programming, you will be able to write small programs yourself, as well as have all the tools needed to proceed to more advanced study or larger program development.

Installing Python and PyCharm

To write your own programs in Python, there are two main pieces of software that you will need to know how to set up: **Python** itself, and an environment for using Python called **PyCharm**.

First, you need to install Python on your computer. This means that you will download a whole set of files that will let you write and run Python programs on your computer. Once you have installed these files, you will be able to execute ".py" files, run an interactive window, and execute basically any Python command.

Second, you're going to want an integrated development environment (IDE). Python comes with an interactive program named interactive development and learning environment (IDLE) that will let you do some simple programming, but it's not an IDE and won't provide nearly the range of features provided in an IDE. It is recommended that you get a full IDE, such as PyCharm. This makes it much easier to write, run, and try out your code. You'll have an application that comes up, and you can write your code in that application, manage files, run code, see output, debug, and more all in that same application.

> Whenever you're following instructions about going to websites to download and install software, keep in mind that things can change. Some of the details might no longer be exactly the same. Where to go, or what to do, might change over time. If you find that things aren't exactly like the following instructions, just treat this as an opportunity for problem solving!

Python

To install Python, go to **www.python.org**, the official site for Python. You can find documentation, tutorials, and examples of using Python on the website. But for now, install Python on your computer. Follow the link to the downloads page.

You'll probably see two different options: one for Python version 2 and one for Python version 3. Version 3 doesn't work quite the same way as version 2. Many people who were already invested in version 2—because they had large amounts of software written in Python 2 or were already familiar and comfortable with Python 2—chose to keep maintaining and developing software in version 2. As a result, two types of Python continued to be used: the version 2 branch and the version 3 branch. The similarities between these are much greater than the differences, but there are some differences. Python 3 is the more up-to-date version, and for people who aren't tied to any old code from Python 2, Python 3 is better.

Follow the link to the Python 3 page. You don't want to get anything called a "development" version—that's a version still being developed, and not fully tested. Look for whatever stable version is right for your operating system. If you're on a mac, you'll probably want the Mac OS X version. If you're on Windows, get the newest Windows version that your operating system can handle. (For example, if you are running Windows XP or older, you might need to download an older version of Python 3.) There's also a Linux version. Whichever system you're on, download the newest stable release that your operating system can handle. For the most part, this should involve clicking a single link.

The installation process should be straightforward. The downloaded files will probably ask for permission to be installed, and it is strongly recommended that you let them install in their suggested location. Chances are that this will go smoothly, and when it does, you should have Python fully installed on your system.

The first thing you can do is bring up the interactive shell, called IDLE. After your download, you should be able to find a program named IDLE somewhere on your machine. If it's not on the desktop or a start menu, you might need to do a search.

Once you've found IDLE, run it. You should see a window pop up with a name like "Python 3.__ shell." There will be a prompt consisting of several greater-than signs. Basically, any command you type into this window will be interpreted as a Python command and executed.

IDLE is useful, especially for trying out something small. But for most of the development in this course, it is recommended that you get a full IDE. There are many Python IDEs to choose from, but PyCharm is a great IDE. It's simple enough that most people can easily use it for basic Python programming, and it's powerful enough that high-end programmers will still use it. The basic edition is free to download, and it has all the tools you could want for this course, such as syntax highlighting, error checking, auto-completion, and a full debugger.

PyCharm

To download PyCharm, go to its website: **www.jetbrains.com/pycharm**. From there, click on the "Download" link. That should bring you to a page where you can choose which operating system you have—Windows or Mac OS X or Linux—and then click on the free "Community" version of PyCharm to download it. When you click that link, it should download a program that you can run to install PyCharm on your computer. Again, you should let it install into whichever directory it would like.

With PyCharm installed, you should be able to run it. Somewhere on your machine should be a PyCharm application, and you want to run that. When you do, there should be a window that opens, possibly with a "hint" window that you can close. You want to try to get a program running in that PyCharm window. There are two steps.

First, go to the **File** menu in PyCharm. Click on the link **New Project**. When you do that, it should prompt you for the name and location for the new project, along with the interpreter to use. The interpreter should default to the Python version that you just installed. For the project title, it will probably default to one called "untitled." Pick a new name for the project, and feel free to pick a different directory. Finally, click the **Create** link. You will probably need to choose whether the new project is in a new window or not. If you pick a new window, you can start off a project in a clean window.

A "project" is going to be a location where there will be one or more Python files that you are developing. You can think of it more like a directory that will hold Python files. Once you have the directory, you need to create a file that will actually be your program. So, go back to the **File** tab in the PyCharm window, click on **New**, and select **Python File**. It will ask you for a name for the file, and this is where you pick the name for your Python file.

In the main PyCharm window, you should see a mostly blank screen. It might have a single line of Python code. You can ignore that line of code; in fact, you can delete it entirely if you want, or just leave it in. It won't make any difference to your code. That window, though, is where you will type in your program.

Again, let's start with a "Hello, World" program. In that window, type in the following: print ("Hello, World"). As you're typing, you might notice that PyCharm will start filling in things for you—for example, when you open the parentheses, it will automatically generate a close parenthesis, and same with the quotation mark.

Notice that unlike the IDLE window, when you hit enter after this line of code, you don't see the results of this code. To see the results, you have to explicitly tell the computer to run the program. In the PyCharm window, go up to the menu item where it says **Run**, and then select "Run" from that menu. You will have to pick the name of the program you just wrote. When you do, a new window will appear at the bottom of the PyCharm environment. This is the window showing the output. You should see the words "Hello, World" output there, along with something saying "Process finished with exit code 0." That last line just means that the program completed without an error.

You might have noticed that there was a green arrow in front of "Run." After running for the first time, you can click the green arrow at the upper-right corner of the PyCharm window or the green arrow down near the output window to run your code again. The new output will replace the old output, so you won't notice anything new if you rerun the same code. But you can also make a modification to your code—maybe add another print statement or change what this print statement says. Then, hit the green arrow to see the results down in the output window.

You've now created your own Python program and run it in the PyCharm IDE. For most of this course, it is recommended that you do all of your development in the PyCharm IDE. You can write your code, run it to see how it works, go back and modify your code, and run it again. It makes it very easy to make modifications and test them. Even if it feels awkward at the moment, as you create more and more programs, it will become very natural to create new projects and new Python files, and run them.

As you create these files in PyCharm, it is saving a copy of that program as a ".py" file on your computer. If you navigate to the directory where you set up the project, you should see the ".py" file that was created. You are able to execute that file directly, because you have installed Python on your computer. So, if you had a program to print "Hello, World," if you double-click on that file, a window will pop up that prints "Hello, World." The window will disappear as soon as it does that, because the program ends, so it might go so quickly that you don't see it, but there will be a window. As you develop programs in the future, you will be able to run the programs this way, if you so choose.

Take some time to practice creating and running programs in the PyCharm IDE.

Game Design with Functions

I n this lecture, you will learn how to develop a game that is similar to many popular computer games. You will learn how functions directly support a top-down design approach, and you will use stub functions to help you rough in the structure of the program along the way. The game will have the guts for a grid-based matching game, in which you have a bunch of objects arranged in a grid and you try to move things around to match up similar items, at which point the matched-up items disappear.

[THE BASICS OF THE GAME]

> The game we'll develop will have a two-dimensional grid of different objects. In the game, we'll have five objects: the letters Q, R, S, T, and U. It will also have the same familiar game mechanics where objects disappear once we get a certain number of the same object in a row or column.

> On each turn, you get to choose to rearrange the pieces somehow. Different games have different types of moves allowed. We're going to assume that the only move we can make is to swap a piece with an adjacent piece.

> When a move is made, some objects are removed from the grid according to patterns that are made. In our case, we'll remove any cases with three or more of the same object adjacent in the same row or same column. Usually, this is what the player gets points for. Then, the remaining objects rearrange, typically by falling down to fill in the gaps just removed.

> We'll want to fill in gaps at the top with random new objects. The game continues like this until the user meets a goal. For this game, the goal will be to get a predefined number of points.

> This is a somewhat complex piece of software; it's certainly not the kind of thing we want to just sit down and start writing.

[DEVELOPING THE PROGRAM]

> We will design this program using a top-down approach. At the broadest level, we have three basic steps: First, we set up everything, initializing the game. Second, we go into a loop. The condition for the loop makes sure that it's not time to end the game. Finally, within the loop, we go through one round of the game.

> In code, we can, and should, take each of these steps and put in a comment describing what needs to be done and in what order. In this case, we have three comments: one for the initialization, one for the loop, and one for taking a turn.

```
#Initialize
#While game not over
    #Do a round of the game
```

> Each of these general tasks is something that can, and usually should, be encapsulated into a function. To illustrate, every time we have one of these tasks, we'll turn it into a function call. This is the main idea of **procedural programming**, where functions are created to handle all the main tasks.

> The following is what the current code looks like if we introduce the functions. Notice that each of the original lines has turned into one function call. Those actual functions are defined, but don't do anything, because we haven't gotten to that level yet.

```
def Initialize():
    #Initialize game
def ContinueGame():
    #Return false if game should end, true if game is not over
def DoRound():
    #Perform one round of the game
#Initialize game
Initialize()
#While game not over
while ContinueGame():
    #Do a round of the game
    DoRound()
```

> If we are using top-down design in practice, we would define some of the lower levels first, before writing any of this code. In particular, you'll notice that all of our functions have empty parameter lists. That's because we don't understand yet what information we need at those lower levels, so we don't know what information needs to be passed in. Despite that, this code is the "main" program for us.

> The term we use to refer to the little functions that are placeholders for something that should be much bigger is a **stub**, which is a function that doesn't really do what it's intended to do but is just enough that everything around it runs.

> Because we've written some code, the next thing we should do is test it. To test in this case, we want to see if everything is getting called in order. The goal is to have something stable that has been tested.

> Let's look at one of the functions that hasn't been defined yet: initialization. In initialization, we need to set up the grid itself—that is, we need to get all the pieces placed into their starting positions on the grid. We also have to set the user's score to zero because we're just starting the game. And we probably want to initialize other variables, such as one that will help us keep track of which round of the game we are on.

› For one round of the game, we have three basic steps: We have to get the move from the user, update the game based on that move, and then display the new grid to the user.

› This brings us to our "continue the game" check. It turns out that this is going to be a pretty simple check for our game—we just want to see if the user has reached the goal score yet, or not. So, we'll have a conditional that checks whether the score exceeds some maximum, or not, and return true or false for that routine.

› This routine is so simple that each of those commands is basically a line or two of code. We can implement this routine as follows.

```
def ContinueGame(current_score, goal_score = 100):
    #Return false if game should end, true if game is not over
    if (current_score >= goal_score):
        return False
    else:
        return True
```

› We have an if statement that compares current score and goal score and a return of either true or false.

› In the main part of the code, we will make a change to the call to ContinueGame. We set up the score and the goal, and we call ContinueGame with that score and goal passed in as parameters.

› At this point, we should test everything.

› We need to decide how the grid itself will be represented. This is what we would refer to as a data structure. For this game, we can have a pretty straightforward data structure. Basically, we want our grid to have a set of rows and columns, and in each of those rows and columns, we have one object. In this case, an object is just a letter.

› Lists let us store rows and columns nicely. In fact, a grid representation is a list of lists.

› Let's say that our board is an 8-by-8 grid, like a checkerboard. We will thus need a list of 8 rows, each with 8 elements. We will actually set these elements to what is needed for the game in the initialization routine, but to begin with, we will make a list of all these elements.

```
board = [[0, 0, 0, 0, 0, 0, 0, 0], [0, 0, 0, 0, 0, 0, 0, 0],
        [0, 0, 0, 0, 0, 0, 0, 0], [0, 0, 0, 0, 0, 0, 0, 0],
        [0, 0, 0, 0, 0, 0, 0, 0], [0, 0, 0, 0, 0, 0, 0, 0],
        [0, 0, 0, 0, 0, 0, 0, 0], [0, 0, 0, 0, 0, 0, 0, 0]]
```

› The initialization routine is going to have three different parts: initializing the grid itself, initializing the score, and initializing the turn. Later, we might find some other things that we wanted initialized, so we'll have to add them here, too.

› Initializing the grid is a complicated process, and we'll do that in a separate function. For the score and the turn, we will want to set the score to 0 and the turn to 1. These score and turn variables are trickier to set. These are immutable values, so we can't pass them in and change them in the function. What we can do, though, is to make sure, within the function, that we declare them as global variables. This will let us initialize them to their appropriate values.

```
def InitializeGrid(board):
    #Initialize Grid by reading in from file
    print("Initializing grid")
def Initialize(board):
    #Initialize game
    #Initialize grid
    InitializeGrid(board)
    #Initialize score
    global score
    score = 0
    #Initialize turn number
    global turn
    turn = 1
```

```
#State main variables
score = 0
turn = 0
goalscore = 100
board = [[0, 0, 0, 0, 0, 0, 0, 0], [0, 0, 0, 0, 0, 0, 0, 0],
         [0, 0, 0, 0, 0, 0, 0, 0], [0, 0, 0, 0, 0, 0, 0, 0],
         [0, 0, 0, 0, 0, 0, 0, 0], [0, 0, 0, 0, 0, 0, 0, 0],
         [0, 0, 0, 0, 0, 0, 0, 0], [0, 0, 0, 0, 0, 0, 0, 0]]
```

> Notice that because this is a list, it is mutable, and thus we are passing it as a parameter to initialize it. There are different ways we could initialize, but let's assign random objects to each grid cell.

> To assign random objects, we need to use the random module, which is part of the Python standard library. We will import the choice function, which will randomly choose one element from a list. Then, to initialize our grid, we will loop through all 8 rows and all 8 columns and set the element to a random value. We will assume that the possible objects are the letters Q through U, but we could change those values to anything we want.

```
from random import choice
def InitializeGrid(board):
    #Initialize Grid by reading in from file
    for i in range(8):
        for j in range(8):
            board[i][j] = choice(['Q', 'R', 'S', 'T', 'U'])
```

> That's the initialization stage. We can now turn our design to the game round itself. There are four basic parts to a turn: presenting the state of the game, then getting the user's move, then determining the result of that move, and finally incrementing the turn number.

> The top-down approach means that we can create a separate function for each of these main steps. We just call these in order from our "DoRound" routine.

```
def DrawBoard(board):
    #Display the board to the screen
    print("Drawing Board")
def GetMove():
    #Get the move from the user
    print("Getting move")
    return "b1u"
def Update(board, move):
    #Update hte board according to move
    print("Updating board")
def DoRound(board):
    #Perform one round of the game
    #Display current board
    DrawBoard(board)
    #Get move
    move = GetMove()
    #Update board
    Update(board, move)
    #Update turn number
    global turn
    turn += 1
```

> The next unfinished portion of our routine is presenting the board. We're just printing to the screen at this point, so we just need to output each of the grid values, in an orderly format. We'll draw horizontal and vertical lines to separate the individual elements.

```
def DrawBoard(board):
    #Display the board to the screen
    linetodraw=""
    #Draw some blank lines first
    print("\n\n\n")
    print(" -------------------------------")
    #Now draw rows from 8 down to 1
```

```
for i in range(7,-1,-1):
    #Draw each row
    linetodraw=""
    for j in range(8):
        linetodraw += " | " + board[i][j]
    linetodraw+= " |"
    print(linetodraw)
    print(" --------------------------------")
```

› That's our display routine. Let's now address our "get move" routine. For now, we'll just ask the user for a move and return that move. Notice that we haven't said what form a move should take, so for now, the "move" is just a string.

```
def GetMove():
#Get the move from the user
    move = input("Enter move: ")
    return move
```

› Next, we'll turn to the actual turn mechanics, which is embodied in the "update" routine. The turn mechanics are the main thing that define the game. They embody the rules about how the game progresses according to a move. In this case, there are a few parts, each of which will require us to do something.

› First, we'll need to update the board according to our move. In this case, that means swapping one object with an adjacent one. Then, we'll need to repeatedly eliminate pieces and update the board until there's nothing more to be eliminated. We'll have to go through and remove any pieces that are three in a row or three in a column. This will leave some empty spaces, and everything else will need to fall down. Finally, any blank spaces at the top will get filled in with new random objects.

› Putting this into code is straightforward, because each action gets turned into a new function. We stub out these functions, and then we will address each of those functions individually.

```
def SwapPieces(board, move):
    #Swap pieces on board according to move
    print("Swapping Pieces")
def RemovePieces(board):
    #Remove 3-in-a-row and 3-in-a-column pieces
    print("Removing Pieces")
    return False
def DropPieces(board):
    #Drop pieces to fill in blanks
    print("Dropping Pieces")
def FillBlanks(board):
    #Fill blanks with random pieces
    print ("Filling Blanks")
def Update(board, move):
    #Update the board according to move
    SwapPieces(board, move)
    pieces_eliminated = True
    while pieces_eliminated:
        pieces_eliminated = RemovePieces(board)
        DropPieces(board)
        FillBlanks(board)
```

> To determine the swapping, we need to convert a "move" into an actual position, and its adjacent position. To do this, we'll need to determine how to express a move. This decision will affect how we express a move when a person types it in.

> In order to express a position, we'll use a system similar to that used in chess. The columns will be numbered using a lowercase letter from *a* through *h*, and the rows will be numbered using a number from 1 to 8. So, we can express a particular position by a letter-number combination.

> Our move must also say what direction we are swapping. To do that, we'll put a single letter after the space to say whether it is swapping up, down, left, or right (*u*, *d*, *l*, and *r*, respectively). Also, there are some invalid moves.

```python
def ConvertLetterToCol(Col):
    if Col == 'a':
        return 0
    elif Col == 'b':
        return 1
    elif Col == 'c':
        return 2
    elif Col == 'd':
        return 3
    elif Col == 'e':
        return 4
    elif Col == 'f':
        return 5
    elif Col == 'g':
        return 6
    elif Col == 'h':
        return 7
    else:
        #not a valid column!
        return -1
def SwapPieces(board, move):
    #Swap pieces on board according to move
    #Get original position
    origrow = int(move[1])-1
    origcol = ConvertLetterToCol(move[0])
    #Get adjacent position
    if move[2] == 'u':
        newrow = origrow + 1
        newcol = origcol
    elif move[2] == 'd':
        newrow = origrow - 1
        newcol = origcol
    elif move[2] == 'l':
        newrow = origrow
        newcol = origcol - 1
```

```
        elif move[2] == 'r':
            newrow = origrow
            newcol = origcol + 1
        #Swap objects in two positions
        temp = board[origrow][origcol]
        board[origrow][origcol] = board[newrow][newcol]
        board[newrow][newcol] = temp
```

> The next routine that's just a stub and needs to be filled in is "RemovePieces." We need to make sure that we remove any three in a row or three in a column, and we could have both cases.

> We'll create a new 8-by-8 board that we will use to keep track of whether a piece should be removed or not. We'll then update this board by looking at the rows and columns to find three of the same object and mark those spaces if they need to be removed. After we've found all the pieces to be removed, we'll go back and remove them. As we're removing them, we'll increase the score. Finally, we'll return "True" or "False," depending on whether the pieces were removed or not.

```
def RemovePieces(board):
    #Remove 3-in-a-row and 3-in-a-column pieces
    #Create board to store remove-or-not
    remove = [[0, 0, 0, 0, 0, 0, 0, 0], [0, 0, 0, 0, 0, 0, 0, 0],
              [0, 0, 0, 0, 0, 0, 0, 0], [0, 0, 0, 0, 0, 0, 0, 0],
              [0, 0, 0, 0, 0, 0, 0, 0], [0, 0, 0, 0, 0, 0, 0, 0],
              [0, 0, 0, 0, 0, 0, 0, 0], [0, 0, 0, 0, 0, 0, 0, 0]]
    #Go through rows
    for i in range(8):
        for j in range(6):
            if (board[i][j] == board[i][j+1]) and (board[i][j] ==
                board[i][j+2]):
                #three in a row are the same!
                remove[i][j] = 1;
                remove[i][j+1] = 1;
                remove[i][j+2] = 1;
    #Go through columns
```

```
    for j in range(8):
        for i in range(6):
            if (board[i][j] == board[i+1][j]) and (board[i][j] ==
                board[i+2][j]):
                    #three in a row are the same!
                    remove[i][j] = 1;
                    remove[i+1][j] = 1;
                    remove[i+2][j] = 1;
    #Eliminate those marked
    global score
    removed_any = False
    for i in range(8):
        for j in range(8):
            if remove[i][j] == 1
                board[i][j] = 0
                score += 1
                removed_any = True
    return removed_any
```

> The next stub routine to fill in is for dropping pieces. To do this, we'll go to each column and make a list of remaining pieces from bottom to top. We'll then fill in the column with those pieces, putting zeros in at the top.

```
def DropPieces(board):
    #Drop pieces to fill in blanks
    for j in range(8):
        #make list of pieces in the column
        listofpieces = []
        for i in range(8):
            if board[i][j] != 0:
                listofpieces.append(board[i][j])
        #copy that list into colulmn
        for i in range(len(listofpieces)) :
            board[i][j] = listofpieces[i]
        #fill in remainder of column with 0s
        for i in range(len(listofpieces), 8):
            board[i][j] = 0
```

› We have just one more stub function to fill in: filling in any blank spaces with new pieces. In this case, we'll just run through all spaces, and if there's a zero, we'll replace it with a random new piece.

```python
def FillBlanks(board):
    #Fill blanks with random pieces
    for i in range(8):
        for j in range(8):
            if (board[i][j] == 0):
                board[i][j] = choice(['Q', 'R', 'S', 'T', 'U'])
```

› We finally have the whole program finished. We can play it now. And when we do, we probably see some things that we could improve. We can use an iterative improvement process to gradually add on these additional features.

Reading

Matthes, *Python Crash Course*, chaps. 12–14.

Exercises

Imagine that you wanted to create a tic-tac-toe game on the computer. Assume that the board spaces are numbered 1 through 9, with the top row numbered 1, 2, 3; the middle row numbered 4, 5, 6; and the bottom row numbered 7, 8, 9.

Show the code you would write for the following pieces of the program.

    1   Define an initial empty tic-tac-toe board, using a character "." to represent an empty square.

2 A function that takes in a board, a position (a number 1 through 9), and a character "'X'" or "'O'" and updates the board to have that value in the appropriate position.

3 A function that takes in a board and examines the first row. If all elements are "'X,'" or all are "'O,'" then that character is returned. Otherwise, "'.'" is returned.

Game Design with Functions

One of the attractions of computer science, for as long as I can remember, has been games. Video games have evolved a lot from the early days of Pong in the 1970s, into a wide-ranging industry that produces games for desktop computers, video game consoles, and smartphones. Believe it or not, the game industry is now bigger than Hollywood and bigger than the music industry. I find that pretty amazing.

Now, just like making a movie, creating a popular game these days takes a lot of people filling a lot of different roles, including artwork, sound, level design, and production. But, the core of the game is the still the software that controls the game mechanics—what actually happens in the game. And, this part of the game is developed by programmers.

We're going to show how to develop a game similar to a lot of popular casual games. In fact, you've probably played games like this before. We'll see how functions directly support a top-down design approach, and we'll use stub functions to help us rough in the structure of our program along the way.

The game we're going to develop will have the guts for a grid-based matching game. Now, these are games where you have a bunch of objects arranged in a grid, and you try to move things around to match up similar items—at which point the matched-up items disappear. There are lots of variations on these games. Objects on the grid might be pieces of candy—like in Candy Crush, or jewels—like in Diamond Mine, or they could be geometric shapes.

For this lecture, our game will use individual letters for our objects, and we'll see the grid as a text grid printed out to the screen.

Here's the game that we'll develop. We'll have a 2D grid of different objects. In our game, we'll have five objects—the letters Q, R, S, T, and U. And, we'll have the familiar game mechanics, where objects disappear once we get a certain number of the same object in a row or column.

On each turn, you get to choose to rearrange those pieces somehow. Now, different games have different types of moves allowed. We're going to assume that the only move we can make is to swap a piece with an adjacent piece.

When a move is made, some objects are removed from the grid according to patterns that are made. For our game, we'll remove any cases where three or more of the same object are adjacent in the same row or the same column. Usually, this is what the player gets points for. Then, the remaining objects rearrange, typically by falling down to fill in the gaps that just got removed.

We'll want to fill in gaps at the top with random new objects. The game continues like this until the user meets a goal. For us, the goal will be to get a predefined number of points.

Now, this is going to be a somewhat complex piece of software—it's certainly not the sort of thing that we want to just sit right down and start writing.

So, let's see how we can design this program using a top-down approach, modified for teaching purposes. Let's think about what has to happen in the broadest terms first. At this broadest level, we have three basic steps. First, we set up everything—initializing the game. Second, we go into a loop. The condition for the loop makes sure that it's not time to end the game. Finally, within the loop, we'll go through one round of the game. So, that gives us three more aspects that we need to define. Notice that at the top level, we've defined the main tasks to be done, but not the details of how to do them.

Now, full top-down design would mean that we keep going, defining more and more levels before we actually write the code. But, I want to go ahead and show you right now how some of this might look. Let's consider that top level first. In code, we can, and should, take each of those steps and put in a comment describing what needs to be done—in what order. In this case, we have three comments. We have one for the initialization, one for the loop, and one for taking a turn. Now, I want to make a key point here.

Each of these general tasks is something that can and usually should be encapsulated into a function. To illustrate here, every time we have one of these tasks, we'll turn it into a function call. Now, this is the main idea of procedural programming, where functions are created to handle all the main tasks. Here's what the current code looks like if we introduce the functions. Notice that each of our original lines has turned into one function call. Those actual functions are defined but don't do anything, since we haven't really gotten to that level yet.

Now again, if we're using top-down design in practice, we would define some of the lower levels first, before writing any of this code. In particular, you'll notice that all of our functions have empty parameter lists. That's because we don't yet understand what information we need at these lower levels, so we don't know what to pass in and out via parameter.

Despite that, this code that you see here is indeed the main program for us. Since we've written some code, what's the next thing we should do with it? Test it.

To test in this case, we really want to see if everything is getting called in order. So, we'll add a few simple print statements in each of the functions. And, for one of the functions, we do need to return True or False, so we'll have to add that line, even though the function's not really doing anything. So, now let's run this. When we run, we do indeed get an initial line that shows that we're in the initialization function. Then, we enter an infinite loop in which we keep seeing that we're checking whether or not to continue and then performing a round of the game.

OK, so far so good. We should probably also check to make sure that it's working if that one function returns False. So, we change that line of code, run again, and now we just get two lines—one saying that we're initializing and one that we're checking whether to continue. And, we never actually do a round since we know that check returns False.

By the way, the term we use to refer to these little functions that are placeholders for something that should be much bigger is stubs. A stub is just a function that doesn't really do what it's intended to do, but it does just enough that everything around it runs. So, if it needs to return a True or a False, it'll do so, but not according to any real computation. When we're developing a program and have a bunch of function calls to make, we say we're stubbing out the program when we write stub functions for each.

OK. Great. We've now looked at our code, and we have something stable that's been tested. Remember how I talked in an earlier lecture about building code in a pyramid fashion one layer at a time? Well, we just implemented our foundation. It's time to add some more layers onto the pyramid.

Now, let me step back for half a second and make sure that we're on the same page. I'm going to be showing you how this code is developed. As I do so, we'll see a good amount of code—about 200 lines overall. When you see code, I want you to make sure that you understand what you see before going on. So please, any time that we're looking at code, make sure you understand what it's doing before going on further.

OK, so now we want to turn back to our design process. Let's look at one of these functions that hasn't been defined yet—say initialization. In initialization, we need to set up the grid itself. That is, we need to get all the pieces placed into their starting positions on the grid. We also have to set the user's score to zero since we're just starting the game. And, we probably want to initialize other variables, such as one that will help us keep track of which round of the game we're on.

Now, for one round of the game, we have three basic steps. We first have to get the move from the user. Then, we have to update the game based on that move, and finally, we have to display the new grid to the user.

This brings us to our continue the game check. It turns out that this is going to be a pretty simple check for our game. We just want to see if the user has reached the goal score yet, or not. So, we'll have a conditional that checks whether the score exceeds some maximum, or not, and return True or False for that routine.

Now, this routine is so simple that each of those commands is basically a line or two of code. So, let's go ahead and implement this routine. Here's what that code will look like. We have an if statement that compares the current score and the goal score, and will return either True or False. Now, do you see anything about this function that's not so great? Well, the thing that strikes me is that we've got these variables—current_ score and goal_score—but we never really define them anywhere. They're mystery values defined somewhere outside of the function, and we just have to hope that they're set correctly for when we read them.

So, a better option will be for us to pass in these values as parameters. So, here we list these values as parameters to our function. This is good because it means that the functions calling ContinueGame will know that they need to pass in the important values that ContinueGame needs to operate. Also, notice that we've used a default value for the goal score, so if the calling routine just wants to pass in the current score, it can do so. Now, we need to make sure that we have the right data on the calling side and that we're passing it in.

So, in the main part of the code, we'll make a change to the call to ContinueGame. We set up the score and the goal, and we call ContinueGame with that score and goal passed in as parameters.

Now, you might be wondering—why did we create a whole function to determine ContinueGame? Couldn't we have just written all of this into the while loop where we now call ContinueGame? The answer is yes. We could have done this all in one line, but that's mainly because we have such a simple condition to determine whether or not to keep going. Here's what that would look like.

There are two related reasons why we made ContinueGame a function, rather than just putting the comparison directly into the while loop. First, it followed our top-down design approach. In our design, at first, we just knew that we needed a check on whether to continue. Only as we went farther down in the design did we determine what that check should be. Since we're separating different concepts using function calls, using a function makes more sense.

Second, using a function call leaves us the option of having a much more complicated function to determine ContinueGame. For instance, maybe the user has to not only get a certain score but also has to remove all the objects of a certain type from the grid. We could encapsulate that check into the ContinueGame routine. As far as the main program is concerned, it just needs to make sure that it provides ContinueGame with the parameters it asks for, and it doesn't need to worry about how ContinueGame itself is implemented. This top-down design has given us the flexibility to make much bigger changes later on.

Now, we should test everything, just like I've shown you before. For the sake of time, I'm going to skip showing you all the testing done along the way, and I'll show you correct code each time. But realize that when you actually write this code, it's extremely unlikely that you're going to have all of this work right, right off the bat.

OK, that was only one small part of this whole program. Before we go much farther, we first ought to think about what some of the data we'll want to store is. We need to decide how the grid itself will be represented. This is what we would refer to as a data structure, and ways of defining good data structures is a whole topic of its own that we'll come back to in a future lecture. For now, we can have a pretty straightforward data structure. Basically, we want our grid to have a set of rows and columns, and in each of those rows and columns, we have one object. In our case, an object is just a letter.

Now, can you think of where you've seen something that would let us store rows and columns nicely? How might you store something like this? If you remember, we've talked about lists in the past. In fact, we've seen a grid representation as a list of lists. Let's look at how this would appear in code.

Let's say that our board is an 8 by 8 grid, like a checkerboard. We'll thus need a list of 8 rows, each with 8 elements. Now, we'll actually set these elements to what's needed for the game in the initialization routine, but to begin with, we'll make a list of all these elements. This is just going to be a list of 8 lists, each of length 8. Now, there're other ways that we could have created these lists, for instance, by creating loops in which we append lists, but I think writing it like this is just as easy, and it makes the structure clear.

OK, now let's turn back to our top-down design and look at some of our other routines. Let's take the initialization routine again. It's going to have three different parts—initializing the grid itself, initializing the score, and initializing the turn. Later on, we might find some other things that we wanted initialized, and so we'll have to add them here, also.

Initializing the grid is a complicated process, and we'll do that in a separate function—Initialize grid. For the score and the turn, we'll want to set the score to zero and the turn to 1. Now, the score and turn variables are going to be trickier to set. These are immutable values, so we can't pass them in and change them in the function. What we can do, though, is we can make sure, within the function, that we declare them as global variables. This will let us initialize them to their appropriate values.

Now, remember globals are often discouraged, but there's not an easy way to get around using them here. Later on, we'll learn about objects, and how they can be mutable, and thus let us initialize data without using globals.

OK, let's consider now how we might handle the grid initialization itself. Notice that since this is a list, it's mutable, and thus we're passing it as a parameter to initialize it. They're different ways we could initialize.

For instance, we might have a file that specifies an initial configuration. But, for us, let's just assume that we'll assign random objects to each grid cell.

To assign random objects, we'll need to use the random module, which is part of the Python standard library. We'll import the choice function, which will randomly choose one element from a list. Then, to initialize our grid, we'll loop through all 8 rows and all 8 columns, and set the element to a random value. We will assume the possible objects are the letters q through u, but we could change those values to anything we wanted. I chose q through u since those letters appear pretty different from each other visually.

So, that's the initialization stage. We can now turn our design to the game round itself. So let's think about what needs to happen during a turn. There are four basic parts: presenting the state of the game, getting the user's move, determining the result of that move, and finally incrementing the turn number.

Again, the top-down approach means we can create a separate function for each of these main steps. We'll just call these in order from our DoRound routine. One of these, incrementing the turn number, requires just a couple of lines of code, and so we'll actually write that out, rather than creating a whole separate function. And that's it for DoRound—we're done with that routine.

OK, now we turn to the next unfinished portion of our routine—presenting the board. We're just printing to the screen at this point, so we just need to output each of the grid values in a nice orderly format. We'll draw horizontal and vertical lines to separate the individual elements. So, we start by drawing a few blank lines to separate our display from any that might have appeared right above it, and then we'll draw a horizontal line.

After that, we're going to draw stuff for each of the rows. We'll form a single string for drawing each row. Since we want the highest row number drawn first, we'll have a range that's decreasing. Notice that we want to start with row 7, and work our way down to row 0, which means our range will go 7 to −1 by steps of −1. Remember that the last element of the range is the stopping point and doesn't get processed.

OK, for each row we'll have one string that we start out using the empty string. For each column, we'll output a vertical line, followed by the letter designating the object that we have. When we've done this for the entire row, we print out one vertical line to end the string; we print it, and then we print another line of horizontal dashes.

OK, that's our display routine. Let's look now at our GetMove routine. For now, we'll just ask the user for a move and return that move. That's super simple. Notice that we haven't really said what form a move should take, so for now, the move is just a string. We're going to have to work out what form that string should take, shortly.

OK. Let's stop quickly to look at all of our code and check out our progress. We have separate routines for all the various levels we've discussed—from initializing, to checking whether to continue, to doing one round—along with all the routines that those would call. We have one stub function remaining, and that's the Update routine. Of course, that's actually a really important routine. If we run the code at this point, we see a display of the board and can enter a move, but nothing's actually happening.

Now, thinking back to our pyramid model of software construction, we've laid out several layers of the pyramid, and we can test it and make sure that it's all working correctly so far. But, we still have a ways to go. Next, we'll turn to the actual turn mechanics, which is embodied in the Update routine.

The turn mechanics are the main thing that define the game. They embody the rules about how the game progresses according to a move. In this case, there are a few parts, each of which will require us to do something.

First, we'll need to update the board according to our move. In this case, that means swapping one object with an adjacent one. Then, we'll need to repeatedly eliminate pieces and update the board, until there's nothing more to be eliminated. We'll have to go through and remove any pieces that are 3-in-a-row or 3-in-a-column. This'll leave some empty spaces, and everything above will need to fall down. Finally, any blank spaces at the top will get filled in with new random objects.

Again, putting this into code is straightforward, as each action gets turned into a new function. We stub out these functions, and then we'll address each of those functions individually.

To determine the swapping, we need to convert a move into an actual position, and its adjacent position. So to do this, we need to determine how to express a move. Notice that this decision will affect how we expressed a move when a person typed it in.

In order to express a position, we'll use a system similar to that used in Chess. The columns will be numbered using a lower-case letter from a through h. And, the rows will be numbered using a number from 1 to 8. So, we can express a particular position by a letter-number combination. For example, e3 would be one space, and f3 would be the space just to the right.

Now, our moves must also say what direction we're swapping. To do that, we'll put a single letter after the space to say whether it's swapping up, down, left, or right. We'll use *u*, *d*, *l*, and *r* to designate up, down, left, and right. Notice, then, that if we were to say e3r, that's the same as saying f3l. Also, they're going to be some invalid moves. For instance, nothing on row 1 could swap down, and nothing in column h could swap right.

Here's how this code would look. We need to get the row and column number, each of which is between 0 and 7, from the first two parts of the move. For the row, we'll take the second element of the move, convert it to an integer, and subtract 1. We have to subtract one since our indices run 0– 7 instead of 1–8. For the column, we need to take the first element of the move and convert the letter a through h to a number. We'll use a series of if-then-else statements to do this, and because it's kind of messy, we'll pull that into its own function.

Next, we'll need to get the row and column we're swapping to. That'll be based on the third element of the move. We'll determine the new row and column from the original row and column, depending on whether it's *u*, *d*, *l*, or *r*. For example, if the swap was up, then the new row is one higher, but the column remains the same. We can make similar rules for *d*, *l*, and *r*.

Finally, we need to actually swap the objects in the two positions The typical way we swap two objects is to copy one to a temporary position and then move the other object into the original position and then use that temporary to fill in the original. Swapping like this is very common.

So, now we have our swap routine fully finished. We've taken in a move, and we've swapped pieces based on that move. We next need to turn to another routine that's just a stub and fill it in. The next one we have is RemovePieces.

Again, following top-down design, let's think about how RemovePieces should work. Now, this is tricky. We need to make sure that we remove any three-in-a-row or three-in-a-column, and we could have both cases. What we'll do is we'll create a new 8 by 8 board that we'll use to keep track of whether a piece should be removed or not. We'll then update this board by looking at the rows and columns to find three of the same object and mark those spaces if they need to be removed. After we've found all the pieces to be removed, we'll go back and remove them. Again, notice that we should mark them first, then remove them. If we remove them when we first find them, then we might miss some additional cases. As we're removing them, we'll increase the score. And, finally, we'll return True or False depending on whether the pieces were removed or not.

Putting this into code takes several lines, but it's pretty straightforward. We first create a board, Remove, filled with 0—where 0 will indicate not to remove, and 1 will indicate we should remove. We then loop through all 8 rows. In each row, we'll go through the first 6 columns and compare that element with the next two columns over. If they match, we'll mark those elements to be removed. We do the same for the columns. Finally, we go through the entire board, and if there's an element marked to be removed—we change that element to a 0, increment our score, and note that we removed something. Finally, we return the removed value.

The next stub routine to fill in is for dropping pieces. To do this, we'll go to each column and make a list of remaining pieces from bottom to top. We'll then fill in the column with those pieces—putting 0s in at the top.

Again, the actual code for this is relatively straightforward. We'll handle each column separately. In each column, we first make a list of the elements that are non-zero. Then, we go through that list, copying it into the column. Notice that our loop is over the size of that new list. Finally, we fill in the remaining spots in that column with 0s. Notice that our loop range, in this case, starts from the length of the list of remaining pieces and goes to the column length, 8.

We have just one more stub function to fill in. That's filling in any blank spaces with new pieces. In this case, we'll just run through all spaces, and if there's a zero, we'll replace it with a random new piece. So, what should the code for this look like?

This is pretty straightforward code, again. We loop through all the spaces on the board. If we have an if statement to check whether the space is empty, that is, if it has a value of zero. Finally, if it does, we generate a random piece in its place.

Hooray! We finally have the whole program finished. We can go ahead and play it now. And, when we do, we probably see some things that would be nice to improve. For instance, it would be nice to know the current score. We can use an iterative improvement process to gradually add on these additional features. For instance, we can print out the score when we print out the board. And, it's nicer to have the rows and columns labeled. These are relatively simple improvements that make the game easier to play.

We could also give instructions more clearly when getting the move. It would help to give some instructions about how to enter a move. It's a very simple improvement—just adding some print statements.

Maybe we should check to make sure the user enters a valid move. Now, where do you think we could put a change like that? Well, since we're trying to get a valid move, we could make a change to the GetMove function. So, we probably ought to think about how we would redesign this function.

Our function already gives instructions—that's the print statements—and it already gets a move. So the new thing we need to add is a loop to continue asking for a move until the user enters a valid one. We'll need a loop, and within that loop, we'll need to ask for another move. The condition for the loop will be that the current move is not a valid one. Now, that check will probably require a routine of its own. So, let's modify our GetMove function and add some comments. We divide it up into three parts—giving instructions, getting a move, and then looping until the move is valid. We'll also create a new stub function for IsValid to test whether a move is valid. Notice that since IsValid will return True at the moment, this code doesn't actually behave any differently than what we had before.

OK, now, how would you write the IsValid function? Remember, before you just write code—stop and think about what it means for a move to be valid, the categories of things that could go wrong, and then about the various checks that you would need to put in to verify that. Here are three things we could check to see if it's a valid move. First, make sure that they entered a 3-character move. If not, the move's invalid, so we return False.

Next, make sure that the individual parts of the move are valid—that they entered a valid row, a valid column and a valid direction. So, we make sure that the column is between a and h, that the row is between 1 and 8, and that the direction is either *u*, *d*, *l*, or *r*.

And third, we can check that the swap direction is valid for the given row and column. If the piece is in the first column, we can't swap left. And if it's in the last column, we can't swap right. The same thing goes for the top and bottom rows. We've now got three nice checks to make sure that the user doesn't enter invalid moves that could cause the program to crash.

There are other ways that we could improve on the program. Maybe we want to do something more advanced, like give an additional type of move. For example, maybe we want to allow the user to have a bomb that destroys lots of pieces or a laser that removes an entire row or an entire column. Maybe removing certain combinations of pieces gives an additional bonus or a new type of piece. Maybe we change from having five types of regular pieces to having more.

Or, maybe we want to change when the game ends, for example, giving the user a certain number of turns or even building in a loop that lets the user continue playing if their points, after a certain number of turns, exceeds a predefined score.

The point is, now that we have this working version, we could augment it to add any of the features we'd like. Let me encourage you to try this out on your own. Think of some feature you would like to see added, then look for a way to add that feature yourself.

OK. We've written a program almost 250 lines long. About a third of our lines are comments and blank lines, but remember that these are very important to helping us develop and understand our code.

Grid-based game mechanics give us a way of demonstrating how top-down design and the use of functions go hand-in-hand. Top-down design provides a conceptual separation between different levels of design, so that one level doesn't have to worry about those just above or just below it. Functions like DoRound, DropPieces, RemovePieces, and so on ensure that we can put this abstraction into practice. By using stubs, we're able to design, write, and test our code in stages without having to generate every piece of it at once. Then, as we fill in the stubs with the real code, the whole program gradually comes together.

In the next lecture, we'll talk about a different form of software design. One that still makes heavy use of functions, but it's kind of the opposite of top-down—we call it bottom-up. And, instead of games, we'll consider some other fun stuff—graphics and robots. I'm looking forward to seeing you then.

14

Bottom-Up Design, Turtle Graphics, Robotics

In bottom-up programming and software design, you start with pieces of code you already understand how to use and use those to build upward toward more complex projects. Bottom-up design tends to promote the reuse of ideas and working code from the lower levels, which should yield savings in the amount of work it takes to develop. Bottom-up design works especially well when we already understand our building blocks and when there is no clear or obvious top-down plan for how to build something better. As you will learn, one area of technology where bottom-up software design works well is robotics.

[TURTLE GRAPHICS]

> To illustrate **bottom-up** programming for things like robots, we're going to use a simple module that will let us simulate a robot motion. The name of this is the turtle module, and it's one of the modules installed automatically with the Python standard library. The turtle module lets us create what are called **turtle graphics**, which are relatively simple line drawings but can be lots of fun on their own.

> A simple turtle graphics program in Python looks like the following. It's a program to create a square spiral. From the "turtle" module, we import the "forward" and "left" commands, and then for every *i* within a given range is movement forward and then a left turn. The little shape that moves around the screen and traces out a path as it moves is called a turtle.

```
from turtle import forward, left
for i in range(1,100):
    forward(2*i)
    left(90)
input()
```

> Even though this isn't a real robot moving around, we can treat the turtle like a robot. It'll have some of the same basic commands that a real robot would have.

> For our example, the turtle will have only six basic commands: move forward or backward, turn left or right, and raise or lower a pen it carries. When the pen is down, wherever it moves is traced out as a graphic on the screen. When the pen is up, it moves without tracing an image.

> These commands, and many others, are all part of the "turtle" package. The "forward" and "backward" commands take in a parameter that says how far to move in pixels, where a pixel is just one dot on the screen. Images that you see are made up of a bunch of pixels arranged in a large grid.

> The commands "left" and "right" cause the turtle to turn in place, either to the left or to the right, with the number of degrees to turn passed in as a parameter. The two controls for the pen are simply "pendown" and "penup."

> The turtle will start in the center of the screen, facing to the right, with the pen down.

> These are the most basic commands. For a real robot, you'll often have something similar—a few basic motion commands—that you will have to put together to do something more complicated.

> For example, let's say that we want to draw a square. We can imagine what we need the turtle to do: go forward for a while, turn 90 degrees (counterclockwise), go forward the same amount, and so on, until the square is completed.

> The following is what this will look like in code.

```
from turtle import forward, backward, left, right, penup, pendown
forward(100)
left(90)
forward(100)
left(90)
forward(100)
left(90)
forward(100)
input()
```

> First, notice that we can use a "from turtle import *" command to get all six commands from the turtle module. We'll make the square 100 units long on each side. So, drawing the square means that we move forward 100 units, turn 90 degrees, etc., until we've drawn all four sides. We are going counterclockwise, so we turn left.

> When we run the program, the turtle goes around and draws all four sides, creating a square. The turtle (the triangle-looking thing) is back at the center of the screen, although now it's facing down instead of to the right.

> Here's where bottom-up design comes into play. We just created a sequence of code that will create a square. We can package those commands together to create a new routine called "drawSquare." We simply define a function, called "drawSquare," and put the code we just wrote into the body of the function. Then, when we call the "drawSquare" function, we get the same behavior as before.

```
from turtle import forward, backward, left, right, penup, pendown
def drawSquare():
    forward(100)
    left(90)
    forward(100)
    left(90)
    forward(100)
```

```
      left(90)
      forward(100)
   drawSquare()
   input()
```

> This is an example of bottom-up design. We took some simple things that we already knew how to do—in this case, moving forward and turning left—and we put those together to create something more complicated—in this case, making a square.

> If we call the "drawSquare" function a second time, it creates a second square, just below the first one. Remember that when we finished drawing our square, the turtle was pointing down, instead of to the right. So, when we called "drawSquare" a second time, it drew another square. For both the first and second square, the square was drawn to the front left of the direction the turtle was originally facing.

> There are several ways we can improve the square program. And we can also create other shapes, such as a triangle or rectangle. And if you explore some of the other turtle commands listed in the library, you can get other features.

[ROBOT PROGRAM]

> One great, if perhaps surprising, way to think about the turtle library is as a good proxy for robot motion. So, we're going to look at how we could control a robot to have it explore a room—the same way a robot vacuum cleaner might, for example. We'll assume that we have the basic turtle commands—forward, backward, turn left, etc.—and will build from the bottom up from those basic commands to define the robot's paths to cover a whole room.

> In addition to movement, most modern robots also have sensors. Sensors can help detect if there's a potential problem or some other event. For example, mobile robots will often have sensors to detect how close a wall is or if they've bumped into something.

› Our turtle is obviously not a real robot, and it does not have sensors. However, we can just define a sensor function that will act like a sensor for our on-screen turtle.

› This sensor we define can tell us if we're too close to an obstacle. If we call "sensor," it should return "True" if we're too close to an obstacle or "False" if we're not. So, the sensor we define is very similar to proximity sensors that you could find on a real robot.

› Our code will start by importing two modules. First, we're going to be using turtle pretty heavily, so we'll import all the turtle functions, indicated with an asterisk. Second, we're going to want some random functions, so we'll import the random module, too. Next, we'll set up variables to say that the room we're operating in is a simple square, going from -250 to 250 in both *x* and *y*. And we'll assume that we should say we're too close to the edge if we're within a proximity of 10.

```python
from turtle import *
import random
xmax = 250
xmin = -250
ymax = 250
ymin = -250
proximity = 10
def sensor():
    if xmax - position()[0] < proximity:
        #Too close to right wall
        return True
    if position()[0] - xmin < proximity:
        #Too clsoe to left wall
        return True
    if ymax - position()[1] < proximity:
        #Too close to top wall
        return True
    if position()[1] - ymin < proximity:
        #Too clsoe to bottom wall
        return True
```

```
#Not too close to any
return False
```

> The sensor function itself will use the position command from the turtle library to compute how far away the turtle is from each of the walls. If the turtle is within proximity of any of the four walls, the sensor function returns "True," indicating that the sensor had triggered. Otherwise, it returns "False."

> Robot vacuums typically have just a few basic types of motion. It can travel in an ever-increasing spiral, and in fact it usually starts out in a spiral. It travels in a straight line, in some seemingly random direction. It also moves parallel to a wall that it is close to.

> We're going to try to build up these patterns for our turtle. For all of them, we only want to continue the pattern until the sensor triggers a proximity warning, at which point we have to do something else.

> Let's start by thinking about how we'd build the easiest of these— traveling in a straight line in a random direction. How would we use our "forward" and our "left" or "right" commands to pick a random direction, and then head in that direction, until the sensor triggered? Remember that we have the random module available to us, too.

> The following is one way to describe this. We define a function named "straightline." Notice that we've included a docstring, stating what the function does. The first action is to pick a random direction to go.

```
def straightline():
    '''Move in a random direction until sensor is triggered'''
    #Pick a random direction
    left(random.randrange(0,360))
    #Keep going forward until a wall is hit
    while not sensor():
        forward(1)
```

> The turtle will turn left by some random amount between 0 and 360 degrees. We use "randrange" from the random module to pick the number of degrees and pass this to the "left" function. The second part of the function just continues in a straight line until the sensor returns "True." Notice that we only move forward one unit at a time before we check the sensor again.

> If we run this code, we see that the turtle heads off in some random direction, until it hits the "edge" of the square room that it's in.

```
def straightline():
    '''Move in a random direction until sensor is triggered'''
    #Pick a random direction
    left(random.randrange(0,360))
    #Keep going forward until a wall is hit
    while not sensor():
        forward(1)
    straightline()
```

> Next, let's define a spiral function. We could use the spiral that we defined earlier, but that's a square spiral—it would be better to have something more circular. Mathematically, this is going to be trickier.

> The following is a spiral function we could use. We've defined a parameter, called "gap," that will tell us how tight the spiral should be. We set a default value in case we don't want to actually specify it, though. The way the spiral works is that at any one time, we pretend we're on a circle of some radius, and we move one unit along that circle's circumference. Then, we increase the radius so that it increases slightly with every step. We keep doing this until our sensor function says it's time to stop.

```
def spiral(gap = 20):
    ''Move in a spiral with spacing gap'''
    #Determine starting radius of spiral based on the gap
    current_radius = gap
```

```
while not sensor():
    #Determine how much of the circumference 1 unit is
    circumference = 2 * 3.14159*current_radius
    fraction = 1/circumference
    #Move as if in a circle of that radius
    left(fraction*360)
    forward(1)
    #Change radius so that we will be out by 2*proximity
      after 360 degrees
    current_radius += gap*fraction
```

> The code shows how the math works.

> If we run this code, we see that the turtle indeed is going to spiral out.

```
def spiral(gap = 20):
    ''Move in a spiral with spacing gap'''
    #Determine starting radius of spiral based on the gap
    current_radius = gap
    while not sensor():
        #Determine how much of the circumference 1 unit is
        circumference = 2 * 3.14159*current_radius
        fraction = 1/circumference
        #Move as if in a circle of that radius
        left(fraction*360)
        forward(1)
        #Change radius so that we will be out by 2*proximity
          after 360 degrees
        current_radius += gap*fraction
spiral()
```

> How might we build a pattern for wall-following? In this case, we'll want to find which of the four walls is closest and then set our direction to be parallel to that wall. Note that we'll want to use the turtle function named "setheading," which allows us to give a direction: 0 is to the right, 90 is up, 180 is left, and 270 is down.

› The following is one way to define a function we can call "followwall."

```
def followwall():
    '''Move turtle parallel to nearest wall for amount
      distance'''
    #find nearest wall and turn parallel to it
    min = xmax - position()[0]
    setheading(90)
    if position()[0] - xmin < min:
        min = position()[0] - xmin
        setheading(270)
    if ymax - position()[1] < min:
        min = ymax - position()[1]
        setheading(180)
    if position()[1] - ymin < min:
        setheading(0)
    #Keep going until hitting another wall
    while not sensor():
        forward (1)
```

› At this point, we were able to build up three different motion patterns: random straight line, spiral, or wall-following. Let's build up from here to create a new routine, "backupspiral," which will move us backward for some amount and then spiral outward.

› The following is the code.

```
def backupspiral(backup = 100, gap = 20):
    '''First move backward by amount backup, then in a spiral
      with spacing gap'''
    #first back up by backup amount
    while not sensor() and backup > 0:
        backward(1)
        backup -= 1
    #Determine starting radius of spiral based on the gap
    spiral(gap)
```

› Now we have several different motion patterns. We can put these together to build up a plan to explore a room. Imagine again that the turtle is a robot vacuum that's going to just keep going around cleaning up. We want something that will keep picking one of these motion patterns at random and using it to explore the room. The following is one way to implement this.

```
speed(0)
#Start with a spiral
spiral(40)
while (True):
    #First back up so no longer colliding
    backward(1)
    #Pick one of the three behaviors at random
    which_function = random.choice(['a', 'b', 'c'])
    if which_function == 'a':
        straightline()
    if which_function == 'b':
        backupspiral(random.randrange(100,200), random.
            randrange(10,50))
    if which_function == 'c':
        followwall(random.randrange(100,500))
```

› If we run this code, we start out in a spiral. One we've spiraled all the way out to where we come in proximity with a wall, we start taking random motions, according to one of our three patterns.

```
speed(0)
#Start with a spiral
spiral(40)
while (True):
    #First back up so no longer colliding
    backward(1)
    #Pick one of the three behaviors at random
    which_function = random.choice(['a', 'b', 'c'])
    if which_function == 'a':
        straightline()
```

```
if which_function == 'b':
    backupspiral(random.randrange(100,200), random.
        randrange(10,50))
if which_function == 'c':
    followwall(random.randrange(100,500))
```

Reading

Zelle, *Python Programming*, chap. 9.

Exercise

Write a function, "drawA," using turtle commands to draw the letter *A*.

Hint: Make the sides of the *A* at a 60-degree angle to the horizontal. This will make the shape of the *A* an equilateral triangle, which may be easier to draw.

Suggestion: Make the turtle finish in its original orientation, shifted over slightly from the last point on the *A*.

Bottom-Up Design, Turtle Graphics, Robotics

Once you understand how to write functions and how to use modules, you're ready for a style of programming and software design called bottom-up. In bottom-up, you start with pieces of code that you already understand how to use, and you use those to build up toward more complex projects. As you might guess, bottom-up design is kind of the opposite of top-down design, where we started with an overall goal and broke it up into its different parts.

To see how bottom-up works, think back to the analogy we used for top-down design: planning a dinner. The top-down approach to this problem is to say, "I'm planning a dinner, so I'll need an appetizer, a main dish, and a dessert," and so on. However, another way to approach cooking is to say, "OK, I have some flour, sugar, and so on, and I know how to mix ingredients into a batter, and I also know how to bake, and I know how to make frosting. So, if I combine all of those together, I can create a delicious dessert." Only later might you be in a position to say, "Well, I know how to make a dessert, and also an appetizer and a main course. If I combine all of these, I can put together a great meal."

Now, bottom-up design has one big advantage—you're starting from common patterns that you already know how to use, and that lets you reuse ideas. In the dinner example, you might be able to use the fact that you know how to cook pasta to create a pasta salad appetizer, or a spaghetti and meatballs main course, or even make something like noodle pudding for desert. So, your ability to cook pasta could potentially get reused many times, across all three courses.

When we're writing code, bottom-up design means that we can take sections of code that we know work, and we can combine them together to get something that has new functionality. Bottom-up design also tends to promote the reuse of ideas and working code from lower levels, and that should yield savings in the amount of work it takes to develop.

Bottom-up design works especially well when we already understand our building blocks, and when there's no clear or obvious top-down plan for how to build something better. Early voice-controlled digital assistants on smartphones are an example. I'm talking about things like Siri, the pleasant voice on an iPhone, that you talk to in order to find out things like how late the oil change place is open, or where you can get a good sandwich for lunch.

Now, putting together a voice-controlled digital assistant took a lot of parts, but most of those parts already existed before Apple made Siri. There was already voice recognition software. There was already the ability to run a search. There was already software that could convert text into speech. Now, I don't mean to minimize the work that it took to make a great product; there was a whole lot of effort and ingenuity that was needed to bring all those pieces together. But that's the point—by starting with some great pieces that already work, a bottom-up approach can create something that's even better.

Another area of technology where bottom-up software design works well is robotics. Now, to illustrate bottom-up programming for things like robots, we're going to use a simple module that'll let us simulate a robot motion. The name of this is the turtle module, and it's one of the modules installed automatically with the Python standard library. The turtle module lets us create what are called turtle graphics, which are relatively simple line drawings, but can be lots of fun on their own. The first turtle programs, dating all the way back to the mid-1960s, were actually based on a physical object that moved around like a robot, but turtle graphics has been adapted for use in various programming languages such as Logo, a teaching language, and Python.

So, let's see what a simple turtle graphics program looks like in Python. Here's a program to create a square spiral. It's just a few lines of code, but you can get an idea of what's going on. From the turtle module, we import the forward and left commands, then for every *i* within a given range, we move forward and then turn left. The little shape that moves around the screen and traces out a path as it moves is what we call the turtle.

Now, even though this isn't a real robot moving around, we can treat the turtle like a robot. It'll have some of the same basic commands that a real robot would have. For example, the turtle will only have six basic commands: move forward or backward, turn left or right, and raise or lower a pen that it carries. When the pen is down, then wherever it moves is going to trace out a graphic on the screen, and when the pen is up, it moves without tracing an image on the screen.

These commands, and many others, are all part of the turtle package. The forward and backward commands take in a parameter that says how far to move in pixels, where a pixel is just one dot on the screen. Images that you see are made up of a bunch of pixels, arranged in a grid. The commands "left" and "right" cause the turtle to turn in place, either to the left or to the right, with the number of degrees passed in as a parameter. The two controls for the pen are simply "pendown" and "penup." The turtle will start in the center of the screen, facing to the right, with the pen down.

Now, these are our most basic commands. For a real robot, you'll often have something similar, a few basic motion commands that you'll have to put together to do something more complicated. So, let's see how we can put these together to do something more complicated. Let's say that we want to draw a square. We can imagine what we need the turtle to do: we want it to go forward for a while, turn 90°, go forward the same amount, and so on until the square is completed. And, by the way, I'm going to be going counterclockwise in my examples because computer graphics has traditionally used counterclockwise orientations. The reason for that, which you don't need to understand for this lecture, is so that cross products between convex edges, defined by the right-hand rule, will generally point up.

Let's see what this will look like in code. First, notice that we can use a "from turtle import" command to get all six commands from the turtle module. We'll make the square 100 units long on each side. So, drawing the square means that we move forward 100 units, turn 90°, et cetera, until we've drawn all 4 sides. We're going counterclockwise, so we turn left.

Notice that I put a line, "input," at the end. This is just to keep the program running until I press a key. If you don't put something like this in, the graphics screen will draw, but then the program will finish, and it'll immediately disappear. And so, by waiting for input, it'll keep the image on the screen just until I type something in or stop the program.

All right, so now when I run the program, I see that the turtle goes around and draws all four sides. We've created a square. The turtle—that's that little triangle-looking thing—is back at the center of the screen, though notice that now it's facing down instead of to the right.

Here's where bottom-up design comes into play. We just created a sequence of code that'll create a square. Now, we can package those commands together and create a new routine called "drawSquare." We simply define a function called "drawSquare," and we put the code that we just wrote into the body of the function. Then, whenever we call the "drawSquare" function, we get the same behavior as before.

This is an example of bottom-up design. We took some simple things that we already knew how to do—in this case, moving forward and turning left—and we put those pieces together to create something more complicated—in this case, making a square.

What happens if we call the "drawSquare" function a second time? Well, it creates a second square, just below the first one. Remember that when we finished drawing our square, the turtle was pointing down, instead of to the right. So, when we called "drawSquare" a second time, it drew another square. For both the first and second square, the square was drawn to the front left of the direction that the turtle was originally facing.

Let's look at a couple of ways we can improve the square program. First, maybe we don't want the turtle to face a different direction at the end than it did at the beginning. As you develop more code, you'll see that it's often good to finish something by returning to as near a state as you can to where you started out. So, if we have a function that should draw a square, it would be nice to just draw the square and have the turtle right where it was when we began. So, to draw this square to the screen and return to our original state, we'll add in one more left-hand turn at the end of the function. If we run the code now, it'll draw the square, and the turtle ends up pointing to the right, just like it started. So, calling "drawSquare" again will just trace right over the previous square.

OK, how about another improvement? I picked a square size of 100 in this case, but what if you wanted a different size? How might you modify the code to easily allow that? Well, we can modify the "drawSquare" routine to take in a parameter that we'll name "size." Then, when we draw each edge, we'll use our size parameter to draw it using whatever value we've specified in the line where we called "drawSquare." Notice that we can set a default value for size of 100, in case a user doesn't want to specify it. However, the user, in this case, did specify a size of 50.

You can imagine doing something similar to create other shapes. How about a triangle? Try making an equilateral triangle, where the length of a side is passed in. Now, as a hint, think about how much you would need to turn each time as you're drawing. Well, we can define "drawTriangle" to have sides the same length as before. So, the code is basically the same as to draw a square, but we're going to be turning 120° each time, and obviously we're only going to draw three edges.

Now, how about a rectangle? How could you create a routine to draw a rectangle when both the horizontal length and the vertical height are needed? Here, instead of one parameter for size, we can take in two parameters: one for length, one for height. Then we draw, just like for a square, but we make sure to draw using length for the horizontal motions, and height for the vertical motions.

Each of those shapes can be encapsulated into its own function, and then we can build up from there. Say we wanted to build something like a house picture, just a square with a triangle on top—that'd be a good start. We could create a "drawHouse" function that first draws a square, and then moves the turtle up to the top of the square, and then draws a triangle. See if you can write something like this. Remember, the shape will always be drawn assuming the turtle is pointing to the right, so if you move the turtle, you want to make sure it's pointing in the right direction before you draw.

OK. Notice that our "drawHouse" function includes "drawSquare" and "drawTriangle," with commands for transitioning between them in the middle. Here, we draw the square first. Then, we reposition the turtle by turning 90° left, going to the top of the square, and turning 90° right. Then, we draw the top, by calling "drawTriangle." And then, finally, we reposition back to the start, by turning right 90°, moving to the bottom of the square, and turning back left 90°. Now, have some fun with this; you can get the turtle system to draw all sorts of shapes for you. And, if you explore some of the other turtle commands listed in the library, you'll see you can get other features like filled-in areas.

Let's look at another example of how we can use bottom-up design and turtle graphics to build up a program. This time, our end goal will be a program where we read in a number from a user, and we convert it into groups of five, where we have four vertical lines crossed by a single line that's diagonal. Now, these are called tally marks, or slash marks, or hash marks—the name varies. So, someone entering the number 13 would have two groups of five, followed by three more.

OK, using bottom-up design, let's see if we can put together the commands we need to represent numbers with tally marks. A single tally mark is simple—just a vertical line. To make a vertical line from the turtle's starting position, we'll turn left 90° and then move forward. I'll make the tally mark 20 pixels tall. Now, after making the tally, I need to return back to my original position. So, in this case, I'll just go retrace my steps by going backward and then turn to the right. Let's run this and test it. Sure enough, it creates a vertical tally mark.

OK, now, let's say that we want to create a second tally mark. We need to move over to the right a few spaces and then draw another tally. When we move right, we don't want to actually draw a line, we just want to move over. So, what we'll do is we'll tell the turtle to pick up the pen, then move five spaces to the right, and then put the pen back down. After that, we can draw another tally mark. Again, we have some new functionality. In this case, we're shifting over to the right, and so we can incorporate that into a function of its own called "shiftRight." Since we're building bottom-up, another option is to incorporate the right shift into the tally mark drawing routine. In this case, the turtle automatically moves over once the tally mark is drawn.

Let's see what other functionality we can put together. Normally, as we're tallying, every five tally marks will be marked with a diagonal slash through the previous four. So, let's see how we can create that diagonal slash. After our last tally, we've already moved over one space, so this is where we'll put the end of the slash. Let's think about how we would want the slash to look. If we don't want the slash to go all the way from the bottom, we need to go up a little bit first. So, we'll turn left, pick up our pen, and go up by a little bit—say, 3 pixels. Then, we'll put our pen down so that we can draw our slash backward through the previous four slashes.

Let's think here a little more about how to draw that diagonal line. If the slashes are 20 units tall, and we want to start and stop 3 units from the ends, we want a slash mark that's 14 units tall in the vertical direction. We're also starting 5 units from the right-hand tally mark, and so we want to go 5 units past the leftmost tally mark. The tally marks themselves are a total of 15 units apart, so we're going to go 25 units in the horizontal direction.

But, instead of writing a function to calculate the distance and angle, which can introduce some rounding errors, we could instead just look at our current position in the graphic, using the "pos" function. Position returns the x, y value of the turtle, so we can get the x value by taking position-sub-0, or the y value by taking position-sub-1. Then, the "goto" function will move us precisely to the new location on the coordinate system, which we can reach by moving $-25, 14$ away from the current position. Finally, we'll return to our starting location by undoing those motions, going back to the starting position, and then moving back to the bottom of the screen. And, last but not least, we'll shift over to the right again. In fact, to leave a gap for the next set of tallies, we'll do a double shift over. Now, if we test this out, drawing four tally marks and a slash, we see that the code performs just like we'd hope.

Now, we can build up from here a little bit more. It seems useful to create a single function to draw five tallies, so we'll put that into a function of its own. Once we can draw a group of five tally marks, we can repeat that as many times as needed. We'll create a function, "drawTallies," that takes any number in as a parameter, *n*. First, we'll be drawing as groups of five tallies over and over, until we can't draw any more. Sounds like a loop, right? So, one way that we can do this is to have a "while" loop that continues as long as the number that we pass in is, at least, five. Each iteration of the loop, we'll draw five tallies and reduce *n* by 5. When that loop finishes, *n* is 4 or less. So, we have some single tally marks still to draw at the end, and we can create another loop to draw all the single tally marks, reducing *n* by one each time, and this will continue as long as *n* is greater than or equal to one.

We can ask the user for the total number of tallies to draw. Then, we just call "drawTallies" for that number. If we run this code, we see that it works just fine. For example, let's type in 23. We see that we get four groups of five, plus three more tallies.

Notice what we've done here. We took very basic commands, and we used them to build up more complex functionality. We started with the very simple turtle commands—forward, backward, left, right, penup, and pendown—and we used those commands to get some slightly more complex operations: making tally marks, shifting over, and making a diagonal slash. Then, we combined those commands together to make something even more complicated, a function that lets us input any number and see the tallies drawn for it.

This is typical for bottom-up design. If you think about it, bottom-up design isn't necessarily that different from top-down design. Both can give your code a very well-organized structure, and both have different levels of detail. In the end, the code might not look all that different from code developed using a top-down approach, but the mindset in developing it is somewhat different. Bottom-up also makes it easier to see how certain functionality can be reused. For instance, in the example we just saw, we used the "shiftRight" command in a couple of different places—after drawing an individual tally mark, and again, twice, after drawing a slash mark. Turtle graphics can be a whole lot of fun, so I'd encourage you to try playing with it some more. The turtle module contains 175 different commands that you can use.

Again, one great, if perhaps surprising, way to think about the turtle library is as a good proxy for robot motion. So, for the rest of the lecture, we're going to look at how we could control a robot to have it explore a room, the same way a robot vacuum cleaner might. We'll assume that we have the basic turtle commands—forward, backward, turn left, et cetera—and we'll build bottom-up from those to define the robot's paths to cover a whole room. In addition to movement, most robots these days also have sensors. Sensors can help detect if there's a potential problem or some other event. For example, mobile robots will often have sensors to detect how close a wall is, or if they've actually bumped into something.

Now, our turtle is obviously not a real robot, and so it doesn't have sensors. However, we can define a sensor function that will act like a sensor for our little on-screen turtle. This sensor that we define can tell us if we're too close to an obstacle. If we call "sensor," it should return true if we're too close to an obstacle, or false if we're not—that's all. So, the sensor that we define is very similar to proximity sensors that you could easily find on a real robot. Isn't programming cool?

So, our code is going to start by importing two modules. First, I'm going to be using turtle pretty heavily, so I'll import all the turtle functions, indicated with an asterisk. Second, I'm going to want some random functions, so I'll import the random module also. Next, I'll set up variables to say that the room we're operating in is a simple square, going from −250 to 250 in both x and y, and I'll assume that I should say I'm too close to the edge if I'm within a proximity of 10.

The sensor function itself will use the position command from the turtle library to compute how far away the turtle is from each of the walls. The sensor function, then, is pretty simple. It computes how far away the turtle is from each wall, and if it's within proximity from any of the four walls, it returns true, indicating that the sensor had triggered. Otherwise, it returns false.

OK, so we have a sensor that we can check any time we want, just by calling "sensor." If you've ever watched a robot vacuum, you might have noticed that it typically has just a few basic types of motion. It can travel in an ever-increasing spiral, and in fact, it usually starts out in a spiral. It can also travel in a straight line, basically a random direction. And, finally, it can travel right along a wall, parallel to the wall. So, we're going to try to build up these patterns for ourselves, for our turtle. For all of them, we only want to continue the pattern until the sensor triggers a proximity warning, at which point we have to do something else.

OK, so let's start by thinking about how we'd build up the easiest of these—traveling in a straight line in a random direction. How would we use our forward and our left or right commands to pick a random direction, and then head in that direction until the sensor triggered? Remember that we have the random module available to us also.

OK, here's one way that we could describe this. We define a function named "straightline." Notice that I've included a docstring, stating what the function does. The first action is to pick a random direction to go. So, the turtle will turn left by some random amount between 0 and 360°. We'll use and range from the random module to pick the number of degrees, and then we pass this to the "left" function. The second part of the function just continues in a straight line until the sensor returns true. Notice that we only move forward one unit at a time before we check the sensor again. We wouldn't want to travel too far, or we might accidentally crash. Now, this is essentially saying that we're going to keep monitoring our sensor as we move, and stop as soon as it goes off. Now, if we run this code, we'll see that the turtle heads off in some random direction until it hits the edge of this square room that we're in.

OK, that function was pretty straightforward. Now, let's define a spiral function. We could use the spiral that I defined earlier, but that's a square spiral—it would be better to have something more circular. Mathematically, this is going to be trickier. Here's a spiral function that we could use. I've defined a parameter, called gap that will tell us how tight the spiral should be. I set a default value in case we don't want to actually specify it. The way that a spiral works is that, at any one time, we going to pretend that we're on a circle of some radius, and we're going to move one unit along that circle's circumference. Then we increase the radius so that it increases slightly with every step, and we keep doing this until our sensor function says it's time to stop.

Now, the code shows how the math works. We compute the circumference, and then we figure out what fraction of the circumference one unit is. That gives us the fraction of 360° that we need to turn. So, we turn left by that amount, and we go forward one unit. We then increase the radius for the next step. We know how much to increase by taking the fraction and multiplying by the gap. So, if we run this code, we see that the turtle is indeed going to spiral out.

OK, we've built up two of the three motion patterns we've seen before. So how might we build a pattern for wall following? In this case, we'll want to find out which of the four walls is closest and then set our direction to be parallel to that wall. Note that we'll want to use the turtle function named "setheading" which allows us to give a direction—zero is to the right, 90 is up, 180 is left, and 270 is down. So, given that, and having already seen how we computed distance to the walls in the sensor function, how might we set up this wall-following function?

Here's one way to define a function that I've called "followwall." Notice that what we do is we first set up motion parallel to the right-hand wall, and store the distance to that wall in a variable: min. Then, we check the distance to each of the other walls. If they're closer than the closest one so far, we set our heading parallel to that wall, and we update minimum. So, in the end, we'll be facing parallel to the nearest wall, and if we're in a corner, it'll be parallel to one of the two walls that are nearest. Then, we just keep moving forward, just like we were in the "straightline" in a random direction function, until the sensor tells us that we're too close to a wall.

So, at this point, we were able to build up three different motion patterns: a random straight line, a spiral, or a wall following. So, let's build up from here to create a new routine: "backupspiral." Now what this will do is it will move us backward for some amount, and then spiral outward. You can see the code here—we just try to move backward for a while before starting the spiral. Now, the reason for having this routine is that it will sometimes help us to move away from an edge before we start a spiral so that the spiral doesn't just end right after it begins. Again, we'll set some default value for the backup amount.

So, at this point, we have several different motion patterns. Imagine that you're at a ministry of silly robot motions, and you want to create something silly. See what you can come up with.

We can put these together to build up a plan to explore a room. Imagine again that the turtle is a robot vacuum that's going to just keep going around, cleaning up. We want something that'll keep picking one of these motion patterns at random and using it to explore the room. Now, think about how you might do this yourself. How would you choose to combine these pieces we have to explore the room? One thing to keep in mind—when you have a sensor triggered, you probably want to go backward one step before trying anything else, otherwise you'll start out already in proximity of the wall, and you'll probably stop immediately.

Well, this is the way I chose to implement it. I set the speed to zero. If you've looked at the turtle module documentation, zero is the way to tell the turtle, "Move as fast as you can." So, I start out by spiraling out from the starting position. When the spiral stops, it means that we've hit a sensor warning, so we're near a wall. Now, we have an infinite loop, the first part of which will bring us backward one unit—that should get us away from whichever wall we got too close to. Then, we select one of our three motions using "which_function," whose value is assigned by the "random module.choice" command. We either go in a straight line in a random direction, we back up and then do a spiral, or we follow along a wall. Notice that if we're going in a spiral, we have two randrange commands for setting a random amount we'll back up—and I just chose for it to be between 100 and 200—and a random gap between spiral loops—and I chose that to be between 10 and 50.

So, if we run this code, we start out in a spiral. One we've spiraled all the way out, we come to proximity with a wall, and then we start taking random motions according to one of our three patterns. We could have picked a different way to combine these basic elements together—this was just the method that I chose. You can try experimenting. For example, maybe don't allow a spiral. Or see what happens if you only follow random straight lines.

Programming for turtle graphics has deep similarities with programming for control of robot motion. Both use many of the same commands, and both benefit from a bottom-up process for software design. Anytime someone is working with existing things to bring together something brand new; it's an example of bottom-up design. It's also a terrific approach for beginners to build their skills in iterative fashion, building on what you already know to put together more complex projects. So, I encourage you to practice a bottom-up approach whenever you can— it's a great way of generating new ideas.

In the next lecture, we'll see how we can go beyond the turtle to develop even fancier graphics, the type you might use in the graphical user interface of a game or in productivity software.

15

Event-Driven Programming

A picture is worth a thousand words. Actions speak louder than words. And the same can be true in programming and computer interfaces: What we see in a graphical user interface (GUI), and what we do inside that graphical interface, can be more important than words. In this lecture, you will explore this visual, action-oriented style of programming: how to write a graphical user interface and how to use event-driven programming, a style of programming that responds to mouse clicks and other events within the graphical interface. To do this, you will be introduced to a package called pyglet.

[PYGLET]

> Pyglet is a Python package created to help support development of games and other audiovisual environments. It provides functions that let you create windows, display images and graphics, play videos and music, get input from the mouse, etc.

> There are a few other game-development packages people also use—pygame is one that's well known—and there are other modules that do individual things that pyglet does, but pyglet packages these functions together nicely and is easy to install. Just go to the pyglet site (bitbucket.org/pyglet/pyglet/wiki/Home), or you can find pyglet through a web search.

> If you're using pip to install modules such as pyglet, you should be able to install pretty easily. Remember that you can go to the command line, to the directory where Python is installed, and type "python –m pip install pyglet" and it should install for you.

> Once you have pyglet downloaded, be sure to run the command: "import pyglet." Only if you don't have pyglet installed will you see a response, so any error message probably means that pyglet hasn't yet installed properly.

[EVENT-DRIVEN PROGRAMMING]

> One form of graphics that is familiar to everyone on a computer these days, in practice if not by name, is the **graphical user interface** (GUI, or "gooey"). The way a GUI works is entirely based on what is called **event-driven programming**.

> To understand the contrast, let's think about how we've been programming up to this point. We've been writing commands, and we expect to start at the first command and follow the commands in sequence, one after the other. Things like conditionals, loops, or function calls might make us jump to a different line of code, but we're basically going along in a definite sequence, where we always know which line of code we will execute next. We can refer to this as a sequential program.

> Event-driven programming is different. Instead of the program deciding when to ask a user for input, events outside the program determine what the program does next. An event is anything that happens where we want the program to respond. In a GUI, an event might be not only pressing a key on the keyboard, but also clicking a button on the screen, entering data into a box on the screen, moving the mouse, etc. For each of those events, the computer program needs to respond—it needs to do something—maybe just update a variable or maybe print to the screen.

> Robots often use event-driven programming, which allows them to respond to events in their environment. For a robot, events might be data that comes in from a sensor—for example, the robot detecting it's about to hit a wall. When the sensor gets this information, it needs to send it to the program to respond.

> The same kind of monitoring is always underway in the GUI of a computer. In any kind of event-driven programming, whenever the program runs,

there is an **event monitor** that runs continuously in the program. There are many other terms for the event monitor—such as a main loop, or an idle function, or a control function—but the job of the event monitor is to take in events and make sure that the appropriate function gets called in response to the event.

› There's more than one way to monitor events. Sometimes the event monitor uses what are called "interrupts." Basically, it just sits there until something interrupts it with an event. Other times, the event monitor actively "polls" the various devices—that is, it actively checks to see whether there is a keyboard event, a mouse event, etc. But you don't have to worry about whether polling or interrupts are monitoring events in your own programs—just know that the event monitor is indeed going to be getting the events.

› When the event monitor gets an event, it needs to do something to handle the event. In a GUI, if someone clicks the mouse, the event monitor should call whatever function has been designated to handle mouse clicks. These functions that get called are known as "event handlers."

› The event handler's main job is to take in events and then call what is known as a **callback function** corresponding to that event. The callback is just a function to execute in response to an event, at which time we go back to the event handler to get the next event.

› To write an event-driven program, there are a few stages. The callback functions have to be defined on their own. These are defined just like other functions. The only difference is that different callback functions have to be ready to handle the appropriate type of parameters for the type they are. For example,a callback that handles a key being pressed on the keyboard needs to be able to take in the key that was pressed as a parameter.

```
#define functions to be used as callbacks
#initialization:
    #set up any variables, data, etc.
    #register callbacks
    #start up event monitor
```

› For the main body of the program, there's usually some initialization work that's done, just like any sequential program. As part of this initialization, callbacks need to be "registered." "Registering" a callback function is how we say what function will be called for each event that we want to respond to. So, we have to write functions for each possible event. The final step of the sequential part of the program is to start up the event monitor.

› Once the event monitor is started, it keeps running indefinitely. As events occur, it keeps calling the different callback functions. The real actions of the program happen in the callback functions.

› There's not a single, universal way that event-driven frameworks work. The way the callbacks are registered, the parameters they need to take in, and the way the event handler is started will all vary depending on what event-driven framework you're using.

› In Python, the pyglet framework is great for event-driven programming. Other frameworks are structured somewhat differently.

› Let's look at a basic pyglet program. After we download pyglet, we import pyglet using the import command. Then, we can set up a window. This window command is pyglet.window.Window, and that lets us pass in parameters that define the window. In this case, we set width to 400 and height to 300 and a caption of "TestWindow." Finally, we have the command pyglet.app.run. This last command is there to start the event handler.

```
import pyglet
window = pyglet.window.Window(width=400, height=300,
  caption="TestWindow")
pyglet.app.run()
```

› When we run this, we get a window of size 400 pixels by 300 pixels, and the name on the window is "TestWindow."

› After we set up a window, we need to register some callback functions. In addition to keyboard commands, pyglet can get input from the mouse and display images.

> We can use this functionality to develop the grid-based game we developed in Lecture 13—the one where we would move some letters around and if you had three in a row or in a column, they'd disappear. With the tools in pyglet, we can easily make a graphical version of the game.

```python
from random import choice
import pyglet
window = pyglet.window.Window(width=400, height = 450,
  caption="GameWindow")
Im1 = pyglet.image.load('BlueTri.jpg')
Im2 = pyglet.image.load('PurpleStar.jpg')
Im3 = ('OrangeDiamond.jpg')
Im4 = pyglet.image.load('YellowCircle.jpg')
Im5 = pyglet.image.load('RedHex.jpg')
def InitializeGrid(board):
    #Initialize Grid by reading in from file
    for i in range(8):
        for j in range(8):
        board[i][j] = choice(['A', 'B', 'C', 'D', 'E'])
def Initialize(board):
    #Initialize game
    #Initialize grid
    InitializeGrid(board)
    #Initialize score
    global score
    score = 0
    #Initialize turn number
    global turn
    turn = 1
    #Set up graphical info
def ContinueGame(current_score, goal_score = 100):
    #Return false if game should end, true if game is not over
    if (current_score >= goal_score):
        return False
    else:
        return True
```

```
def SwapPieces(board, move):
    #Swap objects in two positions
    temp = board[move[0]][move[1]]
    board[move[0]][move[1]] = board[move[2]][move[3]]
    board[move[2]][move[3]] = temp
def RemovePieces(board):
    #Remove 3-in-a-row and 3-in-a-column pieces
    #Create board to store remove-or-not
    remove = [[0, 0, 0, 0, 0, 0, 0, 0], [0, 0, 0, 0, 0, 0, 0, 0],
      [0, 0, 0, 0, 0, 0, 0, 0], [0, 0, 0, 0, 0, 0, 0, 0], [0, 0,
      0, 0, 0, 0, 0, 0], [0, 0, 0, 0, 0, 0, 0, 0], [0, 0, 0, 0,
      0, 0, 0, 0], [0, 0, 0, 0, 0, 0, 0, 0]]
    #Go through rows
    for i in range(8):
        for j inpyglet.image.load range(6):
            if (board[i][j] == board[i][j+1]) and (board[i][j] ==
              board[i][j+2]):
                #three in a row are the same!
                remove[i][j] = 1;
                remove[i][j+1] = 1;
                remove[i][j+2] = 1;
    #Go through columns
    for j in range(8):
        for i in range(6):
            if (board[i][j] == board[i+1][j]) and (board[i][j] ==
              board[i+2][j]):
                #three in a row are the same!
                remove[i][j] = 1;
                remove[i+1][j] = 1;
                remove[i+2][j] = 1;
    #Eliminate those marked
    global score
    removed_any = False
```

```python
        for i in range(8):
            for j in range(8):
                if remove[i][j] == 1:
                    board[i][j] = 0
                    score += 1
                    removed_any = True
        return removed_any
    def DropPieces(board):
        #Drop pieces to fill in blanks
        for j in range(8):
            #make list of pieces in the column
            listofpieces = []
            for i in range(8):
                if board[i][j] != 0:
                    listofpieces.append(board[i][j])
            #copy that list into colulmn
            for i in range(len(listofpieces)):
                board[i][j] = listofpieces[i]
            #fill in remainder of column with 0s
            for i in range(len(listofpieces), 8):
                board[i][j] = 0
    def FillBlanks(board):
        #Fill blanks with random pieces
        for i in range(8):
            for j in range(8):
                if (board[i][j] == 0):
                    board[i][j] = choice(['A', 'B', 'C', 'D', 'E'])
    def Update(board, move):
        #Update the board according to move
        SwapPieces(board, move)
        pieces_eliminated = True
        while pieces_eliminated:
            pieces_eliminated = RemovePieces(board)
            DropPieces(board)
            FillBlanks(board)
```

```python
@window.event
def on_draw():
    window.clear()
    for i in range(7,-1,-1):
        #Draw each row
        y = 50+50*i
        for j in range(8):
            #draw each piece, first getting position
            x = 50*j
            if board[i][j] == 'A':
                Im1.blit(x,y)
            elif board[i][j] == 'B':
                Im2.blit(x,y)
            elif board[i][j] == 'C':
                Im3.blit(x,y)
            elif board[i][j] == 'D':
                Im4.blit(x,y)
            elif board[i][j] == 'E':
                Im5.blit(x,y)
    label = pyglet.text.Label('Turn: '+str(turn)+'   Score:
      '+str(score), font_name='Arial', font_size=18, x=20,
      y = 10)
    label.draw()
@window.event
def on_mouse_press(x, y, button, modifiers):
    #Get the starting cell
    global startx
    global starty
    startx = x
    starty = y
@window.event
def on_mouse_release(x, y, button, modifiers):
    #Get starting and ending cell and see if they are adjacent
    startcol = startx//50
    startrow = (starty-50)//50
    endcol = x//50
    endrow = (y-50)//50
```

```
    #Check whether ending is adjacent to starting and if so,
      make move.
    if ((startcol==endcol and startrow==endrow - 1)
      or (startcol==endcol and startrow==endrow+1) or
      (startrow==endrow and startcol==endcol-1) or
      (startrow==endrow and startcol==endcol+1)):
        Update(board,[startrow,startcol,endrow,endcol])
        global turn
        turn += 1
        #See if game is over
        if not ContinueGame(score):
            print("You won in", turn, "turns!")
            exit()
#State main variables
score = 100
turn = 100
goalscore = 100
board = [[0, 0, 0, 0, 0, 0, 0, 0], [0, 0, 0, 0, 0, 0, 0, 0],
        [0, 0, 0, 0, 0, 0, 0, 0], [0, 0, 0, 0, 0, 0, 0, 0],
        [0, 0, 0, 0, 0, 0, 0, 0], [0, 0, 0, 0, 0, 0, 0, 0],
        [0, 0, 0, 0, 0, 0, 0, 0], [0, 0, 0, 0, 0, 0, 0, 0]]
#Initialize game
Initialize(board)
pyglet.app.run()
```

> The new code, using event-driven programming, is shorter than the code for the text-based game. Creating fancier interfaces doesn't have to be a huge amount of code; you can create a lot of flexible functionality easily if you have the right library—in this case, pyglet.

> Pyglet is designed to support game development and can do lots of other stuff you might want to explore. It can generate two- and three-dimensional plots, graphs, and charts. It also can play sounds and music, display images, and handle events. Pyglet lets you use a graphics library called OpenGL, which lets you make all kinds of complex three-dimensional graphics.

[TKINTER]

> Tkinter, a module that is part of the Python standard library, is useful for creating GUIs with buttons, boxes, and sliders. TK is a cross-platform toolkit that has been ported to many programming languages. Tkinter provides a binding between Python and the overall TK toolkit. The fact that it's cross-platform means that it's available for and works on most platforms.

> Although TK itself is not part of Python, it's released with Python, and the Tkinter module is built on top of it, providing an interface between Python and TK. This lets Python programmers have relatively easy access to a powerful cross-platform GUI library.

> Tkinter relies on object-oriented programming, so some of the coding might look strange on first viewing. But there is more than one way to do event-based programming, and this example will give you a sense of how an object-oriented approach to event-based programming differs, yet is also fundamentally the same.

> The following is a small program to demonstrate some really basic TK commands. It'll create two buttons: "increase" and "decrease." When you hit a button, you see a value printed out. If "increase" is hit, we double the value. If "decrease" is hit, we halve the value.

```python
import tkinter
class Application(tkinter.Frame):
    def __init__(self, master=None):
        tkinter.Frame.__init__(self, master)
        self.pack()
        self.increase_button = tkinter.Button(self)
        self.increase_button["text"] = "Increase"
        self.increase_button["command"] = self.increase_value
        self.increase_button.pack(side="right")
        self.increase_button = tkinter.Button(self)
        self.increase_button["text"] = "Decrease"
```

```
            self.increase_button["command"] = self.decrease_value
            self.increase_button.pack(side="left")
        def increase_value(self):
            global mainval
            mainval *= 2
            print (mainval)
        def decrease_value(self):
            global mainval
            mainval /= 2
            print (mainval)
    mainval = 1.0
    root = tkinter.Tk()
    app = Application(master=root)
    app.mainloop()
```

> Tkinter uses event-driven programming, just like pyglet. We start by importing the tkinter module.

> Classes are a way of grouping things together in object-oriented programming. We'll define a class that inherits from tkinter ".Frame." The section of code that is indented is what is going to describe our window and how it works. Inside of here we'll set up our buttons and the callbacks that go with each one. These things that appear in the window that a user can interact with and generate events are called **widgets**. Besides buttons, TK provides all kinds of widgets—text boxes, sliders, and so on.

> When this object is initialized, it sets up the shape of the window—that's the line "self.pack()." Tkinter will pack the widgets into the window for you with some pretty simple commands. You can create sub-windows and pack those together to design the layout the way you want.

> That routine to create the widgets creates two widgets in this case: the two buttons. Each is created by four lines of code. The first button is the "increase" button. The first line of code for that section just tells TK that we're creating a button, which we refer to by the local variable increase_button. The button is an "object," and objects will contain data called **attributes** and functions called methods.

› The second line of code for this button says that the button should display the text "increase," and it does this by setting the "text" attribute of increase_buttton.

› The third line registers our callback by setting the "command" attribute of increase_button. It says that when the button is pressed, we should call the "increase value" function.

› The fourth line says to place the button at the right of the window. It does this by calling the "pack()" method that's part of the increase_button.

› The increase value function will take a value named "mainval" (a global variable, in this case), multiply it by two, and print the new value to the output window.

› A second button is also created. The format is the same, but this one is labeled "Decrease," will call the "decrease_value" function, and is at the left of the screen. The decrease_value function is just like the increase_ value one, but it divides by two instead of multiplying by two.

› The last part of the code, in the main part of the code, will start the event handler. Specifically, there are lines to set up TK. Note that the class we just created is going to be the one defining our window and then starting the event manager—that's the final line in the code. If we run this code, we see a window come up with two buttons, doing just what we said.

Reading

Gries, *Practical Programming*, chap. 16.

Exercises

1   Using the pyglet library, write a program that draws a window and draws an image wherever a mouse is clicked.

2   Using Tkinter, create a window with a single button. Each time the button is pressed, some phrase—such as "Hello!"—should be printed several times, once more than the previous one. So, the first press should print "Hello!" once, the second press should print "Hello!" twice, etc.

Event-Driven Programming

Y ou've heard phrases like, "A picture is worth a thousand words," or "Actions speak louder than words." Well, the same thing can be true in programming and in computer interfaces. What we see in a graphical user interface, and what we do inside that graphical interface, can be more important than words. We're going to explore this visual, action-oriented style of programming: how to write a graphical user interface, also known as a GUI; and how to use a style of programming that responds to mouse clicks and other events within the graphical interface, a style known as event-driven programming. To do all of this, we're going to make use of a package called pyglet.

Pyglet is a Python package created to help support development of games and other audio-visual environments. It provides functions that let you create windows, display images and graphics, play videos and music, get input from the mouse, et cetera. There are a few other game development packages that people also use—pygame is one that's well known—and there are other modules that do individual things that pyglet does, but pyglet packages these functions together nicely and it's easy to install. Just go to the pyglet site on bitbucket.org, and you can always find pyglet through a web search.

If you're using pip to install modules such as pyglet, you should be able to install pretty easily. Remember that you can go to the command line, then to the directory where Python is installed, and type "python –m pip install pyglet"—that's P-Y-G-L-E-T—and it should install for you. Once you have pyglet downloaded, be sure to run the command "import pyglet." Only if you don't actually have pyglet installed will you see a response, so any error message probably means that pyglet hasn't yet installed properly.

Now, one form of graphics familiar to everyone on a computer these days, in practice if not by name, is the graphical user interface—that's

G-U-I or GUI. And the way a GUI works is entirely based on event-driven programming. To understand the contrast, let's think about how we've been programming up to this point.

We've been writing commands, and we expect to start at the first command and follow the commands in sequence, one after the other. Things like conditionals, or loops, or function calls might make us jump to a different line of code, but we're basically still going along in a definite sequence where we always know which line of code we'll execute next, so we can refer to this as a sequential programming.

Event-driven programming is different. Instead of a program deciding when to ask a user for input, now events outside of the program determine what the program does next. An event is anything that happens where we want the program to respond. In a GUI, an event might not only be pressing a key on the keyboard, but also clicking a button on the screen, or entering data into a box on the screen, or moving the mouse. For each of those events, the computer program needs to respond; it needs to do something—maybe just update a variable, or maybe print to the screen. Robots often use event-driven programming, which allows them to respond to events in their environment. For a robot, events might be data that comes in from a sensor—for instance, the robot detecting it's about to hit a wall. When the sensor gets this information, it needs to send it to the program to respond.

The same sort of monitoring is always underway in the graphical user interface of a computer. In any kind of event-driven programming, whenever the program runs, there's an event monitor that runs continuously in the program. There are lots of other terms for the event monitor—a main loop, or an idle function, or a control function. Regardless of which term is used, the job of the event monitor is to take in events and make sure that the appropriate function gets called in response to the event.

There's more than one way to monitor events. Sometimes the event monitor uses what are called interrupts. Basically, it just sits there happily until something interrupts it with an event. Other times, the event monitor actively polls the various devices—that is, it checks to see, "Is there a keyboard event? Is there a mouse event?" et cetera. But you don't have to worry about whether it's polling or interrupts that are monitoring events in your own programs—just know that the event monitor is indeed going to be getting the events.

Now, when the event monitor gets an event, it needs to do something to handle it. In a GUI, if someone clicks the mouse, the event monitor should call whatever function has been designated to handle mouse clicks. These functions that get called are known as event handlers. The event handler's main job, its whole purpose for being there, is to take in events and then call what is known as a callback function corresponding to that event. The callback is just a function to execute in response to an event, at which time we go back to the event handler to get the next event. We sometimes say the event handler is invoking the callback function. It makes it sound almost magical.

To write an event-driven program, there are a few stages. The callback functions have to be defined on their own. These are defined just like all the other functions we've seen. The only difference is that different callback functions have to be ready to handle the appropriate type of parameter for the type they are. So, a callback that handles a key being pressed on the keyboard needs to be able to take in the key that was pressed as a parameter.

For the main body of the program, there's usually some initialization work that's done, just like any sequential program. As part of this initialization, callbacks need to be registered. Registering a callback function is how we say what function will be called for each event that we want to respond to. So, we have to write functions for each possible event. The final step of the sequential part of the program is to start up the event monitor. Once the event monitor is started, it keeps running indefinitely. As events occur, it just keeps calling the different callback functions. The real actions of the program happen in those callback functions.

Now, there's not a single, universal way that event-driven frameworks work. The way the callbacks are registered, the parameters they need to take in, and the way the event handler is started will all vary depending on what event-driven framework you're using. In Python, the pyglet framework is great for event-driven programming. But, realize that other frameworks will be structured somewhat differently.

So, let's look at a basic pyglet program. After we download pyglet, we import pyglet using the import command. Then, we can set up a window. This window command is: "pyglet.window.Window," and that lets us pass in parameters that define the window. In this case, I set a width to 400 and a height to 300, and a caption of "TestWindow." Finally, I have the command "pyglet.app.run." This last command is there to start the event handler. Now, when we run this, what do you think we'll see?

Well, we get a window, of size 400 pixels by 300 pixels, and the name on the window is "TestWindow." We don't really have anything else at this point, and we didn't define any callback functions, so our program doesn't actually do much of anything, but you can see that we set up a window just like that.

Let's print some text in this window. In pyglet, text is printed in what's known as a label. We'll create a label, in this case, one that just says "Howdy!" We can set some details about the label: the font style—in this case, that's Times New Roman; the size of the font, which is 18 in this case; and the place we want the font to appear—in this case, we're at $x = 50$ pixels and $y = 150$ pixels. That'll be just a little bit over in the horizontal direction and up about halfway in the vertical direction.

Now, in pyglet, x and y values are given in terms of the number of pixels from the lower left corner, with x in the horizontal direction and y in the vertical. But, that's not universally true in graphics. In fact, it's fairly common in other frameworks to start from the upper left-hand corner and have y be the distance down the window. That's mainly due to a historical artifact of how graphics used to be created, but the idea has persisted. Also, sometimes x and y are not specified in pixels but rather in values relative to the current width and height. For example, there might be $x = 0$ on the left-hand side and $x = 1$ on the right-hand side, so you specify positions in between as a floating-point number between zero and one.

Now, after we set up a window, we need to register some callback functions. The first callback we'll need is for whenever we open or refresh, a window and the code looks kind of weird. The way we register a callback is with this: "@window event line." That says that we're about to define how to respond to a particular window event. The next line defines the "on_draw" function, and that means that this is the function that's going to be called when a draw event occurs in the window. Now, that might seem weird. What is a draw event? And does a user create a draw event?

Well, no, a user doesn't create a draw event, at least not directly. Remember that event-driven programming is a general idea, not one specific only to user input. In this case, the event that we're registering a callback for is whenever it's time to draw the window. As you might guess, that'll happen automatically when we first create a window, and it might happen at other times, too, like if we refresh a window, or if we have some other callback function that says, "We need to draw the window again."

So, let's look at the commands in the callback function itself. We have two of them. First, we have something that clears the window: "window. clear." We clear the window each time so that we have a nice blank canvas to work off of. After that, we have another command that draws the label: "label.draw." Notice that we took the variables we defined before—window and label—and we're calling a function by putting a dot after them and then the function name. You've seen this before, for example when we close a file. It's also an example of how we call functions in objects, which we'll discuss in later lectures.

So, what this code should do is create our window, and then clear it and draw the label inside of it. And indeed, that's exactly what it does. You might want to try messing around with this a little bit yourself. Try changing the font size and the position of the label. Or try changing the font itself and the words printed. Or, here's a challenge: try printing a second label to the window, maybe putting "Howdy" in the top left, and "World" in the lower right. Can you do this? Well, here's one way you might have done that. We'll create two labels, label1 and label2, each with different text at a different position. Then, in our draw function, we'll draw both labels.

Let's see now how we might handle a different event, say a keyboard press. This is not a string that a person types in, it's the physical key being pressed down. The event is triggered when a key is pressed down, not because it's typed in. Believe it or not, you can even get another event when the key is lifted back up again.

So, we need a callback to handle keyboard presses. The pyglet function we need is known as "on_key_press." In the code here, we define the function to change the label that's shown. Before the key press, the label's text will be, "Nothing pressed so far." When there is a key press, the event handler will call the "on_key_press" callback. It'll reset the label's text to be, "You pressed a key." Now, if we run the code, we see that the window with the text, "Nothing pressed so far," comes up. As soon as we press a key, we get the new message, "You pressed a key."

Now, the parameters are of two types. The first parameter, symbol, gives the key that was pressed. So, the symbol can be all sorts of things, like a letter, or an arrow key, or the enter key, or the delete key. The second parameter is the modifier, but we're going to ignore modifiers here. Just so you know, a modifier is a key held down in combination with another key—the shift key, or control key, or function key are all examples of this. You can even have more than one modifier active when you press a symbol key.

So, let's focus on symbol keys and say that you want to print out a key that was pressed down. As I said, this is not a string, so we can't check to see if the symbol is equal to A or something. Instead, we have to compare it to some special value that indicates the key. We can put in a check to see if the symbol variable in the callback function is equal to the special value designating that the A key was pressed. That value, which is "pyglet.window.key.A," is kind of long to keep typing. So, I'm going to go ahead and import "pyglet.window.key" on its own, to make it easier to refer to. I've changed the text to be printed to show the key pressed, and I output "unknown" otherwise.

Now, we could start checking for other key presses also, like the return key—key.RETURN—or the left arrow key—key.LEFT. See if you can modify the code to note when the return key or left arrow keys are hit. Again, the code for return is key.RETURN, with return all capitalized, and the code for left arrow is key.LEFT, with left all capitalized. Here's the code. We just add a couple of "elif" statements onto the "if" statement. If we run this code, we can see that the text changes as I hit different keys. It will tell me if I hit the A key, the left arrow, the return key, or some other key it doesn't know about.

Let's see some of the other things pyglet can do. Besides keyboard commands, it can get input from the mouse. It's really similar to what we saw before with the keyboard. One callback function is "on_mouse_press," and that'll happen whenever a mouse button is clicked down. The parameters passed in are the position of the mouse, x and y, when the button was pressed down; a button value that indicates which mouse button was pressed down; and then modifiers that indicate if there's a key being held at the same time, just like for the keyboard. So, the code you see here will indicate where a mouse button was pressed down, and write that text to the screen.

There's also a simple mouse motion command, "on_mouse_motion," that gives the current x and y position, along with the change in position that's seen in the x and y direction from the last update. If we change the callback we saw earlier to "on_mouse_motion," we can print out the current position of the mouse as we move around. There's a mouse event for releasing a button—that's "on_mouse_release." And there's a mouse event for dragging the mouse—that's "on_mouse_drag." You can see here the format needed for each of those events.

Let's see one more thing that pyglet can do, and that's display images. To use images, there are two stages: reading in an image, and then displaying an image. To read an image in, we'll use the "pyglet.image. load" command. Pyglet can load several image formats, but we'll stick to .JPG, or jpeg files. If you look at the example here, I'm loading in a file called BlueTri.jpg. That's a file I created and put in the directory where my Python code is saved. It's a small 50 × 50 image of a blue triangle on a white background, and I'm calling the loaded image file Im1—that's my shorthand for Image 1.

To display this, I use a command called "blit." Blit is short for "block image transfer," which refers to whenever two bitmaps are combined together. And that's what we're doing here—combining our jpg with the graphical window that it's going to appear inside. So, I write, "Im1.blit," and then pass in the parameters of where the lower left corner should be. If I run the code, sure enough, I get a window, and I see the image displayed right where I wanted it to be.

All right, let's put this functionality to use. Let's bring back the grid-based game that we developed in Lecture 13. This is the one where we would move some letters around, and if you had three in a row or in a column, they'd disappear. With the tools in pyglet, we can pretty easily make a graphical version of the game. Let's see how. I'll give you just a little warning—I'm going to move through this pretty quickly, so you might want to pause and think about each part that I show you instead of just rushing through it.

Here's the code from the game again. We're going to make some modifications to the way we draw the screen, and later to the way we get input. In the past, we had a "DoRound" function, and that would take care of one round: getting the user input, making the results of the move, and updating the turn. We now have to put this into an event-driven programming framework.

Drawing the board will no longer be something we call directly, but it needs to happen in response to events. We'll have an "on_draw" callback function in pyglet that should draw our current board. Likewise, we're going to get moves via the mouse. So, we don't call a "getmove" function any more, but rather we get our move by looking at where the mouse motion should be.

Let's look at the drawing function first. Instead of printing a list of characters to the screen, now we'll draw a set of shapes. So, I've created several .JPG files that can correspond to the various types of pieces. I'll load each of these into a separate image. Each is a 50 × 50 image, so my 8 × 8 board will need to be at least 400 pixels × 400 pixels. I'll create a 400 × 450 window to make sure I have enough space to write some info at the bottom of the screen.

To draw the window itself, we'll write the "on_draw" function. We start by clearing the window. We then loop through the board and draw the corresponding image per piece. Since each image is 50 × 50, we offset in *x* and *y* by 50 for every row and column. And, when we draw each image, we pick one of the five images, depending on the piece that's there. At the bottom, we create a label in which we print out the turn and the score.

OK. Now, getting a move is going to be done through a combination of functions. We'll let the player click on one square, and then try to drag it to an adjacent cell and release, in order to make a move. To find the initial cell, we'll have to get the square in which they click the mouse, and so that will be the "on_mouse_press" callback. Basically, all we need to do at this point is store the starting point. We don't even know if it's a valid move yet until we figure out where the player releases the mouse.

Now, finding the final cell will happen when the mouse button is released, and that will be the "on_mouse_release" command. So, let's look at this code a little bit closer. First, we convert our window positions to row and column positions on our grid—this is just mathematics. Since every grid cell takes up 50 pixels, we divide by 50 to get the position in the grid. Notice that we're using the double slash instead of a single slash for division. You might remember that this is integer division, and it returns the integer part of the quotient, ignoring any remainder. Also, notice that since we left a gap at the bottom of the screen to write the score, we have to subtract 50 from the *y* value. Now, we do this for both the start position and the end position, and this gives us our row and column for each one. And we then check to see if we had a valid move. Basically, we need to either have the same row with the column different by exactly one, or the same column with the row different by one. If that's the case, then we have a valid move.

For a valid move, we call update, passing in the board and the move. And we also update the turn and check to see if we won, and thus can stop. Now, one thing that's different here is the way we specified the move. In the text-based version of the game, our move was a letter for the column and a number for the row, and then a direction for where to swap. This was only done to make things easier for the user to type in. But all that first part, where we get the original row and column and have to call "ConvertLetterToCol," and then go through all these "if-elif" statements—all of that's totally unnecessary now. Now that we have a graphical interface, there's no need for any of it. We already have the beginning and end positions. Instead, we can just pass in the row and column for the beginning and end. We do this as a single list, containing four numbers: the starting row and column, and the ending row and column.

The update function doesn't actually do anything with this move besides pass it on to the "SwapPieces" function. That's where we need to make a change. Look at the old "SwapPieces" function. Think about how to update it to make use of the way we specify the move now. Now remember, we already have the beginning and ending positions—they're just the four elements of the list that we pass in as move. So, we can delete that whole first part of the function, everything except the swap part itself. We then need to make a change to the swap part.

And, here's what that looks like. It's the same set of commands that we had before. We're going to swap by putting the first piece into a temporary variable, then moving the second piece into the first slot, then moving from the temporary variable into the second slot. The only difference from what we had in an earlier version is that we're using the indices passed in as the move parameter in order to reference the rows and columns. So, move-sub-zero and move-sub-1 are the original row and column, while move-sub-2 and move-sub-3 are the new row and column.

The only other change is that in the main part of the code, we need to end by starting the event handler. This goes in the main function. That's the "pyglet.app.run" command—the rest of the code is the same. So, if we run this, we can see all the elements, and we can use our mouse to choose which one to move where. For example, if we take this square, and we move it over to this other one, we line up several pieces in a row, they disappear, and the board updates.

Now, compared to a professional game, this probably looks kind of clunky. We aren't focused on graphic design, and I'm not much of an artist, and there's much more that could be done to make it look pretty. We could add additional things like flashes when something's deleted. Each improvement to the look of the game is just more code.

Anyway, the key code for the game is what we already have right here. And what's really surprising is this—the new code, using event-driven programming, is actually shorter than the code for the text-based game. Remember, we were able to get rid of a lot of code to do things like convert letters to columns, and there were several routines no longer called that we can just delete. So, creating fancier interfaces doesn't have to be a huge amount of code—you can create a lot of flexible functionality easily if you have the right library. In this case, that was pyglet.

Pyglet is actually designed to support game development and can do a lot of other stuff that you might want to explore. It can generate 2-D and 3-D plots, graphs, and charts; it can play sounds and music; display images; and, of course, handle events. Pyglet lets you use a graphics library called OpenGL, and that lets you make all sorts of complex 3-D graphics. Now, 3-D graphics could easily be a whole course of its own. The point here is that you can build on pyglet, or find another module to handle events and do whatever you want to do.

Now, speaking of finding another module, let me mention a part of the Python standard library called Tkinter, which is useful for creating graphical user interfaces with buttons, boxes, and sliders. TK is a cross-platform toolkit that's been ported to many programming languages. What Tkinter does is provide a binding between Python and the overall TK toolkit. The fact that it's cross-platform means it's available for, and it works on most platforms—Windows, OS X, and Linux. And, although TK itself is not part of Python, it's released with Python, and the Tkinter module is built on top of it, providing an interface between Python and

TK. This lets Python programmers have relatively easy access to a powerful cross-platform GUI library.

Tkinter relies on object-oriented programming, so some of the coding might look a little strange on first viewing. But there's more than one way to do event-based programming, and this example will give you a sense of how an object-oriented approach to event-based programming differs, yet is still fundamentally the same.

Here's a small program to demonstrate some really basic TK commands. It'll create two buttons: increase and decrease. When you hit a button, you see a value printed out. If increase is hit, we double the value; if decrease is hit, we halve the value—simple. I'll highlight the various parts of this code, and if you're interested in finding out more about the details, you should be able to investigate more on your own. Again, remember that some of this will make a little more sense after we've talked about object-oriented programming.

Tkinter uses event-driven programming, just like pyglet. We start by importing the Tkinter module. Classes are a way of grouping things together in object-oriented programming. We'll define a class that inherits from "tkinter.Frame." This section of code, all the indented stuff, is what's going to describe our window and how it works. Inside of here, we'll set up our buttons and the callbacks that go with each one. Now, these things that appear in the window that a user can interact with and generate events with are called widgets. Besides buttons, TK provides all sorts of widgets—textboxes, sliders, and so on. When this object is initialized, it sets up the shape of the window—that's the line "self. pack." Tkinter will pack the widgets into the window for you with some pretty simple commands. You can create sub-windows and pack those together in order to design the layout the way you want.

That routine to create the widgets creates two widgets in this case— the two buttons. Each is created by four lines of code. The first button is the increase button. The first line of code for that section just tells TK that we're creating a button, which we refer to by the local variable increase_button. The button is an object, and objects will contain data called attributes, and functions called methods, and this is what we'll discuss when we talk about object-oriented programming. The second line of code for this button says that the button should display the text "increase," and it does this by setting the text attribute of increase_ button.

The third line registers our callback by setting the command attribute of increase_button. It says that when the button is pressed, we should call the "increase_value" function. Finally, the fourth line says to place the button at the right of the window. It does this by calling the pack method that's part of the increase_button. The "increase_value" function will just take a value named mainval, multiply it by two, and print the new value to the output window. Mainval is a global variable in this case.

A second button is also created. The format is the same, but this one will be labeled "decrease," and it will call the "decrease_value" function, and it's at the left of the screen. The "decrease_value" function is just like the "increase_value" one, but it divides by two instead of multiplying by two.

Finally, the last part of the code, in the main part of the code, will start the event handler. Specifically, there are lines to set up TK, note that the class we just created is going to be the one defining our window, and then starting the event manager—that's that final line of code. If we run this, we do indeed see a window come up with two buttons, doing just what we said.

Now, even though that code looked quite different from the event-driven programming in pyglet, you can see that the concepts are similar. We still have an event handler that will run until an event occurs. We have callback functions that are registered to the different events. In pyglet, the events were basic user input—pressing a button, moving a mouse, and so on. In Tkinter, the events are tied into the widgets—like buttons, sliders, and so on—so that the programmer sets things up, and then those events get called. Both modules also support graphical display, with pyglet focused more on basic graphics like images and 3-D graphics, and Tkinter focused more on creating interactive windows with widgets. To gain greater familiarity with these approaches, I'd encourage you to play around with pyglet, Tkinter, or a similar package, and explore some ways to make programs that you've already written more graphical.

Event-driven programming is widespread, used in everything from robotic sensors, to network data communication, to graphical user interfaces, including many that appear on the web. Event-driven programming is usually what's responsible whenever you press buttons, or fill out a form with boxes where you enter data and then press a button, or move a slider, or hit enter on a text box. All of those will trigger some event in the program.

The same kind of graphics-based functionality is also present in everything from software applications on a computer to apps downloaded on a smartphone. Best of all, as we've seen, event-driven programming can make possible much more impressive graphical displays without necessarily requiring a lot more work.

In our next lecture, we're going to be using programming to create graphical displays of data, as well as explore how we can create simulations of data that may be difficult or impossible to obtain directly. Far more than most people realize, computer simulations of many kinds influence everything from public policy to our personal lives, so I'll look forward to showing you more then.

Visualizing Data and Creating Simulations

O ne particularly useful aspect of computation is to simulate what might happen in the real world, test scenarios, and understand the range of options. Visualizing data is a key part of this. Taken together, the decisions made based on simulations have consequences measured in the trillions of dollars, are sometimes matters of life and death, and affect practically everyone on the planet. Computers are famous for handling data, but data visualization and data simulation are two areas that often go under-recognized. In this lecture, you will learn how to do both.

[DATA VISUALIZATIONS]

> One of the best packages to create visualizations of data is matplotlib. It has a very wide range of capabilities and is probably the most well-known and popular Python package for creating plots, graphs, and charts from data.

> The first step is to install matplotlib. One option is to use pip. If pip is installed, you should be able to go to your Python directory in the command line and type "python −m pip install matplotlib." If you aren't using pip, you can find out the details of how to install matplotlib at the matplotlib.org website. Installing matplotlib will require installing several other libraries, too.

> With matplotlib installed, let's start by making a basic display. We'll first import pyplot from matplotlib. Then, we'll use the pyplot.axes function, which basically says that we're going to have a data plot that uses axes. We could provide parameters to specify the appearance and range of these axes, but we don't provide any parameters—we can just use the defaults.

> Finally, once we've created a data plot, we'll need to show it, so we call show.

```
from matplotlib import pyplot
pyplot.axes()
pyplot.show()
```

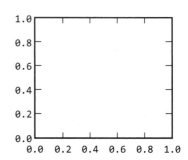

> If we run this, we see that matplotlib has created a plot with axes in the range of 0 to 1 in both *x* and *y*. And it includes some graphical tools at the bottom that let you interact with the chart by zooming in, moving around, or saving it.

> We learn how to use graphical tools like this by looking at the documentation. In particular, the API is the application programming interface. The API documentation lists the various commands that are provided and the details of how each is used.

> For matplotlib, you can see the key plotting commands if you follow the link at the top of the page to "pyplot." That gives you a whole list of commands provided in pyplot, and if you click on each of them, it will give you a more detailed description of what the command does and what parameters it takes in.

> The plot command can take in few lists. The first one gives all the *x*-values. The second one gives all the *y*-values. In this case, we're using the *x*-values from 0 to 5, and then for the *y*-values, we're using the square of the *x*-values.

```
from matplotlib import pyplot
pyplot.plot([0,1,2,3,4,5], [0,1,4,9,16,25])
pyplot.axis([0,5,0,25])
pyplot.show()
```

> Also, notice that we're now passing a parameter to the axis command. The parameter is a list of four numbers, giving the minimum and maximum extents for the *x*-axis and the minimum and maximum for the *y*-axis. In this case, we say that the *x*-axis will go from 0 to 5 and the *y*-axis will go from 0 to 25. Running this gives the plot we'd expect.

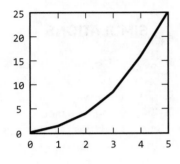

> The following is a more compact version that makes the same plot. Notice that instead of manually making the lists, we made a list of *x*-values using the range command. Then, we built a list of *y*-values by going through the *x*-values and appending the square of that *x*-value onto the list.

```
from matplotlib.pyplot import plot, axis, show
xlist = range(0,6)
ylist = []
for i in xlist:
    ylist.append(i*i)
plot(xlist, ylist)
axis([0,5,0,25])
show()
```

> Also, notice that we're just importing functions from pyplot to make things simpler. Instead of having to write "pyplot" in front of each, we can write "plot," "axis," or "show" directly. And if we run this, we get the same results we had with the previous case.

> There are many ways to improve and change graphs. There are many options in the mathplotlib module—not only for how to do line plots, but also for numerous other types of charts and graphs. It's relatively easy to show many different graphical representations of data, and once you create the representation, it's also easy to incorporate graphical output into any larger program.

[SIMULATIONS]

› Beyond visualizing the data we have, there's also data we would like to have but don't. This brings us to **simulations**. When we talk about simulations, we normally mix two ideas that are very related but distinct. The first idea is a **model**, which tells us what the laws, rules, or processes that we are trying to compute should follow. The actual simulation takes the model and some set of conditions and uses it to determine how the situation develops, usually over time.

› The model is the most important thing about the whole simulation process. If the model is incorrect, it doesn't matter how good the computer is at performing the simulation—it won't get the correct answer. It's also very important to have the correct initial conditions. Sometimes even tiny errors in initial conditions can have large effects later.

› For a typical simulation, we're given a model of behavior and some initial condition. We refer to the overall values we want to simulate as the **state** of the system. The initial conditions will be a starting state (S_0) at a starting time (t_0). Then, we are given some time in the future that we want to simulate to (T).

› We're also given what is called a **time step** (h). The idea is that we're going to take steps forward in time by that amount. That will let us determine a new state at that new time. We'll call this sequence of states S_i and the sequence of times t_i. This will continue until we've reached the total time we want to simulate, T.

› Let's say that we want to see how an account accumulates interest over time. Suppose that we use $1000 to buy a 10-year certificate of deposit that earns 3% per year. We want to see how that grows over time.

> In this context, our model is the increase in interest rate—basically, that our value increases by 3% per year. Our initial state (S_0) is the initial balance, or $1000. And we'll call this year 0—the starting point of the simulation. The simulation will go forward in steps of 1 year, and we'll simulate up to 10 years. So, the simulation loop itself will repeat while t_i is less than 10 and each time will calculate the balance 1 year later.

> The code is as follows. We'll use the variable time to keep track of time (t) and the variable balance to keep track of our state, and we'll initialize each of these to our starting conditions—time 0 and $1000 balance. Each of these is going to be stored in a list—"timelist" or "balancelist"—so that we can keep track of growth over time.

```
#Set initial conditions
time = 0
balance = 1000
#Set list to store data
timelist=[time]
balancelist=[balance]
while (time < 10):
    #Increase balance and time
    balance += balance*0.03
    time += 1
    #Store time and balance in lists
    timelist.append(time)
    balancelist.append(balance)
#Output the simulation results
for i in range(len(timelist)):
    print("Year:", timelist[i], "  Balance:", balancelist[i])
```

> We then have our simulation loop. In the loop, we increase the balance by 3% and the time by 1. We store these in the time and balance lists. And this continues until we've done this for 10 years. At the end, we print everything out.

> If we wanted a graph of the data, it's a simple matter of importing pyplot commands from matplotlib and calling plot and show.

```
from matplotlib.pyplot import plot, show
#Set initial conditions
time = 0
balance = 1000
#Set list to store data
timelist=[time]
balancelist=[balance]
while (time < 10):
    #Increase balance and time
    balance += balance*0.03
    time += 1
    #Store time and balance in lists
    timelist.append(time)
    balancelist.append(balance)
#Output the simulation results
for i in range(len(timelist)):
    print("Year:", timelist[i], "  Balance:", balancelist[i])
plot(timelist, balancelist)
show()
```

> We get an output showing an exponential growth pattern over the years.

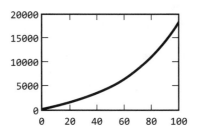

[MONTE CARLO SIMULATIONS]

> The model can be any kind of process. In many scientific simulations, the model is a set of differential equations. But let's focus on a particular class of simulations called **Monte Carlo simulations**. Monte Carlo simulations are based on the idea of simulating lots of random events, but doing it enough times that the overall outcome will be more understandable. A Monte Carlo approach is used in all kinds of simulations, from fluid physics to finance, especially situations in which there is a lot of uncertainty to include.

> Let's look at a simulation of finances, in which you take some set of investments and see how likely they are to meet your retirement goals. Let's start with the previous example, where we examined the growth in a certificate of deposit over a period of time. We can modify the code from that simulation as follows to handle more general investments.

```
from matplotlib.pyplot import plot, show
#Set initial conditions
time = 0
balance = 1000
#Set list to store data
timelist=[time]
balancelist=[balance]
while (time < 10):
    #Increase balance and time
    balance += balance*0.03
    time += 1
    #Store time and balance in lists
    timelist.append(time)
    balancelist.append(balance)
#Output the simulation results
for i in range(len(timelist)):
    print("Year:", timelist[i], "  Balance:", balancelist[i])
plot(timelist, balancelist)
show()
```

> We're going to start by changing the way we compute the change per year. We're going to follow the principle of abstraction to make a separate function that will calculate how the investment will increase (or decrease) in any particular year.

> So, we'll create a function, "ChangeInBalance," that takes in the current balance as a parameter and returns how much it changes 1 year later. In the earlier case, we had a 3% interest rate, so the change in balance is 3% of the original balance. In our simulation loop, each iteration of the loop increases the balance by ChangeInBalance.

```python
from matplotlib.pyplot import plot, show
def ChangeInBalance(initial_balance):
    return initial_balance*0.03
#Set initial conditions
time = 0
balance = 1000
#Set list to store data
timelist=[time]
balancelist=[balance]
while (time < 10):
    #Increase balance and time
    balance += ChangeInBalance(balance)
    time += 1
    #Store time and balance in lists
    timelist.append(time)
    balancelist.append(balance)
#Output the simulation results
for i in range(len(timelist)):
    print("Year:", timelist[i], "  Balance:", balancelist[i])
plot(timelist, balancelist)
show()
```

> Unless we have some "guaranteed" investment, such as a certificate of deposit, the amount that the investment increases or decreases changes with time. Interest rates go up and down, and for investments that are traded, the fluctuations can be quite significant.

> Suppose that we have an investment that we know can fluctuate, but the return will never be negative. Instead of increasing our balance by 3% each year, we might change the balance by a random percentage. A simple way to do this might be to imagine that we can select a maximum level, and a minimum level, and every rate in between is equally likely.

> We could modify our code to pick a random rate of return each year for that investment. We import the random module. We then use the uniform command to pick a random rate in between some maximum and minimum. Let's say that our rate of return will be between 0% and 6%.

```python
import random
from matplotlib.pyplot import plot, show
def ChangeInBalance(initial_balance):
    rate = random.uniform(0.0, 0.06)
    return initial_balance*rate
#Set initial conditions
time = 0
balance = 1000
#Set list to store data
timelist=[time]
balancelist=[balance]
while (time < 10):
    #Increase balance and time
    balance += ChangeInBalance(balance)
    time += 1
    #Store time and balance in lists
    timelist.append(time)
    balancelist.append(balance)
#Output the simulation results
for i in range(len(timelist)):
    print("Year:", timelist[i], "  Balance:", balancelist[i])
plot(timelist, balancelist)
show()
```

> We can run this code and see what the results would be. Every time we run the code, we get a different result. Over the 10 years, the results tend to come out pretty similarly, because the variations will tend to average out.

> If we want to get an even better sense of what the overall performance is likely to be, we can run this code multiple times. To do this, we need to essentially wrap up the simulation into another loop that will run the simulation over and over. And we need to store the results from each time we do that loop.

> We're going to get rid of the lists of the balances year by year and only store the final balances in a list. We'll also generalize things so that the number of years in the simulation and the total number of simulations are single variables that are easy to change.

> We still start with our function that computes the change in balance. We'll then have a loop for however many simulations we need. In each of them, we'll start at time 0, and with a balance of $1000, and simulate for a few years, just like before. We'll store the final balance into the final balances array. After this loop, we can print out all the final balances we found.

```python
import random
def ChangeInBalance(initial_balance):
    rate = random.uniform(0.0, 0.06)
    return initial_balance*rate
number_years = 10
number_sims = 100
final_balances = []
for i in range(number_sims):
    #Set initial conditions
    time = 0
    balance = 1000
    while (time < number_years):
        #Increase balance and time
        balance += ChangeInBalance(balance)
        time += 1
```

```
        final_balances.append(balance)
    #Output the simulation results
    for i in range(number_sims):
        print("Final Balance:", final_balances[i])
```

> Given the results of all those runs, we can replace a simple printout of the values with a histogram to plot the results. The "hist" command in matplotlib will take in a list of results—the final balances, in this case—and plot a histogram. We set the number of bins in this case equal to 20, and we'll run 10,000 experiments.

```
import random
from matplotlib.pyplot import hist, show
def ChangeInBalance(initial_balance):
    rate = random.uniform(0.0, 0.06)
    return initial_balance*rate
number_years = 10
number_sims = 10000
final_balances = []
for i in range(number_sims):
    #Set initial conditions
    time = 0
    balance = 1000
    while (time < number_years):
        #Increase balance and time
        balance += ChangeInBalance(balance)
        time += 1
    final_balances.append(balance)
#Output the simulation results
hist(final_balances, bins=20)
show()
```

> When we run this, we get a wide distribution of results, from cases where we earned small amounts of interest to those where we earned a lot.

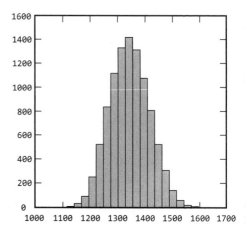

> To understand overall performance, we can compute some basic statistics on the final balances. To help with this, we can use the "statistics" module that's part of the Python standard library. It has functions such as "mean" and "stdev" to calculate the overall mean and standard deviation of a list. So, we can modify our code to import the statistics module, and then at the end of the program, we print out the average and standard deviation from all of our runs.

Readings

Matthes, *Python Crash Course*, chap. 15.

Zelle, *Python Programming*, chap. 9.

Exercise

Imagine that you are rolling 3 dice and are interested in the sum of those dice. Use a Monte Carlo simulation to simulate 10,000 rolls of 3 dice. Use matplotlib to plot a histogram of the results.

Visualizing Data and Creating Simulations

Computers are famous for handling data, but data visualization and data simulation are two areas that often go underrecognized. Let's learn how to do both of these. One of the best packages to create visualizations of data is matplotlib. It has a very wide range of capabilities and is probably the most well-known and popular Python package for creating plots, graphs, and charts from data.

You're going to want to install matplotlib first. One option is to use pip. If pip is installed, you should be able to go to your python directory in the command line and type "python –m pip install matplotlib." If you aren't using pip, you can find out the details of how to install matplotlib at the matplotlib.org website.

OK, with matplotlib installed, let's start by making a really basic display. You can think of this like the "Hello, World" version of matplotlib. We'll first import pyplot from matplotlib. We'll then use the pyplot.axes function, which basically says we're going to have a data plot that uses axes. Now we could provide parameters to specify the appearance and range of these axes. But if we don't provide any parameters, we can just use the defaults. And finally, once we've created a data plot, we'll need to show it, so we call show.

If we run this, we see that matplotlib has created a plot for us with axes in the range of 0 to 1 in both x and y. And, it includes some graphical tools at the bottom that let you interact with the chart by zooming in, or moving around, or saving it.

OK, let's see how to display some data using the plot command. The plot command can take in a couple of lists. The first one gives all the x values. The second one gives all the y values. In this case, I'm using the x values from 0–5, and then for the y values, I'm using the square of the x values.

Also, notice that we're now passing a parameter to the axis command. The parameter is a list of 4 numbers, giving the minimum and maximum extents for the x-axis, and the minimum and maximum for the y-axis. In this case, we say the x-axis will go from 0 to 5 and the y-axis from 0 to 25. Running this code gives the plot just like we'd expect.

Here's a more compact version that makes the same plot. Notice that instead of manually making the lists, I made a list of x values using the range command. Then, I built a list of y values by going through the x values and appending the square of that x value onto the list. Also, notice that we're just importing functions from pyplot, to make things simpler. Instead of having to write "pyplot" in front of each, I can write "plot," "axis" or "show" directly. And, if we run this, we get the same results we saw in the previous case.

Now, there are a lot of ways to improve and change graphs. Say I wanted the plot to be a red line, and each of the points to be marked with a blue cross. And, imagine that I wanted a label for the graph, like "squares." So, in code, we would set some of the parameter values we were letting go to the default previously. We can set "squares" for the label, note that we want a marker that's a plus sign and that the marker should be in blue, and make the color of the graph itself red. For each of these, we list the parameter and the value that we want it to take. And, there's a new command, legend, that we have to import from pyplot. To display the name of the plot, we import the legend command from matplotlib. pyplot. When we run this, we see it that indeed creates a red line with blue crosses marking each data point.

We can also print two plots on the same graph. In this case, we'll create a set of cubes. We'll plot that one in green with green circles marking the data points. All it takes is to create another list of y values and then to call plot a second time, with the parameters for the second plot we want. And, we see a plot of this data, with the cubes and squares drawn in the different colors just like we specified.

We can even have different y-axes for different plots. This gets a lot more complicated to show, but here we have 3 different vertical axes, showing three different data sets being plotted. When we see this plot, we see that we can color code based on the data set; we can show multiple graphs, et cetera.

Let's say that we wanted to graph the amount of a mortgage over time. Here's what the code might look like. We could first get the amount of the mortgage, the interest rate, and the monthly payment from the user. Then, we can generate values for each month. We'll keep this up until we've reduced the mortgage to zero or gone through 30 years. Each month we'll do several things. First, we'll update a month array with a new month. We'll also add on to three other arrays. First, we compute what the amount of interest generated in a month is. We then figure out how much of the payment went to interest vs. principal. Each of these is recorded in a list, as is the amount of the mortgage remaining.

We can easily print out the data using our plot commands. We use a red line to show the remaining mortgage, a blue one for the total principal paid, and a green one for the total interest paid. If we run this, and we enter some basic data, say a mortgage of $100,000, a 5% interest rate, and a paycheck of just $1000, we indeed see a plot showing how these values vary over time.

There are many other options in the matplotlib module. Not only for how to do line plots like this, but also for numerous other types of charts and graphs. The point is that it's relatively easy to show many different graphical representations of data. And once you create the representation, it's also easy to incorporate graphical output into any larger program.

Beyond visualizing the data we have, there's also data we would like to have, but don't. This brings us to simulations. A desire for simulations motivated development of the earliest computers. Harvard's Mark I computer did simulations for the U.S. Navy and the Manhattan Project during World War II. After the war, ENIAC, the first fully electronic computer, simulated ballistic trajectories for the U.S. Army starting in 1946.

Now, when we talk about simulations, we normally mix two ideas, that are very related but distinct. The first idea is a model. A model tells us what the laws, rules, or process that we are trying to compute. The actual simulation takes the model and some set of conditions and uses it to determine how the situation develops, usually over time. So, if we want to simulate a comet in our solar system that might be heading toward Earth, our model would describe gravity of the sun and planets. The initial condition would give the starting position and velocity of the comet. Then the simulation would be used to predict where the comet would be in the future.

The thing to realize is that the model is the most important thing about the whole simulation process. If the model is incorrect, it doesn't matter how good the computer is at performing the simulation—it won't get the right answer. If our model of gravity is wrong, then our prediction about the path of the comet will be wrong. If our model of how a hurricane moves is wrong, then our predictions of hurricane paths won't be accurate. It's also very important to have the correct initial conditions. If we try to predict the path of a comet, but our starting position is wrong, we could end up computing a completely wrong path. Sometimes even tiny errors in initial conditions can have large effects later on.

You've probably heard the phrase "garbage in—garbage out" before. If your model or initial conditions are garbage, the output will be, also. It doesn't matter how great a programmer is, how sophisticated a simulation is, or how powerful a computer is—if the model or initial conditions are wrong, the result is unreliable.

For a typical simulation, we're given a model of behavior and some initial condition. We refer to the overall values that we're wanting to simulate as the state of the system. The initial conditions will be a starting state S_0, at a starting time T_0. Then, we are given some time in the future that we want to simulate to, T. And, we're given what's called a timestep, which is usually stated as h. That's in honor of 19th-century English physicist Oliver Heaviside, who pioneered a widely used step function in calculus. The idea is that we're going to take steps forward in time by that amount, h. That will let us determine a new state at that new time. We'll call this sequence of states S_i and the sequence of times t_i. This will continue until we've reached the total time we want to simulate, T.

Let's say that we want to see how an account accumulates interest over time. Suppose we use $1000 to buy a 10-year certificate of deposit that earns 3% per year. We want to see how that grows over time.

Remember what should be needed for our simulation. In this context, our model is the increase in interest rate: basically that our value increases by 3% per year. Our initial state S_0 is the initial balance, or $1000. And, we'll call this year 0—the starting point of the simulation. The simulation will go forward in steps of 1 year, and we'll simulate up to 10 years. So, the simulation loop itself will repeat while t_i is less than 10, and each time will calculate the balance one year later.

Let's see what the code for that will look like. We'll use the variable time to keep track of time t, and the variable balance to keep track of our state, and we'll initialize each of these to our starting conditions—time 0 and $1000 balance. Each of these is going to be stored in a list—timelist or balancelist so that we can keep track of growth over time. We then have our simulation loop. In the loop, we increase the balance by 3%, and the time by 1. We store these in the time and balance lists. And, this continues until we've gone for 10 years. At the end, we print everything out.

If we wanted a graph of the data, it's a simple matter of importing pyplot commands from matplotlib, and calling plot and show. And, we get an output showing an exponential growth pattern over the years.

The model can be any sort of process. In a lot of scientific simulations, the model is a set of differential equations. But for the rest of this lecture, I want to focus on a particular class of simulations called Monte Carlo simulations. Now, when I say Monte Carlo you might think of the famous casino in Monaco. If you think of casinos and gambling, you should think about probabilities, and how casinos make money. Although the result of any one roll of the dice or spin of the wheel might be random, they know that over time, there will be a certain percentage of the time that they win.

Monte Carlo simulations are based on the idea of simulating lots of random events, but doing it enough times that the overall outcome will be more understandable. A Monte Carlo approach is used in all sorts of simulations, from fluid physics to finance, especially situations in which there's a lot of uncertainty to include. So, in the rest of this lecture, we're going to look at how we'd make a larger program that incorporates uncertainty and allows us to understand the range of possibilities that can occur.

We're going to be looking at a simulation of finances. You might have seen something like this before—where you take some set of investments, and you see how likely they are to meet your retirement goals. Let's start with our previous example, where we examined the growth in a certificate of deposit over a period of time. We can modify the code from that simulation to handle more general investments.

We're going to start by changing the way we compute the change per year. We're going to follow the principle of abstraction to make a separate function that will calculate how the investment will increase, or decrease in any particular year. So, we'll create a function, ChangeInBalance, that takes in the current balance as a parameter, and returns how much it changes one year later. In the earlier case, we had a 3% interest rate, so the change in balance is 3% of the original balance. In our simulation loop, each iteration of the loop increases the balance by ChangeInBalance.

Unless we have some guaranteed investment like a certificate of deposit, the amount that the investment increases or decreases will change itself over time. Interest rates go up and down, and for investments that are traded, like stocks and mutual funds, the fluctuations can be really significant. Suppose we have an investment that we know can fluctuate, but the return will never be negative. Instead of increasing our balance by 3% each year, we might change the balance by a random percentage. A simple way to do this might be to imagine that we can select a maximum level, and a minimum level and every rate in between is equally likely.

We could modify our code to pick a random rate of return each year for that investment. We import the random module. And, then we use the uniform command to pick a random rate in between some maximum and minimum. Let's say our rate of return will be between 0% and 6%. We can run this code, and see what the results would be. Every time we run the code, we get a different result. Now, over the 10 years, it tends to come out pretty similar, since the variations will tend to average out. But, each time we run, we get a slightly different behavior.

Now, if we want to get an even better sense of what the overall performance is likely to be, we can run this code multiple times. To do this, we need to essentially wrap up the simulation inside of another loop that will run the simulation over and over. And, we need to store the results from each time we do that loop.

Let's see what that'll look like. We're going to get rid of the lists of the balances year-by-year and only store the final balances in a list. We'll also generalize things so that the number of years in the simulation and the total number of simulations are single variables that are easy to change. We still start with our function that computes the change in balance. We'll then have a loop for however many simulations we need. In each of them, we'll start at time 0, and with a balance of $1000, and we simulate for a few years, just like before. We'll store the final balance into the final balances array. After this loop, we can print out all the final balances we found.

Given the results of all those runs, we can replace a simple printout of the values with a nice histogram to plot the results. We can use the hist command in matplotlib. That will take in a list of results, which in this case is the final balances, and plot a histogram. We set the number of bins in this case to equal 20, and we'll run 10,000 experiments. You can see that when we run this, we get a wide distribution of results, from cases where we earned small amounts of interest to those where we earned a whole lot.

Furthermore, it's a relatively simple task to make our model more realistic. Say that instead of a random percentage increase between 0 and 6, you instead wanted to pick a random percentage from a normal bell-curve distribution, with an average of 3% and a standard deviation of 2%. How might you do this?

Well, you'd want to change your random function. In this case, we could use the "gauss" or the "normalvariate" function in the random library to create this distribution. In this case, I used "gauss," which is short for "Gaussian"—the normal bell curve distribution that we're familiar with. Because we've separated out the ChangeInBalance routine, it's easy to change to a different model where we calculate the change by some other mechanism.

Say, for example, that we wanted to simulate a stock fund. We could take a historical list of yearly increases or decreases in the S&P 500, and just select one of those. We would need to load in a list of yearly returns, and then randomly select one of the elements of the list, and use that percentage increase or decrease. In this case, I've made a list of 70 years worth of data, and I've hard coded it, but we could read data from a file. Then, we use the "choice" function from the random module to pick one of those 70 returns. If we run this code, we'll see a pretty wide range of outcomes, from ones where we actually lose a little money to ones where we make more than 10 times what we started with.

Let's say that we want to understand that overall performance. We can compute some basic statistics on the final balances. To help with this, we can use the "statistics" module that's part of the Python standard library. It has functions such as "mean" and "stdev," or standard deviation to calculate the overall mean and standard deviation of a list. The larger the standard deviation, the more volatile our investment is. So, we can modify our code to import the statistics module, and then at the end of the program, we print out the average and the standard deviation from all of our runs. If we run this code, we see we get a pretty high balance, and we also a pretty big standard deviation.

Different types of accounts will tend to have different performance characteristics. Stocks will tend to fluctuate a lot in price, but tend to do best on average. Bonds don't do as well as stocks on average, but the drops, as well as gains, will tend to be smaller. Money in cash, like savings accounts, will tend to fluctuate the least, but it'll have the worst average performance. If we have a different set of data, say for bond yields, we can calculate how a bond investment would perform.

So, here I've pulled out a set of bond rates, which I've again hard coded in to the program. I'll pull out a set of bond rates, and see how we might do if we had an account that earned that rate each year, instead of the stock market rate. In fact, we'll simulate both accounts. First, we have a list of historical bond yields. Next, we create a second function to compute the increase in balance for bonds, and we rename the one for stocks so that they're clearly different. So, ChangeInBalanceStocks will compute the change in balance assuming a stock account, and ChangeInBalanceBonds will compute the change in balance assuming a bond account. We'll basically keep track of everything else in pairs. We keep "balance_stocks" for stocks and "balance_bonds" for bonds, and we keep separate lists of final balances for each, as well. We update each one using the appropriate ChangeInBalance function. At the end, we will compute the mean and standard deviation for each of them separately. And, we can show a histogram of these two options, together in one plot. The way we do that is to make a list of the two lists and send that as a parameter.

Now, if we run the code, we'll see a plot showing both stock performance and bond performance. We can see in the histogram that the bonds have a much narrower range of outcomes than the stocks. And, if we look at the statistics that we printed out, we'll see that indeed, our stock funds have a higher average final balance, but also have a significantly higher standard deviation. Now, often people will not have all their money in one kind of account, like all in stocks or all in bonds. A more common approach will be to split the savings into two groups, such as half in a stock account, and half in a bond account. We can easily modify our code to see what that would look like.

Here we've created a third type of account, which we'll call the "mixed" account. We'll keep track of two balances in each iteration: the mixed balance for stocks and the mixed balance for bonds. In this case, I'll assume a 50/50 split between stock and bonds, so each of these will start with $500, keeping the total at $1000. Then, each year, we'll increase the mixed stock and the mixed bond accounts separately. After the new values are determined for each, we can look at the overall balance, and see whether they are out of balance. We can calculate what 50% of the total was—this is the stock amount, and then the difference that we need to move from stocks to bonds or vice versa. Each year we'll do that rebalancing. One other change—rather than computing the two groups totally independently, we'll pick a year at random, and use the stock and bond data from that same year. Stock and bond performance can be related to each other, so we want to make sure we use comparable data for each. That means that we pick one of 35 years, and we pick the stock and the bond data for that year.

Again, running the code will show us a plot and the statistics we calculated. We can see that, like we'd expect, the mixed account will be in between the stock and the bond accounts in terms of average and in terms of standard deviation.

Now, what I've described is a relatively simple analysis, and there are some shortcomings. For instance, I'm just using some approximate overall stock and bond performances—particular types of stocks and bonds will perform differently. My point is not to make you an expert financial analyst, but it's to show you how you can use Monte Carlo simulations like this to analyze even your own accounts. This is exactly the type of approach that financial analysts will use to analyze different scenarios.

Before we go, let's look at one last simulation example, still a financial one, to see how it would work. Let's say that you have some retirement account, and have just retired. Hooray. You want to know if you'll be able to live off of that money during retirement. Now, there is a lot of uncertainty—how much will the account earn? How much will you have to withdraw each year to keep your standard of living, accounting for inflation? And, though it might not be the most pleasant thing to think about, how many years does it need to last?

Let's walk through a simple program to simulate all of these things. The program is similar in a lot of ways to the programs we saw earlier. We'll still have some sets of historical data, for stocks, bonds, and now for inflation. We'll also have functions to determine the increase in a stock account, an increase in a bond account, and the amount of inflation—

all of these just randomly chosen from among the historical examples. Notice that it would be easy to change this if we wanted. For example, if we wanted to assume that inflation was some fixed amount, we'd just change that inflation function to return that amount.

The program itself starts by asking the user to enter some key information. We'll ask how much money is in the account to begin with, what the annual expenses are, and how long the money needs to last.

We'll then set up some initial variables. We'll be keeping a count of how many times the money runs out. We'll assume we have a mixed account that is rebalanced, and we will set some percentage that should be in stocks—in this case, it is set to 50%. Then, we begin our Monte Carlo simulation, with a loop over some large number of scenarios.

Each iteration of this outer loop will be one simulation—what happens to the money in one example. So, we start out by setting the amount in the stock and bond accounts, and the annual expenses. We then loop through all the years, simulating the results from each year.

In this inner loop, representing one year, we first adjust our stock and bond balances based on returns and then rebalance. This is just like we did in the earlier examples, the only difference being that we have the amount to put in stocks as a variable.

After that, we calculate expenses. Each year, expenses should increase with inflation, so we multiply expenses times one plus inflation. Then, we subtract the expenses from our account, splitting the amount taken from stocks and bonds according to the percentage.

Now comes the important check—do we still have money? If our account has gone negative, it means we've run out of money. Oh no! What we'll do in this case is increase our count of running out of money, and then set our time to the maximum so that we won't keep going through this simulation.

At the end of the simulation, we'll check to see if we had a positive balance, and if so, store it in a list.

Finally, after all the simulations have been completed, we'll print out our information. We calculate the percentage of simulations where we had success—that is, where the money lasted as long as needed. For the successful cases, we will calculate the average ending balance and standard deviation, and plot the results in a histogram

OK, so if we run this code, we can enter some data. For example, if we say we have $1 million in the account and average expenses of $75,000, and we want this to last for 25 years of retirement, we can see the results. In this case, we've got about a 2/3 chance of making it. Now, if we do want to make it through retirement, we're likely to have a pretty good size account left over, on average more than $3 million on average, though keep in mind that inflation makes that not as big as it seems. But that 1 in 3 chance of not making it through retirement doesn't sound so great.

If you've ever used an online calculator to show you retirement projections or had a financial advisor show you retirement options, you might have seen results like this before. The code we've been using is a whole lot like what they will use—in fact, this code we have is more sophisticated than the systems that the average person encounters.

You could play around with this—try entering data from your own accounts, and see how it comes out. What happens if you change expenses, or the amount saved, or how long it needs to last, or the percentage in stocks vs. bonds? Can you keep some percentage in cash? And, you now know enough about programming that you can make this more sophisticated if you want to.

Keep in mind that the whole simulation is only as good as the model that we start with. For this case, we have a model based on sampling historical data about stocks, bonds, and inflation to predict the future. There's no guarantee that our model's right. For instance, maybe our model underestimates the possibility of an extreme change in the stock market every so often. That might suggest a sort of fat tail in the distribution instead of a nice bell curve distribution.

Or, maybe the model's ok, but we find ourselves not on track to make it through retirement. In that case, we could run additional simulations to help decide which changes in spending and investment would be most helpful. I'd encourage you to explore these and other computer simulations for yourself.

Overall, it's hard to overstate the importance of computer simulations. In science, where there are many studies on scales of time or space that are extremely large or small, simulations on large supercomputers have increasingly become as important as actual measurement and observation, which can sometimes be either impractical or flat-out impossible.

Predictions that we all rely on about hurricanes and other extreme weather events are based on large computer simulations. Cities and nations regularly use simulations to predict future trends, and to decide how to spend resources and plan for the future. And there are climate simulations, where computers are used to predict the future of our entire planet. Taken altogether, the decisions made based on simulations have consequences measured in the trillions of dollars, are sometimes matters of life and death, and affect basically everyone on the planet.

Simulation was also where, in the 1960s, a programming language called Simula pioneered the use of objects and classes, pointing the way to a new approach to programming that we'll dive into beginning next time: a way to bundle together functions and data that came to be called object-oriented design. I look forward to seeing you there.

17

Classes and Object-Oriented Programming

Object-oriented programming is a newer approach to software that has become widespread since the 1990s. One of its key benefits is called **encapsulation**, which means that all the parts and tools you need get packaged together—encapsulated in a **class**, whose individual instances are known as **objects**. As you will learn in this lecture, using classes and objects will help keep related code together and make it easier for you to design and manage different parts of the software.

[OBJECT-ORIENTED DESIGN]

> An object-oriented approach differs from top-down and bottom-up approaches, which are both task-oriented designs. They tend to focus on the task and how to accomplish the task, either by decomposing the task into more basic tasks or building up from existing tasks we already know how to perform. In computer science terms, both approaches are focused on operations and bundling those operations into more and more sophisticated functions.

> By contrast, neither really focuses on the parts and materials we might need to accomplish any of those tasks. In computer science terms, neither squarely focuses on data.

> Classes and objects allow us to combine operations and data. When they are packaged all together, we have the data we need as well as the operations that work with that data.

> A class can be thought of as the general blueprint for some category, while the objects are specific instances of that category. In other words, the class is a type, while each object is just a variable.

> In object-oriented design, the design decisions we make have to do with what we want to represent and then the data and functions that are needed to represent that thing.

[CREATING CLASSES]

> Let's say that we want to write some software that deals with a bank account. First, we want to think about the types of things we need to know about the bank account and the types of things we'd like to do with it.

> The main thing you need for a bank account is the balance—how much money is in the account. You might want to deposit money, or withdraw money, or maybe just check on how much is in the account.

> In order to create code that lets us manage bank accounts in a compact way, we can introduce the idea of classes. Classes are the containers in which we can package the data and the functions that belong with the data. Classes are basically a new type that a variable can take on, like integers, floats, strings, or lists.

> When we're defining a class, we start with the word "class," followed by the name of the class that we want to use. In this case, we're defining BankAccounts, so we'll name the class "BankAccount," which is followed by a colon. Then, everything in the class definition will be indented from there. The indentation shows that this is the stuff that belongs to that class. Our bank account needs to keep track of the current balance, so that is a data item we have. Indenting in, we call this data item "balance," and we start out by setting it to 0.

```
class BankAccount:
    balance = 0.0
```

> Let's see how we use these classes that we define. First, we can create an instance of the class. Each instance of a class is known as an object. We create an object that's an instance of a class by writing the class

name, followed by parentheses. We can assign this instance to a variable. In this case, we have a class called BankAccount, and we create one instance of the class, which we assign to the variable my_account.

> So, my_account is a single instance of BankAccount. We can then access the attributes of a BankAccount. We do this using a single period after the variable name and then stating the attribute of the class that we want. So, in this case, we write "my_account.balance," and that is going to give us the value of the balance. If we print that variable out, we will get 0, which was the value the balance was set to in the class definition.

```
class BankAccount:
    balance = 0.0
my_account = BankAccount()
print(my_account.balance)

OUTPUT
0.0
```

> Classes are a way of defining a new category of variable. A particular instance of that class is called an object. When we talk about object-oriented programming, we are talking about programming centered around creating and using objects—in other words, defining classes and then using instances of those classes in our programs.

> The idea of classes and objects is common across many languages, but terms for the variables that are within objects vary. In Python, the variables that are inside a class, and help define the class, are called "attributes" of the class. In Java, the parts of an object are called "fields"; in C++, they are called "member variables."

> In Python, some attributes can be set to apply equally across all members of a class, so that every object has that attribute, while other attributes can be defined individually for only some objects. In the previous example, "balance" was an attribute across the entire class—in fact, it was the only attribute of the class.

> To access an attribute within Python, we pick an object in the class and attach a period, followed by the name of the attribute.

> Let's look at our code again. First, we can assign values to the members of an object. After creating my_account, we can set my_account.balance to 100. Then, if we print out my_account.balance, it is 100.

```
class BankAccount:
    balance = 0.0
my_account = BankAccount()
my_account.balance = 100.0
print(my_account.balance)

OUTPUT
100.0
```

> Next, we'll create a second object, called "your_account." We'll set the balance of my_account to 100. If we print out the balance of your_account, the output is 0. We create two separate objects, each of which gets its own place in memory. So, my_account is one object, and your_account is another object. When we set the balance of my_account to 0, it only affects the "balance" attribute of my_account, and there's no change to the your_account balance. So, when we print out the your_account balance, we still get 0.

```
class BankAccount:
    balance = 0.0
my_account = BankAccount()
your_account = BankAccount()
my_account.balance = 100.0
print(your_account.balance)

OUTPUT
0.0
```

[MUTABLE DATA]

> Let's say that we want to keep track of the deposits that were made to the bank account. So, in a bank account, we want to have a list of deposits made. We'll add a new attribute to the BankAccount class, called "deposits," and initialize it to be an empty list. So, BankAccounts now has two attributes: balance and deposits.

```
class BankAccount:
    balance = 0.0
    deposits = []
```

> Let's say that we create a BankAccount object and call it "checking_account." We can access the "deposits" part of the checking_account by writing "checking_account.deposits.append[100.0]," which should append the value 100 into the deposits list. If we print out "checking_account.deposits," we will get a list with 100.0 in it.

```
class BankAccount:
    balance = 0.0
    deposits = []
checking_account = BankAccount()
checking_account.deposits.append(100.0)
print(checking_account.deposits)

OUTPUT
[100.0]
```

> Let's say that we create a second BankAccount called "savings_account." We'll still append 100 into the checking_account list. If we print out the deposits list for the savings account, we get a list that has the 100 in it. We didn't change anything about the list in the savings_account, but it somehow has the value 100 in it.

```
class BankAccount:
    balance = 0.0
    deposits = []
checking_account = BankAccount()
savings_account = BankAccount()
checking_account.deposits.append(100.0)
print(savings_account.deposits)

OUTPUT:
[100.0]
```

> To understand this, we have to see what's happening in memory. Recall that a list is a mutable data type, which means that when we create a list, the variable doesn't store a copy of the list itself—it just has a value that says "the list is here." So, when we create a list, the actual list of elements is stored in one place, but the variable stores "this is the location of the list."

> In this case, the class description that defined "deposits" as an attribute said that deposits will be an empty list, but the problem is that it gives the same location of that empty list to every instance. Every object we create is going to start out with the exact same value for deposits, so it's going to be referring to the exact same list in memory. So, when we append 100 onto the checking_account list, that's the same list as the savings_account would see.

> One way around this is to reset the value of the attribute for a particular object. In the following, we set the value of checking_acount.deposits to be an empty list. This creates a new empty list and sets the value of deposits in the checking account to that list. The "deposits" attribute of the savings_account still points to the original empty list, and if we had other instances of BankAccount, they would, too. But now checking_account has its own deposits list to work with, separate from the rest. So, when we add 100 to the checking_account.deposits list, the savings_account list is unchanged.

```
class BankAccount:
    balance = 0.0
    deposits = []
checking_account = BankAccount()
savings_account = BankAccount()
checking_account.deposits = []
checking_account.deposits.append(100.0)
print(savings_account.deposits)

OUTPUT:
[]
```

> This works, but we could avoid this problem if we could just create a list to begin with that was separate for each object. In fact, there is a better way to approach the issue of attributes.

[METHODS]

> In a Python class, we can have two types of attributes: class variables and instance variables. Everything we've seen so far is a class variable—that is, it's one variable defined for the class. When we create an object—that is, when we create an instance of the class—that instance will get its own versions of the class variables.

> But any initial values set in the class are going to be shared across all instances, which leads to problems with mutable data types. The alternative is to create instance variables, which are created separately for each instance of the class. With instance variables, we never need to worry about the changes to one object inadvertently affecting the attributes of a different object.

> To create instance variables, we need to introduce the topic of **methods**, which are like attributes, but instead of defining data, they define functions. One very special method is the "init" method, which gets its name from the fact that it is initializing an object within the class. The init method is commonly called a **constructor**.

> The init method gets defined much like a regular function, but it's inside the class definition. The init function also has syntax that differs in a few ways from other functions: It starts with a double underscore, then "init," and then another double underscore. It will take one parameter. Then, you have the colon, and the function definition is indented from there. In this case, we'll have one line in the init function: "self.deposits = []."

```python
class BankAccount:
    balance = 0.0
    def __init__(self):
        self.deposits = []
```

> This special init function is a function that is executed whenever a new instance of the class is created. The term for this is **instantiation**. When you instantiate a new object, the Python compiler will find the constructor—that is, the init method—and run it.

> This first parameter, "self," in the init command is also a special one; it's not one you pass in, but it's automatically filled in. The self parameter refers to the current instance of the object. Because of the self parameter, we have a way of clearly referring to things within this particular instance of an object. So, if we write "self.balance," we mean the balance in this one instance.

> In this example, we have a deposits list that we want to be unique for each instance. We write "self.deposits" and set it equal to the empty list. That creates a unique "deposits" attribute for the instance and initializes that deposits list to the empty list.

> If we create two different BankAccount objects, like we did before, this init command is being called for each of them. We can still access the "deposits" attribute of the checking_account, just like before, and append something onto it. But notice that now it does not affect the "deposits" list for the savings account. Our init command created separate instance variables and initialized those individual instance variables independently.

```
class BankAccount:
    balance = 0.0
    def __init__(self):
        self.deposits = []
checking_account = BankAccount()
savings_account = BankAccount()
checking_account.deposits.append(100.0)
print(savings_account.deposits)

OUTPUT:
[]
```

> In general, we should try to use instance variables instead of class variables. So, instead of creating a "balance" class variable, it's better to create an instance variable in the init function, like we did for deposits. Practically, it's not much different, but it helps ensure that we know that the variable is something that can change from object to object. Generally, the only time we should use class variables is when there's some single value, usually one that's not likely to change, that should be the same across all instances of the class.

Readings

Gries, *Practical Programming*, chap. 14.

Lambert, *Fundamentals of Python*, chap. 5.

Zelle, *Python Programming*, chap. 12.

Exercises

For exercises 1 through 3, assume that you have the following class to keep track of inventory.

```
class Inventory:
    item = ""
    barcode = 0
    quantity = 0
    price = 0.00
    sales = 0.00
    def __init__(self, product, bar, pr):
        self.item = product
        self.barcode = bar
        self.price = pr
    def changeprice(self, newprice):
        self.price = newprice
    def sell(self, n):
        self.quantity -= n
        self.sales += self.price*n
    def restock(self, n):
        self.quantity += n
```

1   What would be the output of the following code?

```
widget = Inventory("widget", 1112223334, 10.00)
widget.restock(30)
widget.sell(10)
print(widget.quantity)
print(widget.sales)
widget.changeprice(20.0)
widget.sell(10)
print(widget.quantity)
print(widget.sales)
```

2   What would be the output of the following code?

```
shoes = Inventory("shoe", 12345123245, 30.00)
shoes.restock(100)
shirts = Inventory("shirt", 9876598765, 25.00)
shirts.restock(80)
shoes.sell(10)
shirts.sell(30)
shoes.sell(50)
print(shoes.quantity)
print(shoes.sales)
print(shirts.quantity)
print(shirts.sales)
```

3   Write a method, "print," that will print out information about all the information about the inventory. For example, calling "widget.print()" would print out all the information about name, bar code, etc.

Imagine that you wanted a class to keep track of movies you've watched. You will want to keep track of the name of the movie, the genre, and a numerical rating of how much you liked it.

4   Define a class with attributes for these three characteristics, with some default values.

5   Write a constructor method that takes in values for all three attributes as parameters.

6   Write code that constructs a list of movies by asking a user for the appropriate information, until the user enters a movie with rating less than 0.

Classes and Object-Oriented Programming

Suppose you have to assemble a piece of furniture. The manufacturer might list the tools needed, but it's up to you to get them. You might also have to provide some of your own parts and materials. And, sometimes the instructions might be so bad that you don't even know what tools or materials you need ahead of time. So you have to keep stopping to go find something or just get everything together. Here's the better idea: How about the manufacturer includes, in the package, all the tools and all the materials you need to assemble the product. All in one place. Wouldn't that be a whole lot better?

Clearly, when we have all the necessary tools and parts right there together in one package, life is much easier. And that's the beauty of object-oriented programming, a newer approach to software that has become widespread since the 1990s. One of its key benefits is called encapsulation, and that means exactly what I said—all the parts and tools you need are packaged together—encapsulated in a class, whose individual instances are known as objects.

An object-oriented approach differs from top-down and bottom-up approaches. Both top-down and bottom-up designs are task-oriented. They tend to focus on the task, and how to accomplish the task either decomposing it into more basic pieces or, or building up from existing tasks that we already know how to perform. In computer science terms, both approaches are focused on operations, and bundling those operations into more and more sophisticated functions. In terms of schoolhouse grammar, both top-down and bottom-up are focused mostly on verbs.

In contrast, neither really focuses on the parts and materials we may need to accomplish any of those tasks. In computer science terms, neither one is really focused on the data.

Classes and objects allow us to combine operations and data. Now, packaged all together, we have the data we need, and we have the operations that work with that data. In terms of grammar, we not only bring together all the verbs we want, but we also have all subjects and objects of those verbs.

A class can be thought of as the general blueprint for some category while the objects are specific instances of that category. So, if a class is a dog, then Toto, Lassie, Pluto, and Snoopy are objects in the class. The analogy is not perfect, but in terms of programming, a class Dog, in this case, is a new type of variable, while any particular object such as Toto is a particular variable. In short, the class is a type, while each object is a variable.

In object-oriented design, the design decisions we make have to do with what we want to represent, and then the data and functions that are needed to represent that thing. Let's consider an example—we'll talk about the design, and then we'll see how this gets put into code.

Let's say we want to write some software that deals with a bank account. First, we want to think about the types of things that we need to know about the bank account and the types of things that we'd like to do with it. Let's start really simple. The main thing you need for a bank account is the balance—how much money is in the account. Let's think of things you might want to do with the account. You might want to deposit money, or withdraw money, or maybe just check and see how much is in there. We'll make this a little more complex in a minute, but for now, that should be sufficient.

In order to create code that lets us manage bank accounts in a nice compact way like this, we can introduce the idea of classes. Classes are the containers in which we can package the data and the functions that belong with that data. Classes are basically a new type that a variable can take on, like integers, floats, strings, or lists.

Now, you still might wonder, why don't we just use functions to do everything? The reason is that when you just use functions, the functions have no fixed tie to the data. In contrast, when we create classes we're tying these together—saying that some set of data and some set of functions are designed to work together. Then, if you want to deal with that data, your program already knows to use those functions to do it.

So, we're defining a class, and we start with the word "class," followed by the name of the class that we want to use. In this case, we're defining BankAccounts, so we'll name the class "BankAccount," and that'll be followed by a colon. Then, everything in the class definition will be indented from there. The indentation shows that this is the stuff that belongs to that class. Our bank account needs to keep track of the current balance, so that'll be a data item that we have. Indenting in, we'll call this data item "balance," and we'll start out by setting it to be 0.

Now let's see how we use these classes that we define. First, we can create an instance of the class. Each instance of a class is known as an object. We create an object that's an instance of a class by writing the class name, followed by parentheses. We can assign this instance to a variable. In the case we see here, we have a class called BankAccount, and we create one instance of the class, which we assign to the variable my_account. So, my_account is going to be a single instance of BankAccount. We can then access the attributes of a BankAccount. We do this using a single period after the variable name, and then stating the attribute of the class that we want. So, in this case, we write my_account.balance, and that is going to give us the value of the balance. If we print that variable out, here, we will get 0, which was the value the balance was set to in the class definition.

Let's look more closely at terminology. We first have classes, which are a way of defining a new category of variable. A particular instance of that class is called an object. When we talk about object-oriented programming, we are talking about programming centered around creating and using objects—in other words, defining classes and then using instances of those classes in our programs. The idea of classes and objects is common across lots of languages, but terms for the variables that are within objects vary.

In Python, the variables that are inside a class, and help define the class, are called attributes of the class. If you were in Java, the parts of an object would be called fields. In C++, the parts of an object are called member variables. In Python, some attributes can be set to apply equally to all members of a class, so that every object has that attribute, while other attributes can be defined individually for only some objects.

Now, in the example we just saw, "balance" was an attribute across the entire class—in fact, it was the only attribute of the class. To access an attribute within Python, we pick an object in the class, attach a period, followed by the name of the attribute.

OK, let's look at our code again. First, we can assign values to the members of an object. After creating my_account, we can set "my_account.balance" to 100. Then, if we print out "my_account.balance," it is 100. Let's see if you can figure the next one out. We'll create a second object, called "your_account." I'll set the balance of my_account to 100. What happens if I print out the balance of your_account? The output will be 0. What happens here is that we create two separate objects. Each of these objects gets its own place in memory. So, there is one object my_account and another object your_account. When we set the balance of my_account to 0, it only affects the "balance" attribute of my_account, and there's no change to the balance in your_account. So, when we print out the your_account balance, we still get 0.

Now, this all seems good, and you might think, "Hey, I understand this," but there's a big issue. Let's see how we can extend this class a bit. Say that we want to keep track of the deposits that were made to the bank account. So, in a bank account, we want to have a list of deposits made. We'll add a new attribute to the BankAccount class, called "deposits," and initialize it to be an empty list. So, BankAccounts now has two attributes, balance and deposits. Let's say that we create a BankAccount object and call it "checking_account." We can access the "deposits" part of the checking_account by writing "checking_account.deposits.append[100.0]." That should append the value 100 into the deposits list. Sure enough, if we print out "checking_account.deposits," we'll get a list with 100.0 in it.

Now, let's make this a little trickier. Let's say we create a second BankAccount, called "savings_account." We'll still append 100 into the checking_account list. Now, what if we were to print out the deposits list for the savings account? What do you think we'd get? We get a list that has the 100 in it. Woah. What is going on here? We didn't change anything about the list in the savings_account, and yet it somehow has the value 100 in it.

To understand this, we have to see what's happening in memory. Let's recall the whole discussion of mutable and immutable data types: in particular, remember that a list is a mutable data type. What that means is that when we create a list, the variable doesn't actually store a copy of the list itself, it just has a value that says "the list is here." So, when we create a list, the actual list of elements is stored in one place, but the variable stores "this is the location of the list". In this case, the class description that defined "deposits" as an attribute said that deposits will be an empty list, but the problem is, it gives the same location of that empty list to every instance. Every object we create is going to start out with the exact same value for deposits, and so it's going to be referring to the exact same list in memory. So, when we append 100 onto the checking_account list, that's the same list as the savings_account would see.

Now, this is probably not what we want, so let's look at a couple of ways around this. One way is that we could reset the value of an attribute every time we create an object. Here, we set the value of checking_acount.deposits to be an empty list. Now, when we do this, this creates a new empty list and it sets the value of deposits in the checking account to that list. The "deposits" attribute of the savings_account still points to the original empty list, and if we had other instances of BankAccount, they would too. But, now checking_account has its own deposits list to work with, separate from the rest. So, when we add 100 to the checking_account.deposits list, the savings_account list, is unchanged.

This works, but it'd be nicer if we could just create a list to begin with that was separate for each object so that we never ran into this problem.

In fact, the way I'm going to show you now is the better way to approach the whole issue of attributes.

In a Python class, we can actually have two types of attributes: class variables, and instance variables. Everything we've seen so far is a class variable. That is, it's one variable defined for the class. When we create an object, that is, when we create an instance of the class, that instance will get its own versions of the class variables.

But, any initial values set in the class are going to be shared across all instances, and that can lead to problems with mutable data types like we just saw. The alternative is to create instance variables, and these are variables created separately for each instance of the class. With instance variables, we never need to worry about the changes to one object inadvertently affecting the attributes of a different object. To create instance variables, we will need to introduce the topic of methods. Methods are like attributes, but instead of defining data, they define functions.

One very special method is the init method, which gets its name from the fact that it is initializing an object within the class. The init method is often referred to as a constructor. The init method gets defined much like a regular function, but it's inside the class definition. The init function also has syntax that differs in a few ways from other functions: it starts with a double underscore, then init, then another double underscore. It'll take one parameter. Then, you have the colon, and the function definition is indented in from there. In this case, we'll have one line in the init function: self.deposits equal the empty list. Let me explain how this works.

This special init function is a function that is executed whenever a new instance of the class is created. The term for this is instantiation. When you instantiate a new object, the Python compiler will find the constructor, that is, this init method, and run it. Now, this first parameter "self" in the init command is also a special one—it's not one you pass in, it's automatically filled in. The self parameter refers to the current instance of the object. Because of the self parameter, we have a way of clearly referring to things within this particular instance of an object. So, if we write self.balance, we mean the balance in this one instance.

So, in the example that we have here with the init command for the bank account, we have a deposits list that we want to be unique for each instance. We write self.deposits and set it equal to the empty list. That creates a unique "deposits" attribute for that instance and then initializes that deposits list to the empty list.

If we go ahead and create two different BankAccount objects like we did before, this init command is being called for each of them. We can still access the "deposits" attribute of the checking_account, just like before, and we append something onto it. But, notice that now it does not affect the "deposits" list for the savings account. Our init command created separate instance variables, and initialized those individual instance variables independently.

Generally speaking, we should try to use instance variables instead of class variables. So, instead of creating a balance class variable, it's better style to create an instance variable in the init function, just like we did for deposits. Practically speaking, it's not much different, but it helps ensure that we know that the variable is something that can change from object to object. Generally, the only time we should use class variables is when there's some single value, usually one that's not likely to change, and it should be the same across all instances of the class. The knights of the round table will all be knights, but they may not all be brave.

Now, we can also modify the init function so that it takes in a parameter. Let's say that we want the bank account to be created with some initial balance. We can take that balance in as a parameter. We just list that parameter after the self parameter in the init statement. Remember that self is always going to be the first parameter, and it's not one that we actually pass in. So, the next parameter that we'll take in is initial_amount. And that will be used to set the balance to that initial amount.

Now, when we actually create an object in our program, we can pass this new variable in as a parameter. Here we'll create our checking account by creating a new BankAccount, passing in the parameter of 200. That parameter will be the initial_amount in our init function, and so our balance gets set to 200. Sure enough, when we print out the balance of the account, we see that it's 200.

We can give default parameters here, just like we have for other functions. It would make sense that if we don't have an initial balance specified, that it should be 0, so we'll use that as the default value. Then, we can create a new BankAccount object, either passing in the amount or just leaving that parameter value empty. As we see here, we create a checking account with an initial balance of 200, and a savings account with no initial balance specified. Then, printing out the balances, we see that they are 200 and 0, just like we'd expect.

Besides the init method, we can create other methods in our class. Let's think back to some of the functions that we wanted to do with a bank account. I remember three of them—making a deposit, making a withdrawal, and checking the balance. We call these functions, defined inside a class, methods. The C++ term is member functions. Methods are a part of the class itself and are defined in the context of the class.

We've seen this notation before, like when we worked with files. When we open a file, the thing that we've assigned to a variable is a file object, It not only has the file data but also the file operations that can work on the file. For example, it includes the operation "close" for when you are done with it and write to write data to the file. The close and write methods are part of that file object. As you start looking at Python code, including the code from lots of modules, you'll see these calls to methods all over the place.

Defining a method works just like defining a function, except that it's inside of the class definition. There's one other important difference: Methods always have this first parameter, which by convention is called self. Just like the init method, the self parameter doesn't get explicitly passed in, and it's used to refer to the current instance of the object. Let's see an example, where we want to make a deposit.

We will define a function "makeDeposit" within the class definition. There will be two parameters, "self" and "amount". Inside the function, we will increase the balance of the account by "amount" and we will also append this on to the list of deposits that we've made. Notice that we have to refer to self-dot-balance and self-dot-deposits here.

Here's how we'd actually use this. Let's say we created a checking account with an initial balance of $100, and want to deposit another $50. We would call "checking_account.makeDeposit" and pass in the number 50. Notice that we don't need to pass in "self," since that first parameter of the method is filled in automatically. Then, if we print out the balance and the deposit list, we'd see that the balance is indeed $150, and the $50 deposit is in the list.

Let me give you something to try. Say you wanted the class to include a "withdraw" function that would let you withdraw a certain amount of money. Try writing a "makeWithdrawal" method, and an example of it being used.

Here is what that might look like. Inside the class, we have our method definition for makeWithdrawal. The method takes in two parameters, self and amount. It then decreases the balance by the amount. That's all. If we call this function to withdraw $70, in this case saying "checking_ account.makeWithdrawal (70)," we indeed have the balance reduced from the $150 it was to just $80 left.

Now let's create a way to check the balance. That should be really easy—we've already been doing it. We can just take the account name, and write .dot-balance after it. We could just access the balance directly. And, our line "print [checking_account.balance]" would print out the current balance.

That seems like a nice simple way to access data, and truthfully it is. If you have a really simple class, it might be that this is how you access the attributes. But, in practice, it's probably best not to just access an attribute like that. Let me give you a sense of why another way would be better. Say we had a bank account, that started at $100. Then, let's say we decided to make a deposit. Instead of using that "makeDeposit" method that we just defined, instead, we'll just increase the balance directly. That's doing the same thing, right?

Well, no. In fact, we were doing more than just increasing the balance when we made a deposit; we were also keeping a list of the deposits that had been made so far. When we bypassed the "makeDeposit" method on our own, we created an inconsistency—we did change the balance, but we forgot to update the list of deposits. So, when we print out the results, we see the increased balance, but our list of deposits is empty.

This goes to a principle of good object-oriented design: that we should only deal with the data in an object—I'm talking about the attribute values—through the methods of that object. In our bank account case, that means we should use the makeDeposit and makeWithdrawal commands to add and withdraw money from the account, rather than directly manipulating the balance ourselves.

In Python there is a convention you can use to help encourage this good behavior. The idea is that all the attributes that a person really shouldn't access directly should have a name starting with an underscore. Let's see how this would look in the class definition. The change to what we already have is pretty simple. We just replace "balance" and "deposits" with "_balance" and "_deposits". Everything else works the same.

Now, if we try to have the same code we saw earlier, we get an error. Specifically, we get an "AttributeError" telling us that there is no attribute named "balance." These attributes that we're not supposed to access directly are called private attributes. We could still get around this by putting "_balance" in our code, but we'd, at least, have to be intentionally acknowledging that we're trying to access something that shouldn't.

The problem is that we still want to be able to find the balance in our account, and to get a list of the deposits. So, we'll actually need to create methods to provide this information, rather than accessing the attributes directly. We can do this by creating functions getBalance and getDeposits. Each of these can return the associated data that was meant to be hidden or private. We can then call these functions to get the correct data returned. We can see the balance with getBalance and the list of deposits with getDeposits. And, we never had to directly touch the actual attribute inside the class—we just called these methods to work with that data.

This is another example of abstraction in action. The user of a class doesn't need to worry about the internal structure, but just how to make the calls to get the information needed. For example, maybe instead of keeping a list of deposits, we keep a list of both deposits and withdrawals. When someone asks for the deposits list, we could go through the list and extract the deposits into a separate list that gets returned. It shouldn't matter to the user of the class exactly how that information is stored inside the object.

Also, I want to be crystal clear. It is OK for the attributes of a class to be other classes. Many modules and packages don't just provide functions; they also provide classes that we can use. An example of this is the standard module datetime. Among the classes it provides is one for storing and working with dates.

We could easily incorporate a date class into our BankAccount class. Just to illustrate, consider this example. We first import the date class from the datetime module. Then, in our initialization routine, we can also create a new attribute, opendate. For simplicity, I'll just initialize the date to March 15 of 2011. When we create a checking account and print the opendate attribute, we see that the March 15, of 2011 date is indeed printed.

Notice that we used an object within an object. We can nest classes inside of classes like this indefinitely: a class can have an attribute that's a class, which can have an attribute that's a class, etc., etc. And, the class can be imported from a module—it doesn't have to be something we create ourselves.

Before we finish up, I want to talk for a minute about mutable data. First, I want to show you something about how returned values work, in particular why you need to return a copy of a data list, instead of the actual list of deposits. This sort of thing is not unique to object-oriented programming, but it does tend to come up much more in object-oriented programming.

In our example, we passed back a list of deposits. Let's look at a little code. Let's say that we create a bank account object, make a deposit, and then get a list of deposits. In this case, we've created a checking_account, deposited $50, and then gotten our list of deposits, which we have assigned to the variable x. Now, if we append a value like 1000 on to x, and then later we print out the list of deposits, what do you think will happen? Keep in mind that lists are mutable data types.

The resulting list is going to have both the 50 and the 1000 in the list. Keep in mind that for a mutable data type, like a list, when we pass it back and forth, we are passing something that can be changed. So, when we return our list of deposits from the bank account, we are returning a list that can be changed—anything you do in one place will affect what shows up everywhere with that list. In this case, when we append onto the list in the main code, it's affecting the list that's inside the checking_account object.

Now, this is probably not the way we want this to behave. When we return a list of deposits, we don't want whatever users do with that list to affect what's inside the object. So, how might we do that—how might we return something out of the object that's not going to let people mess with the object's internal information? The solution here is to make a copy of the list, so I'll show you a simple way to make one.

Let's go back to our getDeposits method. We just returned the deposits list that was one of our internal attributes. Here's a new version of that method. We first create a copy of that deposits list. Then, we return that copy. We create the copy using the slicing operations that we can perform on a list. In general, slicing creates a new list by specifying a subset of some other list, where the starting and ending points are specified in brackets, with a colon in between. In this case, leaving the starting and ending points empty means we want to start at the beginning and go to the end. So, when we write "self._deposits[:]," we're creating a new list that's a copy of the entire length of the old one. In other words, we've made a complete copy of the list.

Now, if we return to the same code we had earlier, where we pull out a list of deposits, and we add something to it, we'll see that the original list stored in the object itself is unchanged. Again, although the idea of passing around mutable data is not unique to object-oriented programming, it does come up here a lot more frequently, so you need to be cautious as you pass data around, to make sure you are using copies, whenever you don't want the underlying data to be changed.

Now, one other important thing to note about objects is that all objects are themselves mutable data. So, we can pass in an object to a function, change the object within the function, and return and the object will be changed. Let's look at a quick example.

Let's say we want to create a function to simulate winning the lottery. We take in an account, and we make a $10 million deposit to that account. So, in the code you see here, we have that winLottery function definition, where we bring in an account and call makeDeposit on the account. We then have some code that creates a new checking account, which should have a balance of $0 since we haven't specified a starting balance. We then call winLottery on that checking account. Now, if we print balance of the account, we will get back $10 million. In other words, calling the winLottery command actually changed the value of the account itself. If the checking_account was not mutable, this wouldn't have happened.

Most of the time, it's really nice that objects are mutable. That's what makes it so easy to write a command like winLottery. If only winning the actual lottery was so easy. But, there may be times like we saw when we were returning the list of deposits, where having a mutable data type is not ideal. The key issue is to be aware of what type of data you are using and make sure you make copies when needed.

One other point: In Python, object-oriented programming does not need to replace other ways of programming. You can augment programs you have by including classes and objects. For example, the financial simulation that we made earlier could be converted to an object-oriented approach very easily. We could extend the bank_account class we've been using in this lecture, and let it hold balances of stocks and bonds as separate attributes. We could also create a method to apply one year of interest. This would make our operations in any one loop much simpler.

When object-oriented programming really started taking off in the 1990s, it offered a way of organizing code in ways that people already knew was good, but didn't have the built-in structures to support.

The early promises of object-oriented programming were that it would revolutionize software development, reducing the challenges in design and lead to much more reusable code. And while it might not have achieved the goals of its most optimistic proponents, programmers have found it to be a very useful way to organize their data and operations, and it's become a central part of most modern programming languages. As you develop code, I'd encourage you to use classes and objects as often as you can—whenever data and actions on that data can naturally be grouped together. Using classes and objects will help keep related code together and make it easier for you to design and manage different parts of the software.

In the next lecture, we'll see how encapsulation provides the basis for two other object-oriented features, inheritance and polymorphism, and we'll see more about how we can use object-oriented design as we put together our programs. I'll look forward to seeing you then.

MORE PYTHON PRACTICE

Let me warn you against one thing that can be done with classes. Let's say that we create a checking account, and then we try to set the "name" attribute of the account. Wait a minute—we didn't have a "name" attribute in the account. What do you think will happen? Oddly enough, Python will let you assign something to an attribute that didn't already exist. When this happens, a new attribute is created for just that one object. So, in the code you see here, we assign the name "My Checking Account" to the "name" attribute. We can then print out that name and sure enough, the name is just what we had set. Now, say that we had another bank account, a savings account. If we try to access the name element of the savings account, what will happen? We get an error.

What has happened is that our checking account memory has had an extra attribute, name, added on to it. The attribute is not added to the class, so the savings account doesn't have any corresponding "name" element. We can access "name" just fine in the checking account object, but not in the savings account object.

Now, generally, I'd recommend that you avoid doing things like this. It can be really confusing when you've created one object that has different attributes from all the other objects from that class. But, you should be aware of this, in case you read some code where someone did this, or you accidentally do something like this yourself in your own code—since it's not a bug, the compiler won't catch it for you.

18

Objects with Inheritance and Polymorphism

hildren inherit from their parents the fundamental structure of DNA that makes us human—the fundamental traits that make human bodies work and grow. Inheritance plays a similar role in programming, thanks to object-oriented design and programming. The fundamental idea of object-oriented design is encapsulation, where we put together the data, and functions that work on that data, into a single package. But there are two other aspects of object-oriented programming— inheritance and polymorphism—which you will learn about in this lecture.

[INHERITANCE]

> Imagine that we have a program that we're going to use to keep track of statistics for different players on a sports team. Often, players with different positions will have different statistics that are relevant to them. In football, players on offense will have different statistics than those who play defense.

> For a quarterback, we probably want to know the player's name and team, as well as data like the number of passes attempted, the number of completions, and the number of passing yards. We can set up some functions associated with the quarterback to help us compute percentages and averages, such as the percentage of completed passes or average yards gained per pass.

> For the position of running back, we would want the player's name and team, as well as the number of rushes and rushing yards gained.

> With just these two positions, one possibility would be to create two classes. We could create a "Quarterback" class (which would have attributes for name, team, pass attempts, completions, and passing yards) and a "RunningBack" class (which would have attributes for name, team, rushes, and rushing yards).

> Notice that both quarterback and running back share some attributes. They both have the player's name and the player's team. In fact, this would be true for all the various positions we might want to define.

> So, let's imagine a different organization. Let's say that we have some base type, which we'll call "FootballPlayer," which will have all the attributes common across the various types of players. In this case, that's the player's name and the team. We can then define a Quarterback as a type of FootballPlayer, with some additional attributes: passes attempted, completions, and passing yards. Likewise, a RunningBack is also a type of FootballPlayer with some additional attributes: rushes and rushing yards.

> What we've just seen is called **inheritance**. You can think of the football player as the parent. Then, the quarterback and the running back are children. The children inherit the characteristics of the parent. In this case, the children inherit the name and team attributes defined for the football player.

> We define each of the classes individually. For the FootballPlayer class, we define it the same way we have been. For the Quarterback and RunningBack classes, we put the name of their **parent class** in parentheses. Each of them defines the attributes unique to that class—the attributes that were not in the parent class.

```python
class FootballPlayer:
    name = "John Doe"
    team = "None"
class Quarterback(FootballPlayer):
    pass_attempts = 0
    completions = 0
    pass_yards = 0
class RunningBack(FootballPlayer):
    rushes = 0
    rush_yards = 0
```

> So, we have our FootballPlayer class with a name and team defined, and we set the values to be "John Doe" for the name and "None" for the team.

For a Quarterback, we note that it is a child of the FootballPlayer class, and then we define the "pass_attempts," "completions," and "pass_yards" attributes, initializing all of them to 0. For a RunningBack, we again declare that it is a child or the FootballPlayer class, and then we define the "rushes" and "rush_yards" attributes, again initializing them to 0.

› With those classes defined, we can then create an instance of a class. Let's say that we create a player, called player1, that is a Quarterback. We can print the player's name. Becuase we didn't set the name, it uses whatever the default name was for all football players, which we said would be "John Doe"—that is, the quarterback has a "name" attribute because its parent class, FootballPlayer, had a name attribute. We can also print out the pass_yards attribute, which is 0, just like we initialized it to be.

```
player1 = Quarterback()
print(player1.name)
print(player1.pass_yards)

OUTPUT:
John Doe
0
```

› Let's say that instead of a quarterback, we had said that player1 was a RunningBack. We'd still have the name attribute, because a running back is a child of the FootballPlayer class, and FootballPlayer has a "name" attribute. However, if we tried to print off the pass_yards, we'd get an error. Pass yards were defined only for the Quarterback class.

```
player1 = RunningBack()
print(player1.name)
print(player1.pass_yards)

OUTPUT:
John Doe
AttributeError: 'RunningBack' object has no attribute 'pass_
  yards'
```

> Creating different players is straightforward. For example, we can create player1 as a Quarterback and player2 as a RunningBack and set all the values appropriately.

```
player1 = Quarterback()
player1.name = "John"
player1.team = "Cowboys"
player1.pass_attempts = 10
player1.completions = 6
player1.pass_yards = 57
player2 = RunningBack()
player2.name = "Joe"
player2.team = "Eagles"
player2.rushes = 12
player2.rush_yards = 73
```

> It's not just attributes that can be inherited. We can also inherit methods. In the following, we've augmented our classes to include some methods. For the FootballPlayer class, we'll define a method, "printPlayer," that prints out the name and team of the player. We'll also add some methods for the Quarterback and RunningBack classes to compute some statistics specific to those positions. For a quarterback, that will be the completion rate and yards per attempt, and for the running back, that will be the yards per rush.

```
class FootballPlayer:
    name = "John Doe"
    team = "None"
    years_in_league = 0
    def printPlayer(self):
        print(self.name+" playing for the "+self.team+":")
class Quarterback(FootballPlayer):
    pass_attempts = 0
    completions = 0
    pass_yards = 0
```

```
        def completionRate(self):
            return self.completions/self.pass_attempts
        def yardsPerAttempt(self):
            return self.pass_yards/self.pass_attempts
    class RunningBack(FootballPlayer):
        rushes = 0
        rush_yards = 0
        def yardsPerRush(self):
            return self.rush_yards/self.rushes
```

› We can go back to our two players that we defined earlier, and then we can call the methods for these players. Notice that we can call printPlayer for both player1 and player2. Because the method is defined in the parent, it's automatically inherited by the children. We can also call those statistics methods that are specific to each of the children classes.

```
class FootballPlayer:
    name = "John Doe"
    team = "None"
    years_in_league = 0
    def printPlayer(self):
        print(self.name+" playing for the "+self.team+":")
class Quarterback(FootballPlayer):
    pass_attempts = 0
    completions = 0
    pass_yards = 0
    def completionRate(self):
        return self.completions/self.pass_attempts
    def yardsPerAttempt(self):
        return self.pass_yards/self.pass_attempts
class RunningBack(FootballPlayer):
    rushes = 0
    rush_yards = 0
    def yardsPerRush(self):
        return self.rush_yards/self.rushes
```

› When people discuss inheritance, there are different terms used for the different classes. Sometimes, we call the parent class the "base" class, and we call the children "derived" classes. Other times, we call the parent a "superclass" and the children "subclasses." All of these terms refer to the same thing.

› Just like in biology, where you can inherit traits from more than just one parent, classes can inherit properties from multiple parents. But for the most part, you should stay away from multiple inheritance. It can make your code more confusing to follow. Plus, it's very rare that multiple inheritance is actually the "right" solution to your problem.

[POLYMORPHISM]

› The third main feature of object-oriented programming is **polymorphism**, which means that a function, or method, can take on many different forms, depending on the context.

› Let's return to our example with the football players. Let's imagine that we want to assess whether each player is "good" or not, according to some measure we devise. Clearly, the way we determine whether a quarterback is good at throwing is different from the way we determine whether a running back is good at running.

› So, let's say that we'd like to have a method called "isGood" that returns "True" or "False," depending on whether a player is good or not, according to whatever method we devise. We can augment our earlier definitions to include this function.

› Let's put a function "isGood" in the FootballPlayer class. It's not possible to determine whether a generic football player is good or not, given that all we have is a name and team. So, in this case, we'll print out some sort of error message, saying that we called a function that wasn't defined.

```python
class FootballPlayer:
    name = "John Doe"
    team = "None"
    years_in_league = 0
    def printPlayer(self):
        print(self.name+" playing for the "+self.team+":")
    def isGood(self):
        print("Error! isGood is not defined!")
        return False
```

> Let's assume we have two players that we've created, just like before. We're now going to create a "playerlist," and we'll add both player1 and player2 into that list. Then, we'll go through each of the players in the list, using a for statement. For each player, we'll print out the player information using the printPlayer method, and then we'll call isGood and print out whether the player is a good player or not a good player.

```python
player1 = Quarterback()
player1.name = "John"
player1.team = "Cowboys"
player1.pass_attempts = 10
player1.completions = 6
player1.pass_yards = 57
player2 = RunningBack()
player2.name = "Joe"
player2.team = "Eagles"
player2.rushes = 12
player2.rush_yards = 73
playerlist = []
playerlist.append(player1)
playerlist.append(player2)
for player in playerlist:
    player.printPlayer()
    if (player.isGood()):
        print("   is a GOOD player")
    else:
        print("   is NOT a good player")
```

```
OUTPUT:
John playing for the Cowboys:
Error! isGood is not defined!
  is NOT a good player
Joe playing for the Eagles:
Error! isGood is not defined!
  is NOT a good player
```

> When we run this, we get error messages printed. That's what we'd expect.

> An error is not what we want; we want to be able to make comparisons. So, we'll define isGood as a function in each of the children classes. The following is what that will look like. In both of the **child classes**, we'll create a function isGood. For the quarterback, we return whether the yards per passing attempt are above some level. For the running back, we return whether the yards per rush are above some level.

```python
class FootballPlayer:
    name = "John Doe"
    team = "None"
    years_in_league = 0
    def printPlayer(self):
        print(self.name+" playing for the "+self.team+":")
    def isGood(self):
        print("Error! isGood is not defined!")
        return False
class Quarterback(FootballPlayer):
    pass_attempts = 0
    completions = 0
    pass_yards = 0
    def completionRate(self):
        return self.completions/self.pass_attempts
    def yardsPerAttempt(self):
        return self.pass_yards/self.pass_attempts
    def isGood(self):
        return (self.yardsPerAttempt() > 7)
```

```python
class RunningBack(FootballPlayer):
    rushes = 0
    rush_yards = 0
    def yardsPerRush(self):
        return self.rush_yards/self.rushes
    def isGood(self):
        return (self.yardsPerRush() > 4)
```

> Using the exact code as we had before, if we run it now, we get an output without the error messages.

```python
player1 = Quarterback()
player1.name = "John"
player1.team = "Cowboys"
player1.pass_attempts = 10
player1.completions = 6
player1.pass_yards = 57
player2 = RunningBack()
player2.name = "Joe"
player2.team = "Eagles"
player2.rushes = 12
player2.rush_yards = 73
playerlist = []
playerlist.append(player1)
playerlist.append(player2)
for player in playerlist:
    player.printPlayer()
    if (player.isGood()):
        print("  is a GOOD player")
    else:
        print("  is NOT a good player")

OUTPUT:
John playing for the Cowboys:
  is NOT a good player
Joe playing for the Eagles:
  is a GOOD player
```

> When the Python compiler sees the call to isGood, it first looks at the definition of isGood in the child class. If there's not a definition of that method there, it will look at the parent to see if the method is defined there.

> Inheritance is useful if you're defining your own set of classes, but we can actually inherit from any other class. Python even lets you treat basic types like strings or integers as a parent class. Especially useful is the fact that we can use inheritance to create our own exceptions (which are used to catch errors that would otherwise cause the program to crash).

[JSON AND PICKLE]

> JSON and pickle are two important Python modules that make objects much more usable. They are included in the standard library and can help make it easy to handle objects.

> JSON (JavaScript Object Notation) is a way of structuring data in a text format. It uses a syntax for writing objects that's similar to the way objects are defined in Java and Javascript. JSON data is a human-readable string as opposed to binary data. JSON groups information in objects using curly braces, with each attribute written as an attribute name, followed by a colon, followed by the value. The value can be a new object, nested inside the previous object.

> JSON is perfectly capable of representing our objects, and because it's a text format, we can read and write JSON data easily. Plus, it's something that is independent of the language that it was produced in. For this reason, JSON is the most common way that data files are transmitted over the web.

> Python's JSON module includes commands that let us convert data to and from JSON. Basically, the JSON routines let us convert a piece of data into a JSON string. Most, but not all, Python data types can be converted to JSON. The JSON string can be written to or read from a file like any other string.

> Pickle is a module that lets you read and write data other than strings more easily. Pickle lets us read and write data from a file in binary format (which is how most files you encounter every day are stored, from images to word-processing files). And it works for even more data types than JSON.

> Pickle is a Python-specific format, though. If you write a file using pickle commands, it needs to be read by another Python program also using pickle commands. Pickle should not be used for writing data that you need to send to other people, and you should never read pickle-produced files from others unless you are certain of the source, because it's easy for them to contain malicious data.

Readings

Lambert, *Fundamentals of Python*, chaps. 5–6.

Zelle, *Python Programming*, chap. 12.

Exercises

1 Assume that you have a class, "Game," defined as follows.

```
class Game:
    name = ""
    numplayers = 0
```

How would you define the following?

a) A video game class "Videogame" that has the same attributes as a "Game" and also keeps track of the platform that it is.

b) A board game class "Boardgame" that has the same attributes as a "Game" and also has a number of pieces and a size (stored as a list of two numbers: a length and a width).

2 For the "Game" class, assume that there is a method defined.

```
def print(self):
    print(self.name)
    print("Up to ", self.numplayers, "players")
```

How would you define functions so that calling "Videogame.print()" and "Boardgame.print()" give different printouts, reflecting the information they contain?

3 Write code to create a video game, and then print its information out.

4 How would you use the pickle module to save the video game from exercise 3 into a file, "Game.dat"?

5 How would you read in a game saved in "Game.dat" to a variable "savedgame"?

Objects with Inheritance and Polymorphism

Children inherit some really important stuff from their parents. I'm not just talking about eye color or height; I mean the fundamental structure of DNA that makes us human. Children can vary from parents in lots of ways, but the most fundamental traits that make human bodies work and grow are inherited. Believe it or not, inheritance plays a similar role in programming thanks to object-oriented design and programming.

Remember what an object is. An object lets us group both data and functions together into one package. We can put a lot of related data together in that package, along with functions to operate on the data. This gives us a level of abstraction. We don't worry about how the stuff inside the object works, we just worry about what method we can call to work with it. But most importantly, objects let us group together stuff that's related. Also, remember that objects are defined within a class, where an object is an actual instance of that class. My personal bank account might be one of many objects within a class called BankAccount.

Classes, let's recall, are defined by a class name. Inside the class are a set of variables called attributes, and a set of functions called methods. These attributes and methods are actually part of the class. The example here shows a class for recording information about gifts. There's the init constructor that gets called for every new object, as well as several accessor functions. To create an object, we assign a variable a new instance of that class. We can then call the methods on that object or access the attributes of that object. Here, I'm using that gift class to store information about a shirt given to me by my mother on my birthday in 2015. I then change that record so that it's from my sister instead.

This is encapsulation, the fundamental idea of object-oriented design where we put together the data and functions that work on that data into a single package. But there are two other aspects of object-oriented programming, and those are the ones we'll talk about in this lecture: inheritance and polymorphism.

Let's first start by seeing how inheritance works. Imagine that we have a program, and we're going to use it to keep track of statistics for different players on a sports team. Often, players with different positions will have different statistics that are relevant to them. For example, in soccer or hockey, a goalie is going to have saves while other players are going to have goals. In baseball, a pitcher will have different statistics than a batter, and in football, players on offense will have different statistics than those on defense.

I'll use an American football illustration here, though you don't really need to know anything about football to follow along. For a quarterback, we probably want to know the player's name and team, as well as data like the number of passes attempted, the number of completions, and the number of passing yards. Someone who follows this sport closely might want a lot more information, but this is just for illustration.

Now, we can set up some functions associated with the quarterback to help us compute percentages and averages, such as the percentage of completed passes, or the average yards gained per pass. Now, for the position of running back, we would again want the player's name and team, and now the number of rushes and how many rushing yards were gained. We could continue in this way to other positions such as wide receivers, and defensive players, and kickers, and so on.

But let's stay with just two positions. One possibility would be for us to create two classes. We could create a quarterback class and a running back class. The quarterback class would have the attributes for name, team, pass attempts, completions, and passing yards. The running back class would have attributes for name, team, rushes, and rushing yards. But, let's look at this for a minute. Notice that both the quarterback and the running back share some attributes. They both have the player's name and the player's team. In fact, this would be true for all of the various positions that we might want to define.

So let's imagine a different organization. Let's say that we have some base type, which we'll call Football Player. A football player will have all the attributes that are common across all the various types of players. In this case, that's the player's name and the team. We can then define a quarterback as a type of football player with some additional attributes—passes attempted, completions, and passing yards. Likewise, a running back is also a type of football player with some additional attributes—rushes and rushing yards.

What we've just seen is called inheritance. You can think of the football player as the parent, then the quarterback and the running back are the children. The children inherit the characteristics of the parent. In this case, the children inherit the name and team that were defined for the football player.

Let's look at some code, and to keep things simpler, I'm going to illustrate with examples where the attributes are not private. That is, I'm not going to have attributes starting with an underscore. Nor am I going to have accessor functions.

We define each of these classes individually. For the FootballPlayer class, we define it the same way we have been. For the Quarterback and RunningBack classes, notice that we put the name of their parent class in parentheses. Each of them just defines the attributes that are unique to that class—the attributes that were not in the parent class. So we have our FootballPlayer class defined with a name and team, and we set the values there to be John Doe for the name, and None for the team. For a Quarterback, we note that it is a child of the FootballPlayer class, and then we define the pass_attempts, completions, and pass_yards attributes, initializing all of them to 0. For a RunningBack, we again declare that it's a child or the FootballPlayer class, and then we define the rushes and rush_yards attributes, again initializing them to 0.

With those classes defined, we can then create an instance of a class. Say we create a player, called player1, that's a Quarterback. We can print the player's name. Since we didn't set the name, it uses whatever the default name was for all football players, which we said would be

John Doe. That is, the quarterback has a name attribute since its parent class, FootballPlayer, had a name attribute. We can also print out the pass_yards attribute, which is 0, just like we initialized it to be.

Now, say that instead of a quarterback, we had said that player1 was a RunningBack. We'd still have the name attribute since a running back is also a child of the FootballPlayer class, and FootballPlayer has a name attribute. However, if we tried to print off the pass_yards, we'd get an error. Pass_yards were defined only for the Quarterback. Creating different players is straightforward. As we see in this example, we can create player1 as a quarterback, and player2 as a running back, and we can set all of the values of the attributes appropriately.

Now, it's not just attributes that can be inherited. We can also inherit methods. We've augmented our classes here to include some methods. For the FootballPlayer class, we'll define a method, printPlayer, that prints out the name and team of the player. We'll also add some methods for the Quarterback and RunningBack classes to compute some statistics specific to those positions. For a quarterback, that'll be the completion rate and yards per attempt, and for the running back, that'll be the yards per rush.

We can go back to our two players that we defined earlier, and then we can call the methods for those players. Notice that we can call printPlayer for both player1 and player2. Because the method is defined in the parent, it's automatically inherited by the children. We can also call those statistics methods that are specific to each of the child classes. In the example we have here, we call printPlayer for the quarterback, then print out the completion rate and yards per attempt statistics. We then call printPlayer for the running back and print out the yards per rush statistics for that player.

Let me say a brief word about terminology. When people discuss inheritance, there are different terms used for the different classes. Sometimes, we call them parent and child classes, like I've been doing so far. Sometimes we call the parent class the base class, and we call the children derived classes. The idea here is that the parent class is a base that's shared by everything, and then we derive—or pull out—an extension from the base class. Other times, we'll call the parent a superclass and the children will be subclasses. The idea here is that the parent class encompasses all the other classes which are specializations of it. So, whether you hear parent or base or superclass, or you hear child or derived or subclass, just know that they're referring to the same thing.

Now, just like in biology where you can inherit traits from more than one parent, classes can inherit properties from multiple parents. And you'll see some books with a lot of discussion about what's called multiple inheritance, so you might be tempted to try it. But let me give you a piece of advice. For the most part, you should stay away from multiple inheritance. It can make your code more confusing to follow since you have multiple parents that you could inherit different attributes from, leading to conflicts on which one wins out, plus it's very rare that multiple inheritance is actually the right solution to your problem. So it's good to know that multiple inheritance exists, but we're going to avoid situations where one class can have two or more parents.

The third main feature of object-oriented programming is polymorphism. Think about that word. Poly means many, and morph refers to shape, so polymorphism refers to things taking on many shapes. When we use the term polymorphism, what we mean is that a function or a method can take on many different forms depending on the context. It'll be easiest to see it in action.

Let's go back to our earlier example with the football players. Let's imagine that we want to assess whether each player is good or not, according to some measure we devise. Clearly, the way we determine whether a quarterback is good at throwing or not is going to be different from the way we determine whether a running back is good at running or not.

So, say we'd like to have a method called isGood that returns true or false, depending on whether a player is good or not according to whatever method we devise. We can augment our earlier definitions to include this function. Let's put a function isGood in the FootballPlayer class. Now, it's not possible to determine whether a generic football player is good or not, given that all we have is a name and team. So in this case, we'll print out some sort of error message saying that we called a function that wasn't defined.

Now, let's see how we can use this. Let's assume we have two players that we've created, just like before. We're now going to create a playerlist, and we'll add both player1 and player2 into that list. Then, we'll go through each of the players in the list, using a for statement. For each player, we'll print out the player info using the printPlayer method, and then we'll call isGood and print out whether the player is a good player or not a good player. So what happens when we run this? Well, we get the error message printed out, right in the middle, and that should be what we'd expect.

Now, an error is not what we want. We want to be able to actually make comparisons so we'll define isGood as a function in each of the children classes. Here's what that'll look like. In both of the child classes, we'll create a function isGood. For the quarterback, we return whether the yards per passing attempt are above some level. For the running back, we return whether the yards per rush are above some level. So how does this work if we run it now? Using the exact same code as we had before, we now get an output without the error messages. For one of our players, the quarterback, we find that the player is not a good player, while the other player, the running back, is a good player.

What's happened here is that when the Python compiler sees the call to isGood, it first looks at the definition of isGood in the child class. If there's not a definition of that method there, it'll look at the parent to see if the method is defined there.

Now, this is one example of how polymorphism works. When we went through that player list, we were just calling the isGood method on each player but didn't know how it was implemented. In effect, the isGood method was taking a different shape in the different objects— that is, it was polymorphic. This made it a whole lot simpler for us.

We didn't have to call separate loops to call isGoodQuarterback and isGoodRunningBack or anything like that. Instead, we could have a single method defined, and all the objects that inherited from that method would also have that function defined. I want to show you one more modification to the code we just saw so that you can see another example of how polymorphism can work. This is a way of forcing us to use polymorphism.

Let's say that instead of going through the list of players and having an if statement, we instead just called a method called printGood that checked whether the player was good or not and printed the appropriate message. This would mean that we'd want to add that printGood method into the base class FootballPlayer. The printGood method will check whether the isGood method returns true or false and print the appropriate message.

Now, take a close look at the FootballPlayer class. Do you see anything missing? Well, there's no isGood function defined in the FootballPlayer class anymore. I deleted that function to show a bit more about how polymorphism can work. The printGood method is still calling isGood, but isGood is not defined here in this base class. Instead, we have to go to one of the derived classes to actually resolve what the function is supposed to do. Notice that this is forcing us to implement isGood in each of the children classes. Since the printGood method is calling isGood, if the isGood command is not defined in the child, then printGood will crash. But if we run this code, it's going to turn out exactly like what we had before, since we actually did define isGood in each of the child classes.

One term you'll sometimes hear people use when they discuss polymorphism is a virtual function or an abstract interface. Both of those terms give the connotation of something that's not really there. It's a function that's not really defined or an interface that's abstract instead of concrete.

Now, inheritance is useful if you're defining your own set of classes like we've seen in these examples. But we can actually inherit from any other class. Python even lets you treat basic types like strings or integers as a parent class. That's just confusing to me, though, so let's not talk about that. There is one place where inheritance from a standard type is especially useful, though, and that's exceptions. So let me spend just a minute about them.

First, let me remind you of what exceptions are. Exceptions are used to catch errors that would otherwise crash the program. For example, if we had a function to compute a division, we might catch a couple of types of error: a TypeError when the input values could not have a division defined, or a ZeroDivisionError when we try to divide by zero. If we encounter an error on our own, we can raise an exception. But even though there are a lot of exceptions defined, sometimes those exceptions don't really capture the nature of the problem.

We don't have an exception that describes this problem, so we're going to make our own exception, which will also demonstrate inheritance. This exception will be specific to our case, and we'll call it MissingChildMethodError. To create this new type of exception, we create a new class with that name, and list Exception as the parent, thus it inherits all the functionality that the exception class provides. I don't happen to have anything special to do with this exception, so I'll just define the body of the class as pass, meaning it's essentially identical to the generic Exception, but it has a different name. Now, in the isGood method, I can raise MissingChildMethodError instead. And when we run the code, indeed we see the MissingChildMethodError exception listed.

Even better, though, we can now catch that particular exception. If we set up a try-except statement in our main code like you see here, instead of the exception crashing the program, we can handle it. We can print our own nice message, and we can exit cleanly, or we could choose to do something else. The key is that we created our very own exception class, and that let us raise that exception and then deal with it nicely in a try-except block. So what do you think this code will do?

Well, we have a try-except block. The exception occurs in a call within the try statement, so the exception is handled by the except clause, which prints out "Whoops—we forgot to define isGood," and the code exits cleanly instead of crashing. In fact, given that we caught the exception, we could have continued on processing other data, without crashing our program. So that demonstrates just one of the useful ways we can use inheritance to create our own exceptions.

Now that we've seen objects, I want to introduce two important Python modules that make objects much more usable. After all, it's one thing to just write out a number or string, but to write out an object, that's a little bit trickier. Both of the modules that I want to introduce are included in the standard library and can really help make it easy to handle objects. They're called JSON—J-S-O-N—and pickle.

Remember that for our basic routines for reading and writing files, we deal with strings. We write out strings, and we read in strings. As you might imagine, it can be kind of a pain to have to deal so much with strings, especially when we have data in other formats. The idea of taking that data and turning it into a string to save in a file, or reading in strings and pulling out the individual pieces one at a time, can sometimes be overwhelming.

When we have data that's not a string, we need to convert it into one. JSON, which stands for JavaScript Object Notation, is a way of structuring data in a text format. It uses a syntax for writing objects that's very similar to the way that objects are defined in Java and JavaScript. JSON data is a nice, human-readable string as opposed to binary data. JSON groups information in objects using curly braces, with each attribute written as an attribute name, followed by a colon, followed by the value. The value can be a new object itself, nested inside the previous one.

So JSON is perfectly capable of representing our objects, and because it's a text format, we can read and write JSON data easily. Plus, it's something that is independent of the language that it was produced in. For this reason, JSON is the most common way that data files are transmitted over the web.

Python's JSON module includes commands that let us convert data to and from JSON. Basically, the JSON routines let us convert a piece of data into a JSON string. Most, though not all, Python data types can be converted to JSON. The JSON string can be written to or read from a file like any other string.

To use the Python JSON routines, we need to start out by importing JSON at the beginning of our file. We can then create a JSON string by using the command "json.dumps," and then for the parameter in parentheses, we put the data that we want to convert to JSON format. That gives us a string that we can output to a file just like any other. We can add a newline character to separate it from the other strings.

Later, we could read in the file by reading in a line as a string. For basic data types, we can use the "json.loads" command, putting the string in parentheses. The result of that command will be a data element that we can assign to a variable.

Let's first see a simple example. Imagine that we had the following code. We have a length and width defined, as 20 and 15. We open up a file for writing. Then, we create JSON strings for the length, width, and some text, just saying that this is data for an example. Each of those will be written to the file. So this code is creating a file containing three JSON strings. Now, how would we go about reading that and using it?

Well, here's the code to read that file. We open up the same file for reading. Then we read a line, and we use the "json.loads" command to convert it from a JSON string to a data element. We read in the length, width, and description, and then when we print out the description as well as the product of length and width, we get the answers we would expect.

Now, to make the most use of JSON and really see its power, we'll want to use it to store lists and objects. The process for writing will be exactly the same. Typically, when using JSON, the entire file is just one JSON element, so you're just writing one giant JSON string. The big advantage, though, is that it handles all the conversions between the data types and a string for you.

To see how we can write objects, consider our football player objects that were defined earlier. We can write them out by converting each object to a JSON string, which we can then write out. To do this, we don't pass the object to "json.dumps," but rather the object-dot-underscore-underscore-dict-underscore-underscore. Dict will give a dictionary version of the elements of the object, and that's what will get converted to a JSON string. We'll learn more about dictionaries soon. If we look at the actual output file, we can see that basically every attribute has been printed, along with its value. Now, reading in a JSON string into an object is trickier. Basically, each of the attributes will have to be read out of that string and set in the object one by one. It's a little painful, but it can be done.

Now, besides JSON, there's another Python module that's very useful for working with more complex data and which makes it possible to trivially read objects in addition to writing them. Pickle is a module that lets you read and write data other than strings more easily. Pickle lets us read and write data from a file in binary format, which is how most files you encounter every day are actually stored, from images to word processing files. And it works for even more data types than JSON.

Pickle is a Python-specific format. If you write a file using pickle commands, it basically needs to be read by another Python program also using pickle commands. Pickle should not be used for writing data that you need to send to other people, and you should never read pickle-produced files from others unless you're absolutely sure of the source, since it's easy for them to contain malicious data. Let me show you how to use pickle commands to read and write numbers more easily.

We start by importing the pickle object. We also need to change the way we write and read files. When we open a file for writing, or for reading, or for appending, we will need to use not just *w, r* or *a*, but will also need to add a *b* at the end. So to open a file for writing, we'll put *wb* as the second string inside the parentheses following open. Likewise, to read, we would write *rb*, and to append we would write *ab*. The *b* indicates that this will be a binary file—that is, a machine-readable file in binary, not a text-oriented file like those we've had previously. This also means that the pickled files that we will write and read are not ones that we'd be able to understand just by opening them in a word processor or something like we could do with JSON files.

Now, to write a value to the file, we'll write "pickle.dump," and then as parameters, we'll have two things. The first one is the data we're going to output. The data can be almost anything—a string, a number, a list, or an object. Following this, there's a comma, and then the name of the file that we're going to output to.

So, say we wanted to store data that we were keeping about a bank account. Maybe we want to store the account number, and the name of the account holder, and the balance, in that order, and we want it in a file called BankAccount.dat. How would we write that data out using pickle?

Well, first we'd have our "import pickle" command. We'd then open up the BankAccount.dat file for writing, being sure to put *wb* in at the end. Then we'd call the "pickle.dump" command, First, we would dump the account, then the owner, then the balance, each time specifying the file that we're dumping to. Finally, we close that file.

Now, what about reading from a file that was produced with pickle? Basically, we need to read the data out of that file in the same order that it went in. Here's how that works. When we open our file for reading, we have to note that it is *rb* instead of just *r*. The actual command to load the data in pickle is "pickle.load," and then in parentheses is the name of the file. That will pull out the next item that was written to the file. We need to store that item, so we have to assign the value to a variable.

Let's say that we wanted to read in the data for a bank account that we just saved. We can use the "pickle.load" command three times, pulling out the account, then the owner, then the balance. Notice that we're pulling out the data in the order that it was put in.

Let's look at how we'd output the football player objects from before. We can just take each of the objects and dump it straight to the file. That's all. Now, we couldn't actually look at this file like we did with the JSON file since it's in binary. The real advantage of pickle is on the other side. If we then want to read those objects back in, we can just use the "pickle.load" command and we get an object back. Unlike JSON, this is not a string or dictionary that we need to process further. We actually get an object back. And we can take that object, and we can compute with it, calling methods and everything, just like we had before. You see here that we can call things like the printPlayer and isGood methods on the objects.

The nice thing about pickle is that we don't need to worry at all about the details of how that data is getting stored in the file—no conversion to and from strings, no worry about how it's being written, and so on. However, it's not a universal file format, so it's not great, for instance, if you're going to produce data that people are going to download off of a web page. The place to use it is in your own programs, for your own use. For example, it's great to use pickle if you have a program that you need to be able to save and later load.

Traditionally, object-oriented programming is based on encapsulation, inheritance, and polymorphism—in that order. Encapsulation is easily the most important idea of the three since it helps you organize your code so that you don't have to worry about the details inside of an object, only the methods that are used to interact with it.

Inheritance lets you duplicate an encapsulation and pass it on to the next generation. In the early days of object-oriented programming, proponents claimed that inheritance would eliminate the need to rewrite code for new programs. That particular payoff from using inheritance didn't really pan out quite as much as originally hoped, but what object-oriented design does do is it makes it easier on the programmer to understand and revise their own program, and that makes it possible—whatever your own level—to build more complex programs than would otherwise be possible.

And polymorphism, in practice, is always used with inheritance. Polymorphism lets us treat lots of different types of objects the same way. We can write one set of code, calling methods without worrying about the particular way that that method is implemented.

In Python, object-oriented programming is more of an option rather than a requirement. But objects are such a useful way of designing code that objects and classes are pretty pervasive, especially in Python modules. The tkinter module for creating user interfaces relies heavily on inheritance and polymorphism, for instance.

The key in object-oriented design is to consider what the units of description are, and then turn these into classes—checking accounts, for instance, or vehicles, or people. You want to think about conceptual ideas that you can package together nicely in one class. What things are there, and then what operations have to be done to those things is the heart of object-oriented design. Once you've determined the things, and what needs to happen to them, you're on the way to designing a class and implementing it.

In the next lecture, we'll use classes again, no longer just for specific applications such as bank accounts, but for much more general ways of organizing data, known as data structures. I'll see you then.

19

Data Structures: Stack, Queue, Dictionary, Set

An orderly and systematic method of organizing data makes it much easier to actually use that data. Our code can access the data more easily to find the particular part of the data desired, and this lets us create more efficient programs. The term we use in computer science to describe these ways of organizing data is "data structures." As you will learn in this lecture, structuring our data can make it possible to do things that we never could if it's unorganized.

[DATA STRUCTURES]

> Classes and objects are great at tying together different types of data, but object-oriented design is focused more on bundling different types of data together. **Data structures** are focused on how to organize large amounts of the same type of data.

> One of the simplest data structures is what Python calls a "list," and other languages call an "array," which has an order—is linear—and lets us string many distinct things together in sequence (so it's sequential).

> But stringing things together is not the only way we could organize them. We could lay them out in a grid, for example. Either a list that's sorted, or a heap, would make it much easier to get the largest (or, alternatively, the smallest) value.

> Data structures can also be nonlinear and nonsequential. Maybe the data would be better organized around memberships, or geographic location, or a bunch of special-purpose keys associated with each object.

> There are many methods for organizing large amounts of data. For an army, organizing into a hierarchical structure might be great for helping make sure orders get followed. But that might not be a great way of organizing if the goal were to come up with creative ideas. In other words, organization affects operations.

[STACKS]

> Imagine that we have a stack of books. Let's assume that they are heavy books, such that we can only hold one at a time. If we have a stack of these books, there are basically just two things we can do: add a book to the stack or take the top book off of the stack.

> The **stack** data structure is basically just this, only with data instead of books. If we add something new onto the stack, we'll call the operation a "push"; if we remove the top item from the stack, we'll call it a "pop."

> Let's see how this would work with a list and some of the commands already available for lists. First, just to extend the book analogy, let's assume that we've organized our book data into a book class, where we store a title and author per book. We also create three specific books: a long book, medium book, and short book.

```
class book:
    title = ""
    author = ""
long_book = Book()
long_book.title = "War and Peace"
long_book.author = "Tolstoy"
medium_book = Book()
medium_book.title = "Book of Armaments"
medium_book.author = "Maynard"
short_book = Book()
short_book.title = "Vegetables I Like"
short_book.author = "John Keyser"
```

> Our stack of books is going to be represented using a list. The first book in the list is the book on the bottom of the stack, and the last book in the list is the top book on the stack. So, to push a book onto the book stack, we would just use the "append" command on the stack of books.

> We start out with an empty list, which means that we have an empty stack. We then stack the books on top of each other. Let's say that we want to put the medium book down first. We'll append the medium book to the list. Next, we might want to stack the short book, so we append it. Finally, we stack on the long book.

```
book_stack = []
book_stack.append(medium_book)
book_stack.append(short_book)
book_stack.append(long_book)
```

> In memory, this set of books is treated as a list, with the medium, short, and long books listed in order. But we are supposed to think of it conceptually as a stack, with the medium book at the bottom, then the short, and then the long book.

> Now let's say that we want to pop the top book off of the stack. Lists have a built-in method named "pop," which will remove the last item from a list and return it. In this example, we assign the result of the pop to a variable "next_book," which now refers to the long book, because that was the first one on the stack. If we were to print the title and author of next_book, we would see the title and author of the long book. If we were to pop another book off the stack, the next one would be the short book.

```
book_stack = []
book_stack.append(medium_book)
book_stack.append(short_book)
book_stack.append(long_book)
next_book = book_stack.pop()
print(next_book.title+" by "+next_book.author)
```

```
OUTPUT:
War and Peace by Tolstoy
```

> Stacks give us what's referred to as "last in, first out"—that is, the last thing pushed is the first thing popped.

> Inside computers, stacks have a very fundamental use. As we make function calls, the computer memory is storing data in what's referred to as the **call stack**, also known as a "control stack" or "runtime stack" or "frame stack," which consists of function activation records, which keep track of all the variables and data defined in that part of the program.

[QUEUE]

> What if we want a "first in, first out" process? This is what you encounter when people queue up to stand in line—the first one in line is the first one handled.

> We can implement a queue with a list, very similarly to how we implemented a stack. The order of data in the list is the same as in the queue. With a queue, just like with a stack, we can push new objects onto the end of the list using the "append" command. However, instead of popping from the end of the list, we instead need to take off the element at the front of the list.

> Python makes this really easy. The "pop" command can take a parameter, indicating which element gets taken out of the list. If no parameter is given, it defaults to the final element, as we saw with stacks. But for the first element in the list, we just pass in a 0, and the first element is removed.

> Let's look at some code to get the idea. Instead of a stack of books that we are piling up, we have a queue of books. Maybe we buy books one at a time and want to read them in the order we bought them, for example.

› We can build our queue like we built the stack. We start with an empty list we call "book_queue." Then, we add books to book_queue by calling the append methods. This creates the exact same list as we had in the earlier case. The only difference is in how we think about it—as a queue, versus a stack.

› Just like we could pull one item off of the stack, we can also pull one item off of a queue, by calling the pop method on book_queue. Notice the parameter 0 when we call pop. So, this call to pop would pull off the next book in the queue. When we finished that book, we could call pop with parameter 0 again to get the next book in the queue.

```
book_queue = []
book_queue.append(medium_book)
book_queue.append(short_book)
book_queue.append(long_book)
next_book = book_queue.pop(0)
```

[HASH TABLES]

› Another really useful data structure is called a **hash table**, which works by mapping large data values into a smaller set of indices.

› To see how helpful it can be to map like this, imagine that you have a set of friends and they all have phone numbers, but all of them have blocked caller ID. So, when they call, you don't know whose phone number belongs to whom. You'd like to be able to enter a phone number and find who it is.

› It would not be a good idea to create a giant list, where the list element number corresponded to the phone number. So, if Sue Smith had phone number (135) 246-0987, then element number 1352460987 would have the value "Sue Smith." The problem is that most of the list is going to be empty.

> In fact, there will be 10 billion possible phone numbers, so you'd need a list with 10 billion elements. Even if we could store that whole list, maybe you have about 100 friends, so only 100 of those list values will even be filled in.

0000000000	
0000000001	
0000000002	
...	
1352460987	Sue Smith
...	
8647531234	John James
...	
9999999999	

> Here's where a hash table comes in. Instead of a list of 10 billion elements, let's instead take a list of just 100 elements. We'll store each person in a slot that corresponds to just the last two digits of the phone number. So, Sue Smith, because her phone number ends in 87, would go into the list at index 87.

00	
01	
02	
...	
34	John James (8647531234)
...	
87	Sue Smith (1352460987)
...	
99	

> This is a much more compact representation than the first list. But what if two people have the same last two digits to their phone number?

> Imagine that Bill Brown comes along with the phone number (808) 424-1287. He'll end up in the same position as Sue Smith. To resolve this, we can use **chaining**—just making a list of everyone in that slot. So, when we get to a slot, we can't just pull out the name; instead, we have to look at everyone in that list. But it's still much more practical than the giant list.

00	
01	
02	
...	
34	John James (8647531234)
...	
87	Sue Smith (1352460987), Bill Brown (8084241287)
...	
99	

> Imagine that instead of something simple like a phone number, we had some other way of identifying people. For example, maybe each of your friends has a nickname that he or she uses online, and you want to be able to look people up by that nickname. But we need some way of converting the nickname into a number. A function to convert some particular key phrase into a number that can be used to index into an array is called a **hash function**.

> Hash tables can get much more complicated than this, but fortunately, there's a tool in Python that basically implements hash tables for us, and we don't even have to come up with our own hash function. In Python, this tool is called **dictionary**, and the Python command to create a new dictionary is called "dict."

> Compared to the alphabetical list of a traditional dictionary in a book, a hash table is designed to be more efficient. And there are other names for hash tables, including "map," "symbol table," and "associative array."

[SETS]

> A different way that hash tables can be used is accessible with another built-in Python data structure: the **set**. A set is just a collection of items, but it will be stored using a hash table instead of a list so that it does mathematical set operations and checks set membership very quickly.

> In the following, we've created a set of people, and we initialize it with three people's names. Notice that we have the elements of the set inside the curly braces, separated by commas. This code also shows that we can use the "in" statement to check whether or not a particular item is in the set or not. In this case, we check for the string "John." Because that string was part of the set, this code will print out "Yes!"

```
people = {'John', 'Sue', 'Bill'}
if 'John' in people:
    print("Yes!")
else:
    print("No!")

OUTPUT:
Yes!
```

> Note that we could get the exact same effect by using the "set" command, as follows, instead of the curly braces. The set command takes in a list as a parameter, and all the elements of the list get put into the set. One big advantage of the set command over curly braces is that the set command lets us create an empty set. If we just have curly braces, with nothing inside, that will create an empty dictionary, not an empty set. So, if we want to start with an empty set and gradually add things to it, we have to use the set command.

```
people = set(['John', 'Sue', 'Bill'])
if 'John' in people:
    print("Yes!")
else:
    print("No!")

OUTPUT:
Yes!
```

> Sets have some additional operations defined on them that can be very useful. First, sets have an "add" method defined. To add a new element to a set, just call "add" as a method on that set and pass in the new element as a parameter. In the following example, we have a set of friends from work, and we add "Kathy" to that list. You can see from the output that Kathy is added to the set. Likewise, there is a "remove" method defined. In the example, we remove "Fred" from the list.

```
work_friends = {'Sue', 'Eric', 'Fred'}
print(work_friends)
work_friends.add('Kathy')
print(work_friends)
work_friends.remove('Fred')
print(work_friends)

OUTPUT:
{'Fred', 'Eric', 'Sue'}
{'Fred', 'Eric', 'Sue', 'Kathy'}
{'Eric', 'Sue', 'Kathy'}
```

Readings

Gries, *Practical Programming*, chap. 11.

Lambert, *Fundamentals of Python*, chaps. 7–8 and 11.

Exercises

1   Assume that the "Stack" class is defined as in the lecture. What would be the output of the following code?

```
namestack = Stack()
namestack.push("John")
namestack.push("James")
namestack.push("Joseph")
person = namestack.pop()
print(person)
person = namestack.pop()
print(person)
person = namestack.pop()
print(person)
```

2   Assume that the "Queue" class is defined as in the lecture. What would be the output of the following code?

```
namequeue = Queue()
namequeue.enqueue("John")
namequeue.enqueue("James")
namequeue.enqueue("Joseph")
person = namequeue.dequeue()
print(person)
person = namequeue.dequeue()
print(person)
person = namequeue.dequeue()
print(person)
```

3 What would be the output of the following code?

```
cast = {"Cardinal Ximenez" : "Michael Palin", "Cardinal
    Biggles" : "Terry Jones", "Cardinal Fang" : "Terry
    Gilliam"}
cast["customer"] = "John Cleese"
cast["shopkeeper"] = "Michael Palin"
print(cast["shopkeeper"])
print(cast["Cardinal Ximenez"])
print(cast["Cardinal Fang"])
```

4 What would be the output of the following code?

```
primes = {2, 3, 5, 7, 11, 13, 17, 19, 23, 29, 31, 37}
teens = set([13, 14, 15, 16, 17, 18, 19])
print(primes - teens)
print(primes & teens)
print(primes | teens)
print(primes ^ teens)
```

Data Structures: Stack, Queue, Dictionary, Set

An orderly and systematic method of organizing data makes it much easier to actually use that data. Our code can access the data more easily to find the particular part of the data desired, and this lets us create more efficient programs. The term we use in Computer Science to describe these ways of organizing data is data structures. Structuring our data can make it possible to do things that we never could if it's unorganized. Classes and objects are great at tying together different types of data, but object-oriented design is focused more on bundling different types of data together. Data structures are focused on how to organize large amounts of the same type of data.

One of the simplest of data structures is what Python calls a list, and other languages call an array. A list or array has an order, it's linear, and it lets us string together many distinct things together in a sequence, so it's sequential. But stringing things together is not the only way we could organize them. We could lay them out in a grid. If we had a list that's sorted, or a heap, that would make it much easier to get the largest or the smallest value. Data structures can also be non-linear, non-sequential. Maybe the data would be better organized around memberships, or geographic location, or a bunch of special-purpose keys associated with each object.

There are many, many methods for organizing large amounts of data. For an army, organizing into a hierarchical structure might be great for helping make sure that orders get followed. But that might not be the greatest way of organizing if the goal were to come up with creative ideas. To state it simply, organization affects operations. We're going to start with two of the most basic data structures—stacks and queues—which can be implemented using lists. Then we'll move to a couple of non-linear data structures—dictionaries and sets—both of which can be implemented using a hash table.

OK, imagine we have a stack of books. Let's assume that these are heavy books so that I can only hold one at a time. If I have a stack of these books, there are basically just two things I can do: I can either add a book to the stack, or I can take the top book off of the stack. The stack data structure is basically just this only, with data instead of books. If we add something new onto the stack, we'll call the operation a push. If we remove the top item from the stack, we call it a pop. That's all we want to do with a stack—push or pop.

Let's see how this would work with a list and some of the commands already available for lists. First, just to extend the book analogy, let's assume that we've organized our book data into a book class, where we store a title and author per book. We also create three specific books, which I've called a long book, medium book, and short book.

Our stack of books is going to be represented using a list. The first book in the list is the book on the bottom of the stack, and the last book in the list is the top book on the stack. So, to push a book onto the book stack, we would just use the append command on the stack of books, like this: We start out with an empty list which means we have an empty stack. We then stack the books on top of each other. Let's say we want to put the medium book down first. We'll append the medium book to the list. Next, we might want to stack the short book, so we append it. And finally, we stack on the long book. Now, in memory, this set of books is treated as a list, with the medium, short, and long books listed in order. But we're supposed to think of it conceptually as a stack, with the medium book at the bottom, then the short, then the long book.

OK, so now let's say that we want to pop the top book off of the stack. Well, it just so happens that lists have a built in method named pop. Isn't that convenient? Pop will remove the last item from a list and return it. In our example, we assign the result of the pop to a variable next book, and so next book now refers to the long book since that was the first one on the stack. If we were to print the title and author of next book, we'd see that the title and author are those of the long book. If we were to pop another book off of the stack, the next one would be the short book.

The key thing to keep in mind is to think of this as though we're using a stack. Even though the way we actually implement it is with a list, which we use for all sorts of other things, we want to think of it as though it's a stack and just use our push and pop operations. To help force ourselves to use the stack this way, we could even create a separate stack class that just has methods named push and pop so that we're kind of forced to obey the rules of a stack. Stacks give us what's referred to as last in, first out—that is, the last thing pushed in is the first thing popped out. An example of a stack in everyday life is when a workforce has layoffs that are based strictly on seniority—the last people hired are the first ones fired.

The card game Solitaire is a good example of a stack. In Solitaire, you draw cards from a deck, and as cards are drawn, they're placed onto a stack called the waste. We would say they get pushed onto the waste stack. Then during the player's turn, they always have the option of taking the current top card off of the waste stack to play it. We would say that the top card gets popped off of the waste stack.

Let's see how the code for a waste stack would work where we're dealing with a 3-card draw. I'm not going to show a whole Solitaire game here, but just the part dealing with the waste pile. We would first set up our waste pile as a stack. Then, while the player is playing, there are two possible moves that would require something to be done with that stack. One move would be to draw. In this case, three cards are drawn from the deck, and those cards are placed onto the waste pile. So we'll call the push method on the waste pile object three times, once for each card. The other move that involves the waste pile is when a player wants to use a card from the waste pile. In this case, we'll call the pop method on the waste pile object. This removes the top card from the stack and it returns it as current card. The program would then have to handle the card getting played wherever it goes.

Inside computers, stacks have a very fundamental use. As we make function calls, the computer memory is storing data in what's referred to as the call stack. The call stack—also known as a control stack, or a runtime stack, or a frame stack—consists of function activation records, where the function activation record keeps track of all the variables and data defined in that part of the program.

To illustrate, consider a program with functions *a*, *b*, and *c*, where *c* calls *b* and *b* calls *a*. Somewhere in the main code, we have a call to function *c*. When we first start out the main program, our call stack just consists of the main program. When we call *c*, the function activation record for *c* is created and pushed onto the call stack. When it calls *b*, we get a function activation record for *b* pushed on. And when *b* calls *a*, then *a*'s function activation record is pushed on. When we're finished with *a*, its record is popped off the stack. Then, *b* finishes, and its record is popped off. And finally, *c* is finished and its record is popped off, leaving us back in the context of the main program.

Now, what if we want the opposite of a stack, where we want a first in, first out process? This is what you encounter when people queue up to stand in line—the first one in line is the first one handled. A streaming video service may let you create a personal queue of what to watch next. We can implement a queue with a list, very similar to how we implemented a stack. The order of data in the list is the same as in the queue. With a queue, just like with a stack, we can push new objects on to the end of the list using the append command. However, instead of popping from the end of the list, we instead need to take off the element at the front of the list. Python makes this really easy. The pop command can take a parameter, indicating which element gets taken out of the list. If no parameter is given, it defaults to the final element, as we saw with stacks. But for the first element in the list, we just pass in a zero and the first element is removed.

Let's look at one small piece of code just to get the idea. Now, instead of a stack of books that we're piling up, we have a queue of books. Maybe we buy books one at a time and we want to read them in the order that we bought them. We can build our queue like we built the stack. We start with an empty list that we call book queue. Then, we add books to book queue by calling the append methods. This creates the exact same list that we had in the earlier case. The only difference is in how we think about it—are we thinking about it as a stack or as a queue?

Well, just like we could pull one item off of the stack, we can also pull one item off of a queue by calling the pop method on book queue. Notice the parameter zero when we call pop. So this call to pop would pull off the next book in the queue. When we finished that book, we could call pop with parameter zero again to get the next book in the queue.

Just like with stacks, we could create a separate class for queues if we want. That'll help force us to treat the list like a queue. The typical terms we use in programming to describe adding on to a queue or taking the first element are enqueue and dequeue. So our queue class can be defined with an attribute that's just a list that begins empty, along with an enqueue operation that appends to the list, and a dequeue method that just pops off the first element in the list. I've also added a method to tell me if the queue is empty or not. It'll just check the length of the list, and if it's zero, it'll return true.

Suppose we have a business where we sell shrubberies. The business has a list of orders that we want to process on a first-come, first-served basis for as long as the inventory holds out. Here's how a program to implement this might look. We have our queue class that I just discussed, and we'll also have a class defined to hold an order. An order will have a customer name and an amount, which is the number of shrubberies ordered.

The order class is pretty straightforward. In our main code, we'll start out by creating a variable, orders—that will be our queue of orders. There are lots of ways we could generate orders, but for this example, I'm just generating 20 random orders. The for loop will go over 20, and will generate an order for a random amount from 1–200. The customer name will just be Customer followed by the order number. From this, we create a new order, and we add that to our queue by calling the enqueue method on orders.

At this point, we have our queue of orders. We'll then set an inventory amount—in this case, that's 1000 shrubberies—and we'll start processing the queue as long as it's not empty. The first thing we do is get the next order from the queue—that's the dequeue method called on orders. We check to see if we have enough inventory to fill that order. If so, we print a message to go ahead, and fill it and we deduct that amount from inventory. If we don't have enough inventory, we give a message to notify the customer that it won't be filled. Now, if we look at a run of this code, we see that we fill several orders for customers 0 through 8. We don't have enough to fill the orders of the next few, but later we run across a few people who have small orders that we can still fill.

Another place that queues come up is in what's called a buffer for handling software events, such as a mouse movement or a keyboard key being pressed. This buffer is just a queue of the various events. That way, if lots of events happen quickly and they come in faster than they can be handled, you don't lose your data. If you've ever typed something in on a keyboard and you've seen it take a second before it appears on the screen, you've probably seen the hidden effects of a queue somewhere in the system.

Another really useful data structure is called a hash table, and it works by mapping a large number of data values into a smaller set of indices. To see how helpful it can be to map like this, imagine you have a set of friends and they all have phone numbers, but all of them have blocked caller ID so when they call, you don't know whose phone number belongs to who. You'd like to be able to enter a phone number and find out who it is.

Something that would not be a good idea would be to create a giant list where the list element number corresponds to the phone number. So if Sue Smith had phone number 135-246-0987, then element number 1352460987 would have the value Sue Smith. Now, I hope you can see the problem here. Most of that list is going to be empty. In fact, there will be 10 billion possible phone numbers, so you'd need a list with 10 billion elements. That's crazy. Even if we could store that whole list, maybe you have about 100 friends, so only 100 of those list values will even be filled in. Now, here's where a hash table comes in. Instead of a list of 10 billion elements, let's instead take a list of just 100 elements. And we'll store each person in a slot that corresponds to just the last 2 digits of the phone number. So Sue Smith, since her phone number ends in 8 7, would go into the list at index 87. And John James, whose phone number ends in 3 4, would go into the list at index 34.

There are two things that I hope you're thinking—actually make that three—the first one being "I can't believe how cool this stuff is." But more to the point, the first thing I hope you notice is that this is a much, much more compact representation than that first list was. And the next thing that you might have thought was "What if two people have the same last two digits to their phone number?" Imagine that Bill Brown comes along with a phone number like 108-424-1287. He'll end up in position 87—the same position as Sue Smith. To resolve this, we can use chaining—just making a list of everyone in that slot. So when we get to a slot, we can't just pull out the name, we have to look at everyone in that list. But it's still a whole lot more practical than that giant list was.

Now, imagine that instead of something simple like a phone number, we had some other way of identifying people. For instance, maybe each of your friends has a nickname that they use online and you want to be able to look people up by that nickname. Nicknames don't usually have digits you can just pull out to find the index like a phone number did. Instead, we need some way of converting the nickname into a number.

A function to convert some particular key phrase into a number that can be used to index into an array is called a hash function. Let's just say that there's some hash function that when we apply it to the nicknames of your friends will give a value back between 0 and 99. We can put that friend in the slot corresponding to that number. For instance, if Sue Smith has the nickname Superstar and the hash function converts Superstar to the number 71, then we'll put Sue in the 71st element of the hash table. Later on, if we want to find who has the nickname Superstar, we convert that nickname to a number, 71, and then we look in slot 71 to see who's there. If there's a chain, we look at everyone in the chain to find the match.

Hash tables can get a lot more complicated than this. But fortunately, there's a tool in Python that basically implements hash tables for us, and we don't even have to come up with our own hash function. In Python, this tool is called Dictionary, and the Python command to create a new dictionary is called dict. Now, compared to the alphabetical list of a traditional dictionary in a book, a hash table is designed to be more efficient. And there are other names for hash tables, including map, symbol table, and associative array.

To create a dictionary in Python, we use curly braces. When we write "my_dictionary = {}," we're creating a hash table or a dictionary with no elements—with nothing inside of it. We can also set elements of the dictionary at the time we define it. So, if we want a dictionary that lets us store nicknames, we can write it as "nicknames = {}," and then some data inside the curly braces. That data inside of the curly braces gives the nickname and the full name of each person. We just give the nickname, followed by a colon, followed by the real name. And we use commas to separate however many initial data points we want.

We can access an element of the nickname list with a format very similar to the way we find an element of a list. We take the name of the dictionary, which in this case is nicknames, and then in square brackets we give the index. Instead of a numerical value like we had with lists, we'll have the nickname we're looking for as the index. The result is that the code you see here will identify the person who was entered into the dictionary with the given name.

We could also build up our dictionary in a completely different way. Instead of initializing the dictionary with data, we could begin with an empty dictionary and assign new elements to it one by one. The syntax here is, again, very similar to what we'd see in a list. We just put the nickname in the square brackets and assign the real name to that element.

Now, let's be clear about exactly how this is set up. Putting something into a dictionary requires two parts: a key and a value. The key can be any immutable data type, so it's okay to have a string, like we've seen in the nickname example, or an integer, or floating-point number, or even a tuple. However, it's not okay to have a mutable data type, like a list or an object. The value, on the other hand, can be mutable or immutable.

Let me tell you about two more particularly useful things that you can do with a dictionary. Sometimes, we might want to delete an item. To do this, we write del, followed by the dictionary element that we want to delete—that is, the name of the dictionary, followed by brackets, with the key to delete inside of them. In the example we see here, the Superstar nickname is deleted from the dictionary. The second thing that's really useful is a way to check whether or not a key is in the dictionary. To do this, we write the key, then the word in, then the dictionary. And this will be true if that key is currently part of the dictionary, and false otherwise. So again, in the example, if we check for the nickname Cowboys Fan we'll get a true returned. And if we check for Superstar, we get a false returned, since this nickname was just deleted.

Just so you're aware, you can also iterate through all the elements of a dictionary using a for statement. Writing "for x in dictionary" will let x take on the values of all the keys in the dictionary. In the example here, I write "for nickname in nicknames." This means that in the loop, nickname will be the key, and we'll go through every key in the dictionary this way. And notice that when we print out the entries this way, they're not in the same order that they were put in. We put in Sue Smith, then Bill Brown, then John James. But when we print out all the keys, we find Sue Smith first, then John James, then Bill Brown. The reason is that underneath, there's a hash table, and the order is going to be based on the values that the keys were hashed to. That specific information is hidden from us, but we see the effect.

To illustrate a use for dictionaries, let me show you a short program that you could use to handle passwords. Our program is going to be a login part of a program. We'll ask for a username and password, and let someone through only if they have the right combination. Then, if they have three incorrect attempts, we leave the program. In our code here, we begin by setting up the passwords. In this case, our username will be our key, and the password will be the value. We initialize two variables—failed attempts, which will be used to count how many failed login attempts there were; and verified, which will be used to note that someone has logged in correctly.

Our while loop will run as long as we're not yet verified. In the loop, we first get the user name and password. The key line is the next one—the if statement. We first check to see if the username that the person entered is even in our password dictionary. That's the first part of the if condition. Assuming that's true, the second part of the condition is checked, so we find out whether the password associated with that username is true or not. If the condition is true, the user entered a correct username and password combination, so we print a message and mark verified as true. The code will now leave the while loop and go on. On the other hand, if the user entered a bad username or the incorrect password, we print out a warning message and we increase the number of failed attempts. If this was our third failed attempt, we completely exit the program. Take some time to try this out for yourself and see how it runs in practice. Try setting up some different username/password combinations, and then run the code to make sure that it works

One quick warning: Although this general approach is indeed the way that passwords are handled, if we're writing code that will actually be used, we wouldn't list the actual passwords in the code like this. Instead, we would store encrypted passwords. That way, there's never a list anywhere of actual passwords that someone could grab and steal; there's only a list of encrypted passwords.

Now, a different way that hash tables can be used is accessible with another built-in Python data structure, and that's the set. You've learned about sets in math, and this is just a way of getting that same effect. A set is just going to be a collection of items, but it'll be stored using a hash table instead of a list. And this lets it do mathematical set operations and check for set membership really quickly. For instance, we might want to keep a list of the ingredients that are in a particular dish that we're fixing. We can create a set by using curly braces, just like we did with the dictionary. In contrast to a dictionary though, we won't have key-value pairs; but instead, we'll just have the individual items in the set. Let's see what this'll look like.

Here, we've created a set of people, and we initialize it with three people's names. Notice that we have the elements of the set inside the curly braces, separated by commas. This code also shows that we can use the in statement to check whether or not a particular item is in the set or not. In this case, we check for the string John. Since that string was part of the set, this code will print out "Yes!"

Now, note that we could get the exact same effect by using the set command—like you see here—instead of the curly braces. The set command takes in a list as a parameter, and all the elements of the list get put into the set. One big advantage of the set command over curly braces is that the set command will let us create an empty set. If we just have curly braces with nothing inside, that'll create an empty dictionary, not an empty set. So, if we want to start with an empty set and gradually add things to it, we have to use the set command.

Sets have some additional operations defined on them that can be really useful. First, sets have an add method defined. To add a new element to a set, just call add as a method on that set, and pass in the new element as a parameter. In the example you see here, we have a set of friends from work, and we add Kathy to that list. You can see from the output that Kathy is added to the set. Likewise, there's a remove method defined. In the example, we remove Fred from the list, and you can see he's gone. Sets support all the standard set operations, such union and intersection, but the notation is different from what you would see in a math class. Here, we have two sets of friends: one set from the neighborhood containing John, Sue, and Bill; and one set from work containing Sue, Eric, and Fred. Notice that Sue is in both sets.

We can find the people in one set but not the other using the minus symbol. So, when we say "neighborhood_friends - work_friends," we're left with just John and Bill; Sue was removed. We can find the union of two sets using a single vertical bar. In much of programming, the vertical bar means or, and that's how the union works—anyone in one set or the other is in the final set. In this case, we get the union, showing all five unique individuals. We can also get the intersection of two sets using a single ampersand for and, and that's how intersection works. The intersection of the sets are those people in the first set and the second one. In this case, that's just Sue. And finally, to get the list of people in either set but not in both, we use the carat—the little arrow pointing up. This is what's called an exclusive or in logic terms, and it's the same as the union minus the intersection. In the example, this would give us everyone in the set except Sue.

Let's look at an example of how sets can be useful. Let's say that we're fixing a meal and we need to go out and buy ingredients. In the code, we'll have a recipe class that includes a name for the recipe and a list of ingredients needed. The initialization routine will take those items in as parameters. Then suppose our meal has three dishes—an omelet, bread, and cake. Each of those dishes has a list of ingredients, and we form a list of all those dishes.

Now, the next few lines are key. We start out with an empty set for a shopping list. We then go through each of the dishes in the list, and for each one, we form a set from the ingredients in the dish. Next, we form the shopping list by taking the existing shopping list and forming the union with the new set of ingredients. This will add any new ingredients to our list.

When this is finished, our shopping list consists of every ingredient we'll need for the meal. However, we also have several ingredients on-hand already. So, we take the set of these ingredients on-hand and perform a set difference to remove these ingredients from the shopping list. And finally, we print out the shopping list. If you look at the output, you'll see that we have a single list of all the items needed for any recipe, but that are not already on hand.

Data structures provide an organization that lets us perform operations more effectively. The Python list lets us implement stacks and queues very easily, all of which are linear or sequential data structures. Python also provides support for nonlinear, or non-sequential data structures such as dictionaries and sets—both of which are based on the hash table. And this is just the beginning of data structures. In future lectures, we'll see a couple more—graphs and trees—plus there are hundreds of other data structures used for specific applications. The main thing I want you to take away is that by providing some structure to the data, we can speed up some of the operations on that data.

In the next lecture, we're going to look at how we can use algorithms to describe ways of working with these and other data structures to accomplish specific tasks. I'm really excited about this topic, since algorithms are what many people would argue is the heart of computer science. I'm looking forward to you joining me there.

20

Algorithms: Searching and Sorting

lgorithms form the core of computer science. Algorithms are how we describe what we actually want the computer to do. Computer programming is really just the process of taking an algorithm and converting it into a program that the computer understands. The program is the concrete incarnation of the more general algorithm. In this lecture, you will learn more about algorithms, including how they're described and how they're implemented in code. You will also learn a few of the most well-known algorithms for searching and sorting.

[ALGORITHMS]

› Writing a program is essentially the same thing as writing an **algorithm**. The difference is that a program is a specific, concrete implementation in a particular programming language. An algorithm can be thought of as a more general description that's not necessarily tied directly to a particular programming language.

› We do not want to tie algorithms too tightly to any particular programming language, so we typically describe algorithms in a form that corresponds to some programming language but is not actual code in that language.

› One example of such a form is a **flowchart**, where we describe the algorithm graphically. We identify individual steps by shapes that contain text describing the step, with arrows showing how to move from one step to the next.

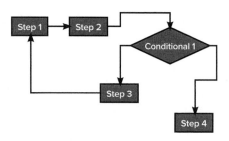

> We can also use **pseudocode** to describe the function of the algorithm. With pseudocode, we give an overview of the various steps of the algorithm and how they relate to each other. Pseudocode looks a lot like regular code in some languages, but many of the details can be eliminated along the way. Conversely, a single step in the algorithm might actually involve several lines of real code. If we design our algorithms well, it should always be straightforward to convert our algorithms into code.

```
1.  Step 1
2.  Step 2
3.  If (condition)
    a.  Step 3
    b.  Go to Step 1
4.  Else
    a.  Step 4
```

[SEARCHING]

> To illustrate how algorithms work and how they're implemented, we're going to start with one of the simplest general algorithms: a **search**. We'll assume that we have some list and want to find whether a particular value is in the list or not. Keeping with the way algorithms are usually developed, we won't worry about exactly what we're searching for.

> Let's assume that we know nothing about this list—it's just a collection of values. We have a value that we're looking for, and we want to return either "True" or "False" in this case. Let's see how we might write some pseudocode for this algorithm.

> There are two pieces of data we need to run our algorithm. First, we need the list itself, which we'll designate as L. Next, we'll need the value we're looking for, which we'll designate as v. The output, the result of our algorithm, is going to be a Boolean value: either "True" if v is in L or "False" if it's not. If we're writing pseudocode, we want to be clear, at the beginning, about what's needed for input to the algorithm and what the resulting output will be.

> Next, we need to outline the steps to be taken. In this case, the idea is simple—we are just going to go through each element of the list, checking to see if there's a match. This is called a linear search: We're just going down the line, looking at each item, one at a time.

> If we find a match, we return "True," but if we get to the end of the list and haven't found anything, we return "False." We can write the pseudocode step by step. We first set a value, i, to be the first index in the list. Then, we go through a loop, as long as i is still within the range of the list. In each iteration, we compare the ith element with our value we are looking for, v. If it matches, we return "True" and are done. If not, we increment i. If we eventually reach the end of the loop, that means we never encountered the value v in the list, so we return "False."

```
Input:
    List of values: L
    Value to find: v
Output:
    True if v is in L, False otherwise

1.  Let i be the index of the first element in the list
2.  While i is less than the size of the list:
    a.  if element i of list L matches v, return True
    b.  otherwise, increment i
3.  return False
```

> It's pretty straightforward to put this algorithm into code. We can create a function that implements this algorithm almost exactly. We take in a list and a value as input. We initialize the index i to 0 and have a loop until i is no longer less than the length of the list. We have an if statement to compare element i of the list with our value, returning "True" if they match or incrementing i if they don't.

> The following example shows how we could use this. We have a list, "favorite_foods," and we call the function we just created on two values. When we look for a value that is in the list, we get a "True" back, and when we look for one not in the list, we get a "False."

```
def isIn(L, v):
    i = 0
    while (i<len(L)):
        if L[i] == v:
            return True
        else:
            i += 1
    return False
favorite_foods = ['pizza', 'barbeque', 'gumbo', 'chicken and
  dumplings', 'pecan pie', 'ice cream']
print(isIn(favorite_foods, 'gumbo'))
print(isIn(favorite_foods, 'coconut'))

OUTPUT:
True
False
```

> There is a built-in function within Python that implements this algorithm for us: the "in" command. So, when we ask whether some value is "in" some list, Python is doing exactly what we just showed in the background—it's just looping over all the elements to see if the one we want is there.

> Let's assume that instead of having a list of values in any order, our list was sorted, from smallest to largest. A command to sort the list would be to call a sort method on the list. But for purposes of writing an algorithm, we can just assume that the list has been sorted.

> There is a better way to write this routine—a way to make use of the fact that our input is sorted to search for the value more efficiently.

> If you had a dictionary and wanted to create a program to look up a word, going through every single word to see if it matches would be inefficient. A more efficient approach would be to start by checking some point in the middle of the dictionary. If that word was not the one you're looking for, then figure out whether it came before or after the word you wanted to find, and then look in the remaining half of the dictionary. You could continue this until you found the value, or else found that it was missing.

> How might we write the pseudocode for this? The input and output is the same as what we had before. We take in a list of values and a value to find and return "True" or "False." The only difference is that the list of values is given in sorted order.

> Now we need to describe the steps of our algorithm very precisely. Our approach will be to gradually narrow down the range of options until we find the one we're looking for. So, at any point, we will have a maximum and a minimum index of where the value might be. At the very beginning, our maximum and minimum indices will be from 0 to the list size minus 1. We'll check those values to make sure it's not matching them.

```
Input:
    List of values IN SORTED ORDER: L
    Value to find: v
Output:
    True if v is in L, False otherwise

1.  Set low = 0 and high = length of list - 1
2.  If L[low] == v or L[high] ==v, return True
```

> At this point, we know that the value we are looking for is somewhere between item "low" in the list and item "high" in the list. We are going to gradually narrow down low and high until either we find the point or there's nothing left between low and high.

```
Input:
    List of values IN SORTED ORDER: L
    Value to find: v
Output:
    True if v is in L, False otherwise

1.  Set low = 0 and high = length of list - 1
2.  If L[low] == v or L[high] ==v, return True
3.  While low < high-1          #Value is between L[low] and L[high]
```

> So, we are going to have a loop that continues as long as low is less than high minus 1. Notice that we want to continue only as long as the high and low indices are at least 2 apart so that there's some potential value in between. Once the high and low values are next to each other, we can quit the search, because there is no possibility of another value in between them.

> Notice that at each iteration of the loop, we still have that same condition: The value we're looking for is either between element low and element high, or it's not in the list. This condition—this thing that's the same every time we go through a loop—is called a **loop invariant**. When we're designing an algorithm, it often is helpful if we can identify such a loop invariant.

> Now we need to decide what's done in each iteration of the loop itself. We will compute a midpoint that's halfway between the high and low point and check to see if it matches the value. Notice that when we calculate the midpoint between low and high, we can do so by finding the difference between low and high, dividing it by 2, and adding it to the low. Notice that because we're dividing by 2, we could end up with a fractional value, which doesn't work for indices. So, we need to make sure that we are doing an integer division—keeping only the quotient but ignoring the remainder.

```
Input:
    List of values IN SORTED ORDER: L
    Value to find: v
Output:
    True if v is in L, False otherwise

1. Set low = 0 and high = length of list - 1
2. If L[low] == v or L[high] ==v, return True
3. While low < high-1          #Value is between L[low] and L[high]
    a. midpoint = low + (high-low)/2            #Integer division
    b. If L[midpoint] == v, return True
```

> Notice that because we know the high and low values are at least 2 apart from each other, high minus low divided by 2 is at least 1. So, the midpoint is guaranteed not to be the same as low or the same as high—it will be a new index somewhere between low and high.

> If the midpoint turns out not to be the actual value, we can at least use the midpoint to narrow our range. We're faced with one of two possibilities: either go forward with the range from low to midpoint or the range from midpoint to high. We can decide which of these is the right sub-range to continue with by comparing the value at the midpoint to the value we're searching for. If the value at the midpoint is less than *v*, it means that we need to use the upper sub-range. So, we can set low to be the midpoint. Going forward, we'll be looking between that midpoint and the high index. On the other hand, if the value at the midpoint is greater than *v*, it means that we should use the lower sub-range. So, we can set high to be the midpoint.

```
Input:
    List of values IN SORTED ORDER: L
    Value to find: v
Output:
    True if v is in L, False otherwise

1.  Set low = 0 and high = length of list - 1
2.  If L[low] == v or L[high] ==v, return True
3.  While low < high-1          #Value is between L[low] and L[high]
    a.  midpoint = low + (high-low)/2          #Integer division
    b.  If L[midpoint] == v, return True
    c.  If L[midpoint] < v, set low = midpoint
    d.  else set high = midpoint
```

> Notice that our loop invariant is maintained. The value we're looking for is either between low and high or it's not in the list at all.

> Finally, if we finish the loop, it means that we narrowed in, and the value we were searching for was not found. In this case, we'll return "False."

```
Input:
    List of values IN SORTED ORDER: L
    Value to find: v
Output:
    True if v is in L, False otherwise

1.  Set low = 0 and high = length of list - 1
2.  If L[low] == v or L[high] ==v, return True
3.  While low < high-1          #Value is between L[low] and L[high]
    a.  midpoint = low + (high-low)/2          #Integer division
    b.  If L[midpoint] == v, return True
    c.  If L[midpoint] < v, set low = midpoint
    d.  else set high = midpoint
4.  return False
```

> This is our algorithm description, and we've described it using pseudocode. The term for this type of search is a **binary search**, where at each iteration, we're reducing the search range by a factor of 2. This is much more efficient than the linear search, where we just looked at one item at a time, one after the other.

> Given an algorithm description, it's pretty straightforward to convert this to Python code. Notice that when we compute the midpoint, we are using integer division—the double slash rather than the single slash—to make sure that we get the integer quotient without any remainder.

```python
def binaryIn(L, v):
    low = 0
    high = len(L)-1
    if L[low] == v or L[high] == v:
        return True
    while low < (high-1):
        midpoint = low + (high-low) // 2
        if L[midpoint] == v:
            return True
```

```
        elif L[midpoint] < v:
            low = midpoint
        else:
            high = midpoint
    return False
favorite_foods = ['barbeque', 'chicken and dumplings', 'gumbo',
  'ice cream', 'pecan pie', 'pizza']
print(binaryIn(favorite_foods, 'gumbo'))
print(binaryIn(favorite_foods, 'coconut'))

OUTPUT:
True
False
```

> When we run this code with a sorted list, we find that we correctly identify when an item is in the list or not. Realistically, we want to make sure that we tested this in a variety of situations.

[SORTING]

> Linear and binary search are two of the simplest and most fundamental algorithms. Some slightly more complex algorithms are sorts. There are many different ways to sort, and different methods will work better or worse in different circumstances.

> What if we have a list of values that are in no particular order? If we want to find values in that list, we're stuck using a linear search. If we had a sorted list, though, we could use binary search and do the checks much faster. Often, if we are working with sorted data, our operations are much easier and simpler than if it's just a random collection of values. Sorting is a key tool.

> Let's compare two basic sorts: **selection sort** and **insertion sort**.

> Selection sort works as follows. We start with a mixed-up set of values that we want to put in order from smallest to largest. Because the first

thing we want is the smallest item, we look through all of our values and find the smallest one. We put that into the first place. We then repeat that process to find the next-smallest item and put that into the second place. Each time, we have to look at all of our remaining items so that we can select the one that is the smallest-remaining item. That's where we get the name "selection sort."

> Another decision that comes up when sorting is whether to move around the original elements of the list or make a copy. Lists are mutable data types, so you have the ability to reorder the elements themselves, if you want.

> If you directly sort the elements of the list, that's called an "in-place" sort. In contrast, an "out-of-place" sort means that you create a new list that's a copy of the original one. In this case, the original list stays unchanged, while we also have a new, sorted, list to work with.

> Choosing whether you want an in-place or out-of-place sort will depend on whether you need to maintain the original order for some reason. If so, you want an out-of-place sort. The more common case, though, is to just do the sort in place.

> In the selection sort, we can sort in place by making sure that every time we place a new element into its final position, we swap it with an existing element.

> Selection sort works, but it spends a lot of time going through the entire unsorted list on every iteration. Insertion sort is a different approach that can be much faster and simpler. For insertion sort, at iteration *n*, we've sorted the first *n* elements. So, the only thing to do on each iteration is add one more element into the right spot.

> With insertion sort, we start with the first item—and only the first item. When we take the second item, all we do is compare it with the first item and insert it in whichever position is correct. We continue making iterations in this way, where each time we take one more value and insert it into the list of sorted items. That's where we get the name "insertion sort."

> Sorting is such a common operation that Python has a built-in sorting function. For a list, we can call a sort method on the list by saying "sort()." This is an **in-place sort**. For an **out-of-place sort**, Python offers a more general command called "sorted()."

Readings

Gries, *Practical Programming*, chaps. 12–13.

Lambert, *Fundamentals of Python*, chap. 3, p. 60–70.

Zelle, *Python Programming*, chap. 13.

Exercises

We will show how to build another sorting routine: the bubble sort.

1 Write a function that takes in a list and an element number, *i*, and swaps element *i* with element *i*+1.

2 Write a routine, "one_bubble_pass," that implements the following pseudocode.

```
one_bubble_pass:
Input:
    List lst
Output:
    Modified list, True if a swap was made, False if not

1.  returnval = False
2.  Loop over all elements except last one in lst
3.  If lst[i] > lst[i+1] then swap elments i and i+1 and set
    returnval = True
4.  Return returnval
```

3 The bubble sort just keeps calling "one_bubble_pass" until no more swaps can be made. Write a routine, "bubblesort," that implements the following pseudocode.

```
bubblesort:
Input:
    unsorted List
Output:
    sorted List

1.  Set flag to True
2.  While flag is True
3.  Set flag = one_bubble_pass
```

Algorithms: Searching and Sorting

When we turn to algorithms, we're entering what's often regarded as the heart of computer science. The concept of algorithms comes to us from the Persian mathematician al-Khwarizmi, who wrote one of the most influential books of all time. Way back in the 9th century, his book systematically described precise procedures for solving equations, and in the process, really revolutionized mathematics. It formed the foundation for much of what we consider mathematics today.

The book was eventually translated into Latin and so its ideas spread from the Middle East throughout Europe. It was so influential that two words that we commonly use today come to us because this book introduced those ideas to the Western world. First, the title of the book contained the term al-jabr, referring to a method that al-Khwarizmi introduced for balancing equations. This word became our own familiar word algebra. The other term that we get from him is based on the author's own name. Al-Khwarizmi became the word algorithm, which is used to refer to a precise set of steps or rules to follow to accomplish some task.

These earliest algorithms offered some general techniques for solving basic arithmetic and algebra problems. If I asked you to tell me how to multiply two numbers, you could probably give me an algorithm—a general set of steps that you can use to multiply any two numbers together. School children usually learned one like this: First you take the ones digit from the first number and you multiply it by each digit of the other number, carrying the tens part over to the next column each time, and so on.

But the idea of laying out a precise set of steps or rules to accomplish a task doesn't apply only to arithmetic. If I asked you to tell me the process for making a sandwich, you could probably give me a precise set of steps to follow involving a bottom slice of bread, some condiments, and so forth. You'd be giving me a sandwich-making algorithm.

As computers have been developed, the idea of algorithms has become more and more important. As I mentioned all the way back at the beginning of this course, computers are not really very smart at all and they can only follow very precise instructions given in very particular ways. So, to get computers to do all the wonderful things we think of them doing, we need to be able to formulate the bigger ideas that we have as these precise sets of instructions—that is, we need to be able to define algorithms.

Now, algorithms really do form the heart of computer science. When we use the term computer science, we're referring to a much bigger idea than just the programming that's been the main focus of this course. We're instead thinking about the broader ideas of how computation works and how we can organize that computation to achieve particular goals. Now, there are lots of different aspects to the study of computer science, but understanding algorithms is particularly important. Algorithms are how we describe what we actually want—in a more general way, what we want the computer to do. Computer programming is really just the process of taking an algorithm and converting it into a program that the computer understands. The program is the concrete incarnation of the more general algorithm.

Researchers in computer science often focus on coming up with new algorithms to solve various problems. The actual programming can become somewhat distinct, even secondary. There are different ways to program an algorithm—different languages to use, and different features of those languages. The key challenge, the important part, is coming up with the general steps to follow to achieve the goal. So for this lecture, we're going to focus on understanding more about algorithms—how they're described, how they're implemented in code, and we'll look at a couple of the most well-known algorithms for searching and sorting.

Let's first talk about what an algorithm really is. A particular analogy that's really useful is to compare an algorithm with a recipe. When we have a recipe, we start with a list of ingredients. We then follow a particular set of steps, performing actions with those ingredients. At the end, we've produced some particular dish. In computer science, our ingredients are the data. The algorithm consists of the sequence of steps that we need to follow. Now, I've used this analogy before to describe programming, and there's a good reason—writing a program is essentially the same thing as writing an algorithm. The difference is that a program is a specific, concrete implementation in a particular programming language. An algorithm can be thought of as a more general description that's not necessarily tied directly to a particular programming language.

Now, you can think of this as writing a recipe where you know the general category of the ingredient—like it's a liquid, or a granular material, or a solid—without needing to know what particular substance it actually is. For example, the basic procedure for making vinaigrette is fundamentally the same, regardless of which specific oil and vinegar are used.

And this is how we typically describe algorithms. We do not want to tie them too tightly to any particular programming language, so we usually describe algorithms in a form that corresponds to some programming language, but it's not actual code in that language. One example of such a form is a flowchart, where we describe the algorithm graphically. We identify individual steps by shapes that contain text describing the step, with arrows showing how to move from one step to the next. Conditionals will have two arrows indicating what to do if the condition is true or false.

Another option is to use pseudocode to describe the function of the algorithm. With pseudocode, we give an overview of the various steps of the algorithm and how they relate to each other. Pseudocode looks a lot like regular code in some language, but many of the details can be eliminated along the way. Conversely, a single step in the algorithm might actually involve several lines of real code.

Now, we've actually been using this idea in the course whenever I've given you an overview of a function before actually showing the code to implement that function. What I've been doing in those cases is describing an algorithm before showing how that algorithm got turned into code. If we design our algorithms well, it should always be straightforward to convert our algorithms into code.

All right, to illustrate how algorithms work and how they're implemented, we're going to start with one of the simplest general algorithms—a search. We'll assume that we have some list and we want to find whether a particular value is in the list or not. Keeping with the way algorithms are usually developed, we won't worry about exactly what we're searching for. So, let's assume that we know nothing about this list; it's just a collection of values. We have a value that we're looking for, and we want to return either true or false in this case. Let's see how we might write some pseudocode for this algorithm.

There are going to be two ingredients—two pieces of data—that we need in order to run our algorithm. First, we need the list itself, which we'll designate as L. Then, we'll need the value we're looking for, which we'll designate v. Now, the output, the result of our algorithm, is going to be a Boolean value—either true if v is in L, or False if it's not. If we're writing pseudocode, we want to be clear, at the beginning, about what's needed for input to the algorithm and what the resulting output will be. Next, we need to outline the steps to be taken. In this case, the idea is simple—we're just going to go through each element of the list, checking to see if there's a match. This is called a linear search. We're just going down the line, looking at each item, one at a time.

If we find a match, we return true; but if we get to the end of the list and we haven't found anything, we return false. We can write the pseudocode out step by step. We first set a value, i to be the first index in the list. Then we go through a loop as long as i is still within the range of the list. In each iteration, we compare the i-th element with our value that we're looking for, v. If it matches, we return true and are done. And if not, we increment i. If we eventually reach the end of the loop, that means we never encountered the value v in the list, so we return false.

Now, it's pretty straightforward to put this algorithm into code. We can create a function that implements this algorithm almost exactly. We take in a list and a value as input. We initialize the index i to 0 and we have a loop until i is no longer less than the length of the list. We have an if statement to compare the element i of the list with our value, returning true if they match or incrementing i if they don't. The example shows how we could use this. We have a list, favorite foods, and we call the function we just created on two values. Sure enough, when we look for a value that's in the list, we get a true back; and when we look for one that's not in the list, we get a false.

Now, there's a built-in function within Python that actually implements this algorithm for us—that's the in command. So, when we ask whether some value is in some list, Python is doing exactly what we just showed in the background. It's just looping over all the elements to see if the one we want is there. Like I said, that's a really simple algorithm and it seems very straightforward. But let's assume that instead of having a list of values in any old order, that instead our list was sorted from smallest to largest. A command to sort the list would be to call a sort method on the list. But for purposes of writing the algorithm, we can just assume that the list has already been sorted. Now, is there a better way that we might write the search routine? Maybe a way that can make use of the fact that our input is sorted to search for the value more efficiently?

The answer is, of course, yes. You're familiar with this already. If I gave you a dictionary and I asked you to create a program to look up a word, how would you do it? Well, going through every single word to see if it matches would be very inefficient. A more efficient approach would be to start by checking some point in the middle of the dictionary. If that's not the word that you're looking for, then you can figure out whether it came before or after the word that you wanted to find, and then look in the remaining half of the dictionary. You could continue this until you found the value, or else found that it was missing.

So, how might we write the pseudocode for this? Well, the input and the output is the same as what we had before. We take in a list of values and a value to find, and we return true or false. The only difference is that the list of values is given in sorted order. So, now we need to describe the steps of our algorithm very precisely. Our approach will be to gradually narrow down the range of options until we find the one that we're looking for. So at any point, we'll have a maximum and a minimum index of where the value might be. At the very beginning, our maximum and minimum indices will be from 0 to the list size −1. We'll check those values to make sure it's not matching them.

So, at this point, we know that the value that we're looking for is somewhere between item low in the list and item high in the list. And we're going to gradually narrow down low and high until either we find the element that we're looking for or there's nothing left between low and high. So we're going to have a loop that continues as long as low is less than high minus one. Notice that we want to continue only as long as the high and low indices are at least two apart so that there's some potential value in between. Once the high and low values are next to each other, we might as well quit the search, since there's no possibility of another value in between them. Notice that at each iteration of the loop, we still have that same condition—the value we're looking for is either between element low and element high, or else it's not in the list. This condition—this thing that's the same every time we go through a loop—is called a loop invariant. When we're designing an algorithm, it's often helpful if we can identify such a loop invariant.

So, now we need to decide what's done in each iteration of the loop itself. We'll compute a midpoint that's halfway between the high and low point, and we'll check to see if it matches the value. Notice that when we calculate the midpoint between low and high, we can do so by finding the difference between low and high, dividing it by 2, and adding it to low. Notice that since we're dividing by 2, we could end up with a fractional value, which doesn't work for indices, so we need to make sure that we're doing an integer division—keeping only the quotient but ignoring the remainder. And notice that since we know that the high and low values are at least two apart from each other, high minus low divided by 2 is at least 1. So, the midpoint is guaranteed not to be the same as low, or the same as high; it'll be a new index somewhere between low and high.

All right, if the midpoint turns out not to be the actual value, we can at least use the midpoint to narrow our range. We're faced with one of two possibilities: We can either go forward with the range from low to midpoint, or the range from midpoint to high. We can decide which of these is the right subrange to continue with by comparing the value at the midpoint to the value that we're searching for. If the value at the midpoint is less than v, it means that we need to look in the upper subrange, so we can set low to be the midpoint. Going forward, we'll be looking between that midpoint and the high index. On the other hand, if the value at the midpoint is greater than v, it means that we should be using the lower subrange, so we can set high to be the midpoint. Notice that our loop invariant is maintained. The value that we're looking for is either between low and high, or it's not in the list at all. Finally, if we finish the loop, it means we narrowed in and the value that we were searching for was not found. And so, in this case, we'll return false.

So, this is our algorithm description, and we've described it using pseudocode. The term for this type of search is a binary search. When you hear binary, you should think two. And notice that at each iteration, we are reducing the search range by a factor of two. This is much more efficient than the linear search that we saw earlier, where we just looked at one item at a time, one after the other. If we had a huge list—say the size of a real dictionary—and we were searching through it, that binary search would be a whole lot faster than the linear search.

Now, given an algorithm description, it's pretty straightforward to convert this to Python code. Basically, every line of pseudocode gets converted into a line or two of Python code, and pretty much every line is taken directly from the pseudocode. Notice that when we compute the midpoint, I'm using integer division—the double slash rather than the single slash—to make sure that we get the integer quotient without any remainder. When we run this code with a sorted list, sure enough, we find that we correctly identify when an item is in the list or not. Now realistically, we'd want to make sure that we tested this in a variety of situations. For example, what if the list was empty?

To handle the possibility of an empty list, we can make one change to the pseudocode at the very beginning. If the list was empty to begin with—that is, if the length was less than 1—then we immediately return false. And that prevents us trying to access an element at index 0, which wouldn't exist. The rest of our testing would address questions like: What if we had just one element or just two? What if the thing we were looking for was the very first one, or the very last one? What if it was a giant list? Realistically, if we were writing an algorithm, we'd need to go through a testing process, just like always. And if we find errors, we might have to adjust the algorithm itself. However, here, I'll just tell you that this code actually does work in those cases.

Now, before we move on from searching, let's make one change. Often, we don't just want to know if something is in the list, we actually want to know where it is in the list. So, what if we wanted to modify our algorithm so that instead of returning true or false, it returned the index that matched the search value? If the value wasn't found, we could return an invalid index, like −1.

First, looking back at the algorithm pseudocode for binary search, think about how you would modify it to return a specific location. The changes are pretty minor. First, we'd want to change the description of the output for the algorithm in the algorithm itself. We're going to be returning the index if we find a match. Notice that we need separate checks for low and high, since they're separate values. If we find a match at a midpoint during the loop, we return the midpoint. And if we didn't find the value at all, we return −1.

Next, we could modify our Python code to reflect this algorithm. Given that new algorithm, how would you modify the code so that we return the index, or −1, if we don't find the value? Here's the code. Notice that our changes directly reflect the changes in the algorithm. We return the index whenever we find a match, or if we get to the end of the routine, we return −1. Linear and binary search are two of the simplest and most fundamental algorithms. Let's turn our attention to some slightly more complex algorithms—sorts.

Sorting algorithms have a long history in computer science, and they're traditionally the main example we use to illustrate the basics of algorithm development and analysis. One of the cool things about sorting is that there are lots of different ways to do it, and different methods will work better or worse in different circumstances. Plus, sorting is something that we're all familiar with in everyday life, so it's easy to make a connection between the ways you might sort things at home and the way you should sort them in a program. In this lecture, I'll introduce a couple of sorting algorithms, and we'll see a couple more next lecture.

We've already seen a hint of the problem we face when sorting, and why sorting can be useful. What if we have a list of values and the values are in no particular order? If we're wanting to find values in that list, we're stuck using a linear search. If we had a sorted list though, we could use binary search and do the checks a lot faster. Often, if we're working with sorted data, our operations are a whole lot easier and simpler than if it's just a random collection of values. Sorting is a key tool in our toolbox that we'll want to understand very well.

I want to compare two basic sorts—selection sort and insertion sort. Selection sort works like this: I'll start with a mixed up set of values that I want to put into order from smallest to largest. Since the first thing I'm going to want is the smallest item, I'll look through all of my values and I'll find the smallest one, and I'll put that into the first place. I'll then repeat that process to find the next smallest item, and I'll put that into the second place. Notice that each time, I'm going to have to look at all of my remaining items so that I can select the one that's the smallest remaining. That's where we get the name selection sort from. Another decision that comes up when sorting is whether to move around the original elements of the list or make a copy. Lists are mutable data types so you have the ability to reorder the elements themselves, if you want. If you do directly sort the elements of the list I gave you, that's called an in-place sort.

In contrast, an out-of-place sort means that you create a brand new list that's a copy of the original one. In this case, the original list stays unchanged while we also have a new, sorted list to work with. Choosing whether you want an in-place or an out-of-place sort will depend on whether you need to maintain the original order for some reason. If so, you want an out-of-place sort. Probably the more common case is to just do the sort in-place.

In the selection sort, we can sort in-place by making sure that every time we place a new element into its final position, we swap it with an existing element. Let's look at the pseudocode for this algorithm. Our input is an unsorted list, and the output is the sorted list. We're going to have a loop that goes from the beginning to the end of the list. Each time, we'll look at all the remaining values, select the smallest one, and then swap that with the index that we're on. It's very simple, but it's also looking at every element, every single pass, so it might not be particularly efficient.

Now, converting our pseudocode to code for selection sort means setting up a loop. The loop we have goes over the full length of the list. Inside the loop, we first find the smallest remaining element. To do that, we'll keep track of the index of that smallest value—that's our min index variable—and we start out by assuming the smallest one is the first one of the remaining list. We then loop through all the other remaining elements, and if we find one smaller than the current minimum, we update min index. Now, once we've done this for all of the elements and found the smallest of the remaining ones, we swap the min index element into the current position that we're trying to fill. We can test this by creating a short list of items in random order. Then we'll call selection sort on this new list, and then print the results. Sure enough, it comes out sorted.

Now, selection sort works but it spends lot of time going through the entire unsorted list on every iteration. Let's try a different approach called insertion sort. For insertion sort, at iteration *n*, we've sorted the first n elements. So, the only thing to do on each iteration is add one more element into the right spot. So, let's see how that'll work.

With insertion sort, I'm going to start with the first item, and only the first item. In this approach, I want to avoid scanning the whole unsorted list.

But since I start with just this one item to work with, for purposes of this first step, it's already in sorted order. When I take the second number, all I do is compare it with the first number, and I insert it in whichever position is correct. I continue to make insertions the same way, where each time I'm going to take one more value and insert it into the list of sorted items. That's where we get the name insertion sort. Now that we've described this algorithm, maybe you want to practice writing pseudocode yourself. Really, take a minute to see if you can sketch out the steps that are needed to run an insertion sort.

OK, let's see what the pseudocode will look like. This might look a little trickier. The input and output are still the same, and we're still going to have a loop where we visit each element. Inside the loop is what's different from selection sort because we want to insert the next element into the already sorted part of the list. So, notice what we do. L[i] is the element i at each iteration, and we copy that element that we want to insert next into a variable, temp. At each iteration, we need to work our way backward down the list to figure out where to insert the current element. This is what our variable j is keeping track of—working our way down the list to figure out where to insert. We'll keep checking whether element j is greater than the value we're trying to insert. If so, we copy that j-th element into the next slot down.

Eventually, we reach either the beginning of the list or an element that's not greater than the temporary element that we're wanting to insert. So, we can put that temporary element into that place. There will be a space just waiting for us there, since we already slid everything else down one. It might help you to look at this pseudocode and try it out for yourself, to make sure you see how this is working.

Now, given that pseudocode, what would the code itself look like? Remember, the pseudocode did almost all the work for us so it should be pretty straightforward to convert the pseudocode into actual code. Here's the code. Now notice, the pseudocode already did almost all the work for us. In fact, it's basically one line of Python for each line of pseudocode. And when we run the code, it does indeed sort our data. Sorting is actually such a common operation that Python has built-in a sorting function for you to use. For a list, we can call a sort method on the list, by just saying sort. That's right. We just call sort and it will sort the list. This is an in-place sort, so what does that mean for the original data? Right, it's been sorted in place. The list is rearranged.

What if we want an out-of-place sort? Maybe we want to keep the original list in its own order, but we also want a sorted version. For those cases, Python offers a more general command called sorted. We can use the sorted function, passing the list in as a parameter. The function returns a sorted list. If we print out the original list, we see it's still in the same order that it was before, and the returned list is in sorted order.

Both the built-in sort command and the built-in sorted command can be modified to sort in reverse order. To do this, we just set the reverse parameter to true when we call the function. You can see here an example of doing a reverse sort on the dataset, in this case, with the out-of-place sort. Python's built-in sort function is famously great and it's even been adapted for use in Android and Java. But how it works combines insertion sort with another basic sorting algorithm called merge sort, which we'll discuss in the next lecture.

Developing algorithms that can be applied to solve problems is a big part of what computer science is all about. And as the search and sort algorithms illustrate, we can design algorithms to address more general problems as well. The process of algorithm design is so critical to programming that most of our code can be thought of as just an implementation of algorithmic ideas. Sorts, in particular, provide an easy way of illustrating many key concepts of algorithm design. Once you understand how various sorts work, you understand a lot of the fundamental ideas in algorithm development that can be used to make more complex programs.

In the next lecture, we're going to expand on algorithms by introducing a particularly interesting idea called recursion, and introduce a couple more sorts that make use of recursive ideas. And we'll see how we can analyze algorithms to compare how well different algorithms perform work in practice. See you then.

21

Recursion and Running Times

One algorithm can take so long to run that it will never complete in our lifetimes, while another one, solving the same problem, might take less than a second. The choice of which algorithm to use can be critical. But how do we know whether or not a particular algorithm is a good one to use in our program? To help answer this question, you will be introduced to an approach known as algorithm analysis.

[RECURSION: MERGE SORT]

› **Recursion** can be, but isn't always, a great way to create efficient code. The great trick in recursion is that a function is calling itself.

› Let's say that we want to print a countdown. We want some function that takes in an integer value and then counts down to 0 from there. That function might look like the following. We define the function countdown, which takes in a number, *n*, as a parameter. That will be the number we are counting down from. We then print out the number that was passed in. Assuming that the number is greater than 0, we are going to call our own self again, but with *n*-1 as the parameter.

```
def countdown(n):
    print (n)
    if n > 0:
        countdown(n-1)
countdown (5)
```

```
OUTPUT:
5
4
3
2
1
0
```

> If you think of the function countdown as "a function that prints all numbers from n down to 0," then this makes a little more sense. When we call countdown with n-1 as the parameter, we're just saying "we are printing the numbers from n-1 down to 0." So, the overall function is "print the number n and then print the numbers from n-1 down to 0." Thinking about the function that way makes a little more sense.

> Of course, there are other, better, ways to count down from n to 0—that's what loops are made for. But this idea of recursion is going to let us do a few things that don't have such a nice non-recursive version, and it will help us organize some of our programming so that even if we can find a non-recursive solution, we'll have a tool for thinking about problems.

> One of the main approaches that can rely on recursion is what's called **divide and conquer**. The idea is that it's easier to deal with two smaller problems rather than one big one. But there's a more particular meaning to the term "divide and conquer" in computing. When we use the term, we mean that we are taking a large data set and dividing it into subsets that we handle independently.

> Let's look at two algorithms that rely on divide-and-conquer approaches, both of which are sorting algorithms.

> First, we have merge sort. Let's assume that we're given some completely unordered set of numbers. We're going to do three steps to get these sorted. First, we'll divide the set of numbers in two—using the first half to form one list and the second half to form the other list.

> The second step is to sort each of those lists. We can use the merge sort routine to sort the lists, and the sorting process is an example of divide and conquer. We're taking one large sorting problem and reducing it to two small sorting problems that we solve recursively. Finally, there's a merge stage, where we'll merge those two sorted lists into one bigger sorted list. To merge, we'll work through both lists, pulling out the smallest one left from whichever list.

> Let's put all of that into pseudocode, which is a great intermediate step for writing algorithms because it lets us specify the key ideas of the steps without also needing to specify all the syntax at the same time. In fact, less detail in pseudocode is sometimes better, because that leaves the programmer more flexibility to determine how to implement an item.

```
Input: unsorted list L, length n
Output: L, with elements sorted smallest to largest

1.  If n <= 1
    a.  Return L            #a list of length 1 is already sorted
2.  L1 = L(0:n/2-1)         L2 = (n/2:n-1)
3.  MergeSort(L1)           MergeSort(L2)
4.  L = Merge(L1, L2)       #Merge will be defined separately
```

> Like other sorts, we'll be taking in an unsorted list and returning a sorted one. The actual routine will start out with a special case, though. We'll first check to see if we have a list of length 1, and if so, we just return that list—because if we have a list of length 1, it's already sorted. Also, if our list has only one element, we can't divide it into two lists, so the rest of the routine isn't going to work.

> We refer to this sort of special case check as a **base case** when we are discussing recursion. A recursive routine that keeps calling itself has to stop at some point, or it will go on forever. The point where it stops is the base case.

> We have a less-than sign in there just in case someone sends us an empty list—there's no reason to try sorting anything less than the base case, either.

> If we have more than the base case—that is, if we have a list of 2 or more elements—we'll go through our three steps. First, we'll form two lists, *L*1 and *L*2, made from half of the original list. We'll then sort each of those lists by a recursive call to this very routine. Finally, we'll merge those lists together.

> In the actual code, we define our function, **mergeSort**, and take the list in as the parameter, *L*. We'll store the length of *L* in a variable, *n*. First, we handle the base case: If *n* is less than or equal to 1, we just return, because the list is already sorted. Otherwise, we'll form our two shorter lists.

```
def mergeSort(L):
    n = len(L)
    if n <= 1:
        return
    L1 = L[:n//2]
    L2 = L[n//2:]
    mergeSort(L1)
    mergeSort(L2)
    merge(L, L1, L2)
    return
```

> Notice two things about the transition from pseudocode to Python syntax in the next lines of code. First, we're using the slicing operation to take a subset of the lists, and we're using *n*/2 as the splitting point. So, we can write ":n/2" for the first sublist and "n/2:" for the second sublist.

> Second, in order for our code to specify that splitting point, *n*/2, we had to use integer division, where we drop the remainder, to make sure that we have an integer result for the index. That integer division is the double slash, as opposed to the single slash for regular division.

> The next two lines are the recursive calls to mergeSort.

› Finally, we have a call to a merge routine, which takes two lists and merges them into a third list.

```python
def merge(L, L1, L2):
    i = 0
    j = 0
    k = 0
    while (j < len(L1)) or (k < len(L2)):
        if j < len(L1):
            if k < len(L2):
                #we are not at the end of L1 or L2, so pull the
                 smaller value
                if L1[j] < L2[k]:
                    L[i] = L1[j]
                    j += 1
                else:
                    L[i] = L2[k]
                    k += 1
            else:
                #we are at the end of L2, so just pull from L1
                L[i] = L1[j]
                j += 1
        else:
            #we are at the end of L1, so just pull from L2
            L[i] = L2[k]
            k += 1
        i += 1
    return
```

[RECURSION: QUICKSORT]

› Another example of a recursive sorting routine is called **quicksort**, because it works quickly on typical cases. In quicksort, the idea is still divide and conquer, but the division is done differently than in merge sort.

> In quicksort, we pick some value to split everything around—typically just the first value in the list. We call this term the **pivot**. We then form two new lists: one with all the values less than the pivot and one with all the values greater than the pivot. Next, we sort each of those lists—again with a recursive call, to quicksort. After that, the whole list is sorted: We have the first list, followed by the pivot, followed by the last list.

> When we write pseudocode for quicksort, the input and output are just like we've had before. We'll take in an unordered list, and our output will be a sorted list. For a recursive routine, we want to have a base case. The base case will be just like in merge sort—we want to return if we have a list of length 0 or 1.

> Next, we pick the first element of the list, the pivot. Then, we form two lists, $L1$ and $L2$—one with elements below the pivot and one with elements above. We then recursively sort the two lists. This is our recursive call, where we call the quicksort function from within the quicksort function. Once the lists are sorted, we form our final list, by joining the two lists and the pivot.

```
Input: unsorted list L, length n
Output: L, with elements sorted smallest to largest

1.  If n <= 1
    a.  Return L              #a list of length 1 is already sorted
2.  pivot = L[0]
3.  Form lists L1 and L2 of remaining elements less/greater than
    pivot
    a.  Set empty lists L1 and L2
    b.  Loop through elements of L from 1 onward
        1.  If the element is less than the pivot, add it to L1,
            otherwise add it to L2
4.  QuickSort(L1) QuickSort(L2)
5.  L = Join(L1, pivot, L2)
    a.  Clear L
    b.  Loop through L1, appending elements on to L
    c.  Append pivot to L
    d.  Loop through L2, appending elements on to L
```

> Let's use the pseudocode to write the code. The following is one way to implement quicksort.

```python
def quickSort(L):
    #handle base case
    if len(L) <= 1:
        return
    #pick pivot
    pivot = L[0]
    #form lists less/greater than pivot
    L1 = []
    L2 = []
    for element in L[1:]:
        if element < pivot:
            L1.append(element)
        else:
            L2.append(element)
    #sort sublists
    quickSort(L1)
    quickSort(L2)
    #join the sublists and pivot
    L[:] = []
    for element in L1:
        L.append(element)
    L.append(pivot)
    for element in L2:
        L.append(element)
    return
```

[ASYMPTOTIC ANALYSIS AND RUNNING TIME]

> In addition to the four different sort routines we've used—selection sort, insertion sort, merge sort, and quicksort—people have also developed a variety of other sorts. Sorting shows that there can be several different, sometimes very different, algorithmic solutions to the same problem.

> Given so many different possible solutions to a problem, how do we choose between them? The best choice of algorithm should be independent of the individual programmer. And because the motivation for much of computing has been increased efficiency, we often use efficiency as the criterion to choose one algorithm over another.

> In the case of sort routines, Python has a built-in sort routine, which uses a combination of a merge sort and an insertion sort. That built-in Python sort is really efficient. In fact, that should usually be the version you use. Most other languages will have some similar built-in sort function.

> To assess efficiency, computer scientists use what's called **asymptotic analysis**. This type of analysis looks at how a function performs as the input size grows larger and larger: How does the running time increase as the input size increases? For the algorithms we've looked at, such as searching in a list or sorting a list, the input size will be the length of the list.

> When it comes to asymptotic analysis, many programmers just need a general idea of practical running time. What will happen if we double the input size? For our searches or sorts, think of having a list twice as long.

> We also have to think about what part of the running time we care about. Do we care about the best case, the worst case, or the average case? Most of the time, computer scientists will analyze the worst case, because they want to make sure that things don't behave too badly. However, depending on the problem, we sometimes care about the best case or average case.

> As we work with various programs, we'll sometimes want to make sure that what we're doing is reasonably efficient. The bigger the data sets we deal with, the more important this is. But even with reasonably sized data sets, the difference in asymptotic complexity can make a big difference.

> The algorithm used in Python's built-in "sort()" function has been cleverly designed to do even better than each of the four algorithms we've been using, at least most of the time. Python's current algorithm uses a combination of merge sort and insertion sort.

> Even though merge sort works better on large problems, insertion sort works faster on smaller problems. The Python sort routine basically uses merge sort for the overall problem, but once it's dealing with sufficiently small problems, it switches to insertion sort.

> The Python algorithm uses recursion whenever there's a merge sort but avoiding recursion whenever there's an insertion sort. It does this because recursion is a useful way of describing certain calculations. In fact, for some calculations, it's the only good way of describing what needs to be done. But there are other times when recursion is possible but should not be used.

> By selecting a different algorithm, we can sometimes turn a problem that seems completely impossible into one that's easily solved. It's worth analyzing your code to determine running time, to make sure that you're not being wildly or unnecessarily inefficient in the algorithm you've chosen to solve a problem.

Readings

Lambert, *Fundamentals of Python*, chap. 3, p. 49–59 and 70–81.

Zelle, *Python Programming*, chap. 13.

Exercises

1   What does the following code do?

```
def dosomething(lst):
    if len(lst) == 0:
        return 1
    else:
        return lst[0]*dosomething(lst[1:])
```

2   Consider the "swap," "one_bubble_pass," and "bubblesort" algorithms defined in the previous lecture's exercises. Considering that the worst case occurs when a list is entirely in reverse order, how would you characterize the running time of each of the three routines?

a)   swap
b)   one_bubble_pass
c)   bubblesort

The options are as follows:

◊   constant time (independent of the number of elements in the list)

◊   logarithmic time (proportional to the log of the number of elements in the list)

◊   linear time (proportional to the number of elements in the list)

◊ $n \log n$ time (proportional to the length times the log of the length of the list)

◊   quadratic time (proportional to the square of the length of the list)

◊   exponential time (proportional to an exponential function of the length of the list).

Recursion and Running Times

Here's something pretty amazing—one algorithm can take so long to run that it will never complete in our lifetimes, while another one, solving the exact same problem, may take less than a second. The choice of which algorithm to use can be critical. So, how do we know whether or not a particular algorithm is a good one to use in our program? The two broad approaches to algorithms that we'll explore in this lecture are iteration and recursion. They're more different than their names may sound.

Recursion is one of the most interesting ideas in computer science. We'll apply recursion to form a couple of sorting algorithms. To do this, we'll initially set up our programs using pseudocode. And, to see how to answer the question of which algorithm is good, we'll use an approach known as algorithm analysis to compare some of the built-in routines that Python provides to support sorting.

Now, recursion can be, but isn't always, a great way to create efficient code. The great trick in recursion is that a function is calling itself. To see what I mean, let me first give you an example of a name that refers to itself. There's a popular package manager for Python that we've talked about before called pip, and pip stands for "pip installs Python" or "pip installs Packages." There's no deep reason to have that name, but it's a playful example of recursion—the name is in the name. Similarly, if we have a program that exhibits recursion, we expect to see a function that calls itself.

Let's say that we want to print a countdown. Now, we've already seen how to do this with iteration; we just use a loop. But let's look now at how we can do a countdown with recursion. We want some function that takes in an integer value, and then counts down to zero from there. Here's what that function might look like. We define the function "countdown," which takes in a number, *n*, as a parameter. That'll be the number we're counting down from—so far, so good. We then print out the number that was passed in. Again, this seems OK. Now, here comes the weird part. Assuming that the number is greater than zero, we're going to call our own self again, but with $n - 1$ as the parameter.

Now, if you think of the function "countdown" as a function that prints all numbers from n down to zero, then this might make a little bit more sense. When we call countdown with $n - 1$ as the parameter, we're just saying we're printing the numbers from $n - 1$ down to zero. So, the overall function is print the number n and then print the numbers from $n - 1$ down to zero. Thinking about the function that way makes a little bit more sense.

Now, iteration is better than recursion for counting down from n to zero; again, that's what loops are made for. But, this idea of recursion is going to let us do some other things that don't have such nice, non-recursive solutions. One of the main problem-solving approaches out there that can rely on recursion is what's called "divide and conquer." The idea is that it's easier to deal with two smaller problems rather than one big one. But, there's a more particular meaning to the term divide and conquer in computing. When we use the term, what we mean is that we're taking a large data set and we're dividing it into two subsets that we handle independently.

Let's look at two algorithms that rely on divide and conquer approaches. Both of these are sorting algorithms, quite different from the ones that we've seen before. I'll explain both of them conceptually first, then we'll write some pseudocode, and then we'll use the pseudocode to write the code that we need in Python.

First, we have merge sort. Let's assume that we're given some totally unordered set of numbers. We're going to do three steps to get these sorted. First, we'll divide the set of numbers in two. That's really easy; just use the first half to form one list and the second half to form the other list. The second step is to sort each of those lists. So, do we have a routine to sort a list? Yes—we have the merge sort routine that we're using right now. The sorting process is going to be an example of divide and conquer. We're taking one large sorting problem and we're reducing it to two smaller sorting problems, and we'll solve each of those recursively. Finally, there's a merge stage, where we'll merge those two sorted lists into one bigger sorted list. To merge, we'll walk through both lists, pulling out the smallest one left from whichever list.

Now, let's put all of that into pseudocode, which is a great intermediate step for writing algorithms since it lets us specify they key ideas of the steps without needing to worry about the details of syntax. In fact, less detail in pseudocode is sometimes better, since that leaves the programmer more flexibility in how to implement an item.

Like the sorts that we've seen in the past, we'll be taking in an unsorted list, and we'll be returning a sorted one. The actual routine will start out with a special case, though. We'll first check to see if we have a list of length 1, and if so, we just return that list. Why do we do that? Well, if we have a list of length 1, it's already sorted, so there's nothing more to do. Also, if our list has only one element, we can't really divide it into two lists, so the rest of this routine isn't going to work. We refer to this sort of special case check as a base case when we're discussing recursion. A recursive routine that keeps calling itself has to stop at some point, otherwise it's going to go on forever. The point where it stops is the base case. Oh, and we have a less-than in there just in case someone sends us an empty list. There's no reason to try sorting anything less than the base case, either.

Now, if we have more than the base case—that is, if we have a list with at least two elements in it—we'll go through our three steps. We'll first form two lists, and I'll call them L1 and L2, made from half of the original list. We'll then sort each of those lists by a recursive call to this same routine, the one that we're writing right now. And, finally, we'll merge those lists together. Merging is another function call that I'll define separately.

So, let's see what the actual code will look like. We define our function, mergeSort, and we take the list in as the parameter L. We'll store the length of L in a variable, n. First, we handle the base case: if $n <= 1$, we just return, since the list is already sorted. Otherwise, we'll form our two shorter lists.

Notice two things about the transition from pseudocode to Python syntax in these next lines of code. First, we're using the slicing operation to take a subset of the lists, and we're using $n \div 2$ as the splitting point. So, we can write colon n over 2 for the first sublist, and n over 2 colon for the second sublist. You might notice that the notation is a little different than in our pseudocode. That's because our pseudocode was written to describe the general case, whereas in Python, the way we write our code is more precise. Second, in order for our code to specify that splitting point, $n \div 2$, we had to use integer division, where we drop the remainder, to make sure that we have an integer result for the index. That integer division is the double slash, as opposed to the single slash for regular division.

The next two lines are the recursive calls to mergeSort. And then, finally, we have a call to a merge routine, which takes two lists and merges them into a third list. Rather than go through pseudocode on this part, I'll just jump straight to some finished code and walk you through it.

In this routine, we're going to keep track of three variables—i, j, and k—that keep track of the index for the L, L1, and L2 arrays. The basic idea is that we're going to go through the L1 and the L2 arrays, pulling the smallest value from between them and putting it into the L array. So, we'll start with a "while" loop that says we continue as long as we haven't hit the end of both the L1 and L2 arrays. First, we'll check to see if we're at the end of the L1 array—that is, if our j index is already at the length of the array. If it's too large, we'll follow the else clause in this statement, and we'll pull a value from the L2 array; otherwise, we continue on.

We next check to see if we're at the end of the L2 array—that is, if the k index is already at the length. If we've hit the length there, we follow an else clause that pulls a value from the L1 array. But, assuming we're not at the end of either L1 or L2, we're going to pull the value from whichever one has the smallest current value. So, we compare L1 sub j to L2 sub k, and we choose which of the two arrays to pull from. If we're pulling from L1, we assign the value in L1 to L, and we increment j to the next index. If we're pulling from L2, we assign the value in L2 to L, and we increment the *k* to the next index. At the end of this loop, since we've added something to L, we increment *i* to the next index for the L array. And we can test this out using the same input that we've used to test earlier sorts. We'll create a list of foods and we'll call mergeSort, printing the results. Indeed, we get a sorted list out, just like we'd expect.

Let's look at one more example of a recursive sorting routine. This one is called quick sort, since it works famously fast on typical cases. In quick sort, the idea is still divide and conquer, but the division is done differently than in merge sort. In quick sort, we pick some value to split everything around, typically just the first value in the list, and we call this term the pivot. We then form two new lists—one with all the values less than the pivot, and one with all the values greater than the pivot. Next, we sort each of those lists, again with a recursive call to quick sort. After that, the whole list is sorted: we have the first list, followed by the pivot, followed by the last list.

Now, let's work through how we'd write some pseudocode for quick sort. The input and output are just like we've had in the past—we take in an unordered list, and our output will be a sorted list. Again, for a recursive routine, we want to have a base case. So, what do you think the base case will be for quick sort? Our base case will be just like in merge sort; we want to return if we have a list of length 0 or 1.

What's next? Well, the next thing we should do is pick the pivot, which we'll just do from the first element of the list. What comes after that? Next, we would form two lists, L1 and L2—L1 with elements that are less than the pivot, and L2 with elements that are greater than the pivot. Now, now that we have L1 and L2, what do we do next? Well, next, we recursively sort the two lists. This is our recursive call, where we call the quickSort function from within the quickSort function. And, once the lists are sorted, what do we do then? Well, then we form our final list, by joining the two lists and the pivot.

Let's use the pseudocode we have to write the code for this. First, give it a try yourself. I'll give you some hints, which you can also pause, to keep you going. So, first, define the function, and handle the check for a base case. Second, just like step two of the pseudocode, set your pivot. Third, you'll want to form two lists, one with values less than the pivot, one with values greater. Start with two empty lists, and then add in elements to one or the other. And then, for the recursive calls, you'll just call quickSort, passing in those two lists that you made. To join the lists, you can start with list 1, append on the pivot, and then append the elements of list 2.

Let's look at a finished implementation, to see one way you might have implemented quick sort. I've included some comments to make sure that we're following. First, we have our function header, defining quick sort with the list L as our parameter. Next, we'll have our base case check: if the length of L < = 1, we're done, so we return. Next, we have our pivot defined, just taking the first element of the list L. All of this, so far, is pretty straightforward from our pseudocode. We next have the lines that form our two sublists. We'll start with two empty lists, L1 and L2, and then we'll have a loop that goes through all the elements, except the first element, in the input list. We write this with a "for" loop—that is, elements from the second one in L until the end. For each of those, we append to either L1 or L2 depending on whether we're below or above the pivot.

All right, next, we have our recursive calls to quick sort: one for L1, and one for L2. And, finally, we have our code to join the two lists. We start out by deleting the elements already in L. Remember that, because we're relying on L being mutable, we can't assign L itself to a new value—we have to just modify the elements in L. Then, we go through list L1, adding its elements to L. Next, we add the pivot. And last, we go through L2, adding its elements to L. Again, if we test this routine out, we'll find that it sorts input just fine.

So, we've now seen four different sort routines: selection sort, where we kept selecting the next smallest value; insertion sort, where we would take the next value and insert it into the sorted list; merge sort, where we divided the whole list into two nearly equal parts and sorted those recursively; and quick sort, where we divided the whole list into smaller and larger parts around a pivot, and then we sorted those recursively. People have also developed a variety of other sorts. Now, what sorting shows very clearly is that there can be several different, sometimes very different, algorithmic solutions to the same problem.

Well, given so many different possible solutions to a problem, let's look at how we choose between them. In practice, sometimes people just choose "what's the easiest thing for a programmer to understand" or "what's the easiest thing to write code for," and these actually aren't bad reasons—you should only write code for things that you understand. But, the best choice of algorithm should be independent of the individual programmer, and, since the motivation for much of computing has been increased efficiency, we often use efficiency as the criterion to choose one algorithm over another.

In the case of sort routines, we already saw that Python has a built-in sort routine, which uses a combination of merge sort and an insertion sort. That built-in Python sort is really efficient. In fact, that should usually be the version that you use. Most other languages will also have some sort of built-in sort function. Now, to assess efficiency, computer scientists use what's called asymptotic analysis. This type of analysis looks at how a function performs as the input size grows larger and larger. We ask, "How does the running time increase as the input size increases?" For the algorithms that we've looked at, like searching in a list or sorting a list, the input size will be the length of the list.

Now we could spend a couple of lectures diving into asymptotic analysis, but, for many programmers, we just need a general idea of practical running time. A good way to think about this is, "What will happen if I double the input size?" For our searches or our sorts, think of having a list twice as long. We also have to think about what part of the running time we care about. Do we care about the best case, or the worst case, or the average case? Most of the time, computer scientists will analyze the worst case, since we want to make sure that things don't behave too badly. However, depending on the problem, you sometimes really care about the best case or the average case.

Let's start by thinking about a search. If I have a list with n items in it, and I do a standard, linear search, in the best case, the item I'm looking for is the very first one in the list. So, I just check one element and I'm done. In the worst case, I go through all n items and I don't find it at all, or I find it in the very last one. On average, I'll have to go through half the items—or n over 2—to find it, if it's in the list at all.

Now, what happens if I have a list twice the size—that is, $2n$? I still have the same situation in the best case: one single check. In the worst case, I have to go through all $2n$ items. And, in the average case, assuming it's in the list at all, I'm going through half of the list, or n items. So, notice that when I doubled the input size, I doubled the worst-case and the average-case search times, and we describe this as a linear process, since the running time is a linear function of the input size. We'll also say it order n, and we'll sometimes write it big O of n. And yes, that's the right term; we call this big O notation.

Now, let's consider binary search, where I divide the list in half each time. Again, the best case is one where the first element I check is the one that I'm looking for. Now, each iteration of the search, I prune away half of the remaining elements. So, in the worst case, I keep dividing by 2 until I'm down to just one element. If I have less than 8 elements, then 3 checks is enough. If I have less than 16 elements, then 4 is enough. And, in general, for a list less than length n, I'll have log base 2 of n checks required. In the average case, I have just one less check, so it's only one less than log base 2 of n checks—basically the same. And, if I double my list size, in the worst case, I have just one more check.

So, mathematicians describe this as a log function, since the running time is a logarithmic function of the input size, and we'll write it as big O of log n. Clearly, if we're choosing between a linear process and a logarithmic process, given a sufficiently large data set, we'll always prefer the log process. If we have the option of a log search, we shouldn't choose a linear one.

Let's use this kind of comparison to see how some of the sorts work, in terms of running time. Let's start with selection sort—that's where we go through the whole list and pull out the smallest element, and then go through again to find the next smallest, and so on. To understand how this runs, we should think of something of size n. On our first iteration, we have to check through all n items in the list, and then perform one swap. The next iteration, we check $n - 1$ items in the list, and perform one swap. Then we check $n - 2$ items, and so on, until finally we're down to just one item left.

So, the total number of checks that we needed in this case was $n + n - 1, + n - 2, + n - 3$ all the way down to 1. This is the sum from 1 to n, which you could do step by step or you could use the summation formula: $n \times n + 1$ over 2. Now, as n gets larger and larger, the only part of that that really matters is the n squared part—the minus n is insignificant compared to the n squared portion. This is called a quadratic running time, or more commonly, big O of n squared. Notice that selection sort always takes the same amount of time, so the best case and the worst case running times are the same.

Now, let's consider insertion sort instead. Remember that we'll always be inserting one new value into an already sorted list. In the best case, the whole list is already sorted, and in this case, we only have to do one comparison for each item, so the whole thing takes order n time. In the worst case, we're in complete reverse order. So, we can insert the first item with no comparisons; the next one, we'll have to compare once; the next one, we have to compare two times; the next one, three times, and so on. And, if you think about it, this is, again, a sum from 1 to n total comparisons. So, in the worst case, insertion sort is approximately n squared—just as bad as selection sort.

Now, let's consider merge sort. In merge sort, we have three steps each time. First, we split the list in two—that's easy, and it just takes a constant amount of time. Then, we sort each of those sublists. Then, we merge the two sublists together again. That merge takes order n time, since we visit each of the elements exactly once. Notice that merge sort is always order n log n; there's no case better or worse than another.

Finally, we have quick sort. With quick sort, if we have a good split at each level, where about half the numbers are above and half are below, the running time is very similar to merge sort, for the same reasons. So, it's order n log n. In the worst case, we have an already sorted, or an already reverse-sorted, list, and we end up operating a lot like a selection sort, so we'd be order n squared. On average, we're nearer to the best case. In fact, quick sort can be implemented very efficiently, so it's often faster than merge sort in practice, even though it could be worse in some cases. If we look at a summary of all of these algorithms, we can get a sense of how they'll behave in various cases. Notice that an insertion sort is order n in the best case. In fact, it's the best of any of these.

Now, as we work with various programs, we'll sometimes want to make sure that what we're doing is reasonably efficient. The bigger the data sets we deal with, the more important this is. But, even with reasonably sized data—like, up to 1000 elements—the difference in asymptotic complexity can make a difference. This is a good place to say a little more about the algorithm used in Python's built-in sort function, since it's been cleverly designed to do even better than each of the four algorithms that we've been discussing individually, at least most of the time. Python, in its early days, used quick sort, before its current algorithm was created by Tim Peters using a combination of merge sort and insertion sort.

Even though merge sort works better on large problems, insertion sort will work faster on smaller problems. The Python sort routine basically uses merge sort for the overall problem, but once it's dealing with sufficiently small problems, it switches to insertion sort. It also has some checks to find out if a portion of the list is already sorted. Lists that are at least partially sorted are more common than you might suppose, especially for data that isn't in absolutely random order. If we think about this in terms of recursion, the Python algorithm is using recursion whenever there's a merge sort, but it's avoiding recursion whenever there's an insertion sort. Why might that combination be a good idea?

Well, recursion is a really useful way of describing certain calculations. In fact, for some calculations, it's the only good way of describing what needs to be done. But, there are other times when recursion is possible, but you should, well—run away. To make this point clear, I'm going to show you a recursive program, and then I'm going to show you an alternative way of computing it that's a whole lot more efficient.

To do this, I'm going to use some Fibonacci numbers. Fibonacci numbers are numbers in a sequence, the Fibonacci sequence, where each number in the sequence is the sum of the two previous numbers. The first two Fibonacci numbers, the zeroth and first Fibonacci numbers, are 0 and 1. Then, we add the two adjacent numbers to get the next number. So, the second one is 0 + 1, or 1. The third one is 1 + 1, or 2. The fourth one is 1 + 2, or 3.

Fibonacci numbers have all sorts of interesting incarnations in math and nature. So, let's see how we might write that as a recursive routine. So, think about this: how would you write a routine, named Fib, where you pass in a number, and it gives you that number in the Fibonacci sequence by making a recursive call. So, passing in 0 or 1 would return 0 or 1; passing in 4 would return 3, and so on.

OK, here's one way you could do this. First, we define Fib, taking in the index n. We first check for the two base cases, if n is 0 or 1. In these cases, we just return 0 or 1. Otherwise, we compute Fib for $n - 2$ and Fib for $n - 1$, and we return that. Now, this code is correct, and it will compute Fibonacci numbers, but it's also horrendously slow. Try printing out Fib of 4 or 5 or 6, and you'll get an answer. But, try printing out Fib of 100, and your computer will take a long time to finish—too long.

The problem here is that each call generates twice the number of function calls as the previous level. So, a call like Fib 100 will generate 2 to the 100th recursive function calls until it reaches the base cases. That's something like a nonillion function calls. Have you even heard of a nonillion? It's a trillion times a trillion times a trillion. So, no wonder that was taking so long; this algorithm is taking exponential time. If we analyzed the running time of the algorithm, we'd have to conclude that it's not very practical. In fact, that's roughly the time it would take one of very fastest current computers if it ran for more than 10 million years.

Now, fortunately, we didn't need to use recursion to compute the Fibonacci numbers. If you look at the computation, you can see that there are a lot of cases where we're computing the same number over and over. Instead of writing a recursive routine, see if you can write a routine that calculates the numbers in order, until you reach the one that you care about. So, you would first compute 0 and 1, then 2, then 3, and so on, until you get the one you want.

Here's a much better way of computing Fibonacci numbers. We create a list, F, initializing the first two elements to 0 and 1. Then, we'll keep adding on elements by adding the previous two together. In this way, we can compute all the way to the 100th Fibonacci number easily. The answer's really big, but at least it's quickly computed. Now, what kind of running time process does this new algorithm have? Think about it, and see if you can figure it out? This is a linear algorithm. The reason is that each of the Fibonacci numbers is computed exactly once. If we want to compute a number twice as big, it takes twice as long. That's a whole lot better than exponential.

Here's the point. By selecting a different algorithm, in this case a linear one that's iterative instead of an exponential one that's recursive, we can sometimes turn a problem that seems completely impossible into one that's easily solved. The recursive approach to the Fibonacci calculation is just not practical, whereas the iterative approach nicely matches how Fibonacci numbers are defined. The lesson to learn is that it's worth analyzing your code to determine running time, to make sure that you're not being wildly or unnecessarily inefficient in the algorithm you've chosen to solve a problem.

Understanding algorithms is of central importance for much of computer science, and the basic problems in searching and sorting that we've seen are the classic examples because they're so widely used. By analyzing the running time of our algorithms, we can make choices that will lead to better code and more efficient use of processor time. Recursion can offer an elegant way of solving some problems for us, but we have to be careful with it. Whenever iteration is possible, it'll usually be more efficient. However, there are cases where recursion is really the only formulation that makes sense. We'll see an example of this in our next lecture, when we discuss graphs, trees, and a couple of recursive algorithms.

22

Graphs and Trees

Graphs offer a structure for capturing an incredibly wide diversity of relationships and the connections that are formed all over. They represent connections between locations, between people, among species, and among data. These and many other relations are well represented on a graph. Once relationships are captured in a graph, algorithms let us use the graph effectively in our programs. In this lecture, you will learn about graphs, as well as trees—a particularly useful type of graph that makes organizing data easier.

[GRAPHS]

› Imagine that you live in a kingdom with five main cities: Rivertown, Hillsview, Brookside, Lakeside, and Forrest City. Three of these cities are connected to each other directly with roads. Lakeside is connected only to Forrest City, and the only other road from Forrest City connects it to Hillsview.

› Whenever you have a bunch of entities—cities, in this case—with connections to each other, you have a data structure that's called a **graph**. In this sense, graphs, which are studied in a field called "graph theory," are used for everything from airplane connections, to ecological webs among species, to social networks.

› In a graph, we call the "things" that we're representing a "vertex" or a **node**. These are the cities in our example. The connections between nodes are **edges**. In our example, these are the roads. Edges let us know that there's a relation between the two nodes—for example, that they're connected by a road.

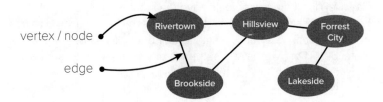

> In terms of writing code, graphs can have more than one representation. For example, there is one that is more global and one that focuses on adjacent neighbors. The more global option is to represent a graph as two lists: one list of nodes and one list of edges.

> Each node will contain information about itself. So, each of our city nodes might contain just the name of a city, or each node could also contain other information, such as city population, GPS coordinates for the city, and so on.

> An edge would have the names of the two nodes—in this case, the two cities that it connects. If it's a weighted graph, the edge would also store a **weight**, which in this case might be the length of that road, in miles or kilometers.

> Let's try to write code to support this. We'll want two classes, one for the nodes and one for the edges. Remember that a class helps us encapsulate the stuff that goes together, so the node class should incorporate the stuff in a node, and the edge class should incorporate the stuff in an edge.

> The node class will have a name for the city and a population. We'll set these with our initialization routine, which sets the instance attributes "_name" and "_pop." This is why we have the "self" reference; each node can have a different name and population. We make sure that we can access the name and population variables through two accessor functions, "getName" and "getPopulation."

› Likewise, our edge class would have the names of two cities, along with the distance along the road. These are set with the "init" initialization routine, which sets local instance attributes for "city1," "city2," and "distance." Then, we have a set of accessor functions to get each city name, or the pair of city names, and the distance.

```python
class node:
    def __init__(self, name, population=0):
        self._name = name
        self._pop = population
    def getName(self):
        return self._name
    def getPopulation(self):
        return self._pop
class edge:
    def __init__(self, name1, name2, weight=0):
        self._city1 = name1
        self._city2 = name2
        self._distance = weight
    def getName1(self):
        return self._city1
    def getName2(self):
        return self._city2
    def getNames(self):
        return (self._city1, self._city2)
    def getWeight(self):
        return self._distance
```

› The following is how we might set up our node list and edge list for the city example. We'll create our five cities, each with some population, and add those to the city list. For example, we create a node for Rivertown with a population of 100 and append it to the cities list.

```python
cities = []
roads = []
city = node('Rivertown', 1000)
cities.append(city)
```

```
city = node('Brookside', 1500)
cities.append(city)
city = node('Hillsview', 500)
cities.append(city)
city = node('Forrest City', 800)
cities.append(city)
city = node('Lakeside', 1100)
cities.append(city)
road = edge('Rivertown', 'Brookside', 100)
roads.append(road)
road = edge('Rivertown', 'Hillsview', 50)
roads.append(road)
road = edge('Hillsview', 'Brookside', 130)
roads.append(road)
road = edge('Hillsview', 'Forrest City', 40)
roads.append(road)
road = edge('Forrest City', 'Lakeside', 80)
roads.append(road)
```

> We'll also create our roads—five of them, in this case—and add them to the road list. For example, we form an edge between Rivertown and Brookside of length 100 and then append that edge to the roads list. It would be simple to add another road between two cities, or another city—just create a new edge or node and append it on.

> In addition to the first method of storing graphs—by keeping a global list of edges—there is a second way: by keeping a list of edges in each node. This second type is called an **adjacency list**.

> The global list of all the edges is probably most useful if you find yourself regularly needing to look at all of the edges. That's the approach commonly used to represent geometric models, like you would have in three-dimensional graphics.

> The second approach—the adjacency list, where you keep a list of the edges within each node—is useful in most typical graph operations, such

as airline connections, social networks, and so on. The adjacency list works well because most graph algorithms are already designed to work just looking at one node at a time and its neighbors.

> There is also a third method to store graphs, called an **adjacency matrix**, in which, instead of list, there are matrix entries that note which nodes are connected. This can be useful for operations where you need to quickly run over many different values or perform certain computations that can be expressed using linear algebra.

> An adjacency matrix can be the most compact form of a graph, especially when there are many edges. This is a key factor when graphs are huge. And it's the fastest of the representations if you need to check whether a particular pair of cities is connected.

> For any given graph, we can define a variety of graph algorithms. Some of these algorithms are simple. For example, returning a list of all the cities adjacent to one city is a very basic algorithm. The representation used to store the graph will determine exactly how the algorithm will perform.

> Graph algorithms let us analyze all kinds of things about the structure of graphs. For example, the **breadth-first search** algorithm lets us analyze how many degrees of separation there are between two people in a social network.

> With roads, we can usually travel the road in either direction—we just say that those nodes are connected. Graphs like this are called "undirected" graphs. A graph where people are friends is undirected: If person A is friends with person B, then person B is also friends with person A.

> However, we can also have cases where two things are linked, but it's not an equal connection between the two sides. For example, imagine cities connected by airline routes. Not all airline routes fly round-trips. Sometimes, a plane will fly from city 1, then to city 2, then to city 3, and then back to city 1. In this case, the edges go from one city to another, but not necessarily the other way around.

> So, there should be an edge from city 1's node to city 2's node, and one from city 2's node to city 3's node, and one from city 3's node back to city 1's node. These are called "directed" edges, and the resulting graph, made up of **directed edges**, is called a "directed graph," or "digraph."

> Web pages and the links between them form a directed graph. If web page A has a link to web page B, there's not necessarily one from web page B back to web page A.

> We say that a graph is **connected** if there is some sequence of edges connecting every pair of nodes. A graph has a **cycle** if there's some way to follow a set of edges and end up back where you started. In our city example, there's a cycle—you could go from Rivertown, to Hillsview, to Brookside, and then back to Rivertown.

[TREES]

> A connected, undirected graph that does not contain a cycle is called a **tree**. Trees are such a useful structure that a whole set of algorithms have been developed just for trees.

> The following is an example of a tree. All the nodes are connected to each other, and there's no cycle in the graph.

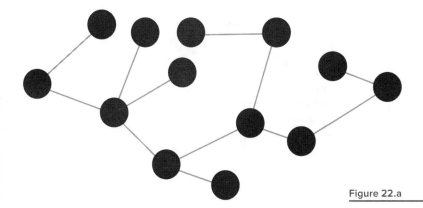

Figure 22.a

> Usually, when we talk about trees, we'll designate one node as the **root**, which can be thought of as the starting point, or the central point. It's the top level of a hierarchy. The rest of the tree can then be arranged in terms of "levels" from the root, where the root is at level 0, and each subsequent level is formed based on how many edges must be followed to get to the root.

> All the nodes connected to the root are considered its children and form the first level. The nodes they are connected to form the second level, and so on. For any node, the node it is connected to at the previous level is called its parent, and the nodes below it are called its children. A typical drawing of a tree will put the root at the top and the children in levels below.

> Because trees have this particular structure, they often have a particular way they are stored in code. Trees almost always use an adjacency list, where the edges are stored inside each node. And they usually store the parent and the children separately. So, any one node will store its own information, along with an index (or some other notation, such as a name) for the **parent node**, along with a list of its children.

> In code, we'll keep a variable to give the parent, and we'll keep a list of variables that are the children. We can add additional children whenever we need to.

```
class node:
    def __init__(self, name, parent=-1):
        self._name = name
        self._parent = parent
        self._children = []
    def getName(self):
        return self._name
    def getParent(self):
        return self._parent
    def getChildren(self):
        return self._children
```

```
        def setParent(self, p):
            self._parent = p
        def addChild(self, c):
            self._children.append(c)
```

> A very common type of tree is called a **binary tree**. In this case, every
  node has no more than two children. We'll usually call them a left
  child and a right child. So, a node will hold a parent, a left child, and a
  right child.

```
class node:
    def __init__(self, name, parent=-1):
        self._name = name
        self._parent = parent
        self._left = -1
        self._right = -1
    def getName(self):
        return self._name
    def getParent(self):
        return self._parent
    def getLeft(self):
        return self._left
    def getRight(self):
        return self._right
    def setParent(self, p):
        self._parent = p
    def setLeft(self, l):
        self._left = l
    def setRight(self, r):
        self._right = r
```

> Binary trees have many uses, but a common one is to store objects in
  sorted order. We call these **binary search trees**. Unlike arrays or lists that
  we might have to sort every time we add a new value, a binary tree can
  keep items always in sorted order. It's usually faster to add an item to a
  binary tree than to add it to an array or list that's been sorted.

> With a binary search tree, at any node in the tree, all the descendants on the left side are less than the node, and all those on the right side are greater than the node. Notice, for example, that 21 is greater than the root, 15, so it's on the right side of the root. It's greater than the next node, 18, so it's also on the right side of it. But it's less than the next node, 23, so it's on the left side of that one.

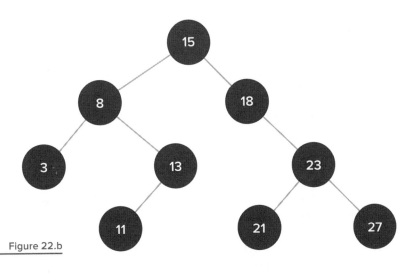

Figure 22.b

> There are various things we can do with a binary search tree, such as print out the entire tree in sorted order. This ends up being basically another sorting routine: We put elements into the binary search tree in order, and then when we print them out, we get a sorted list. If we take our set of nodes, insert them all into the tree, and then print it out, we get a sorted output list. This routine is fast, plus it works really fast, on average, if you have to update the sorted list.

Reading

Lambert, *Fundamentals of Python*, chaps. 10 and 12.

Exercises

1   Consider the parts of a body: head, neck, torso, arms, legs, hands, and feet. Draw a graph showing the connectivity between the parts of the body.

2   From the graph in exercise 1, what is the longest number of edges you would need to follow to go from one body part to another?

3   Is the graph in exercise 1 a tree? Why or why not?

4   Show the binary search tree that you would get by inserting nodes into an empty tree in the following order: 3, 1, 8, 2, 9.

5   Note that instead of storing indices for cities, we could instead store the cities in a dictionary instead of in a list. Following is part of the code used to build a list of cities in the code from the lecture. How would you modify this so that it uses a dictionary of cities instead of a list?

```
cities = []
city = node('Rivertown', 1000)
cities.append(city)
city = node('Brookside', 1500)
cities.append(city)
city = node('Hillsview', 500)
cities.append(city)
city = node('Forrest City', 800)
cities.append(city)
city = node('Lakeside', 1100)
cities.append(city)
...
road = roads[0]
pop1 = 0
pop2 = 0
for city in cities:
    if city.getName() == road.getName1():
        pop1 = city.getPopulation()
    if city.getName() == road.getName2():
        pop2 = city.getPopulation()
```

Graphs and Trees

I magine that you live in a kingdom with five main cities: Rivertown, Hillsview, Brookside, Lakeside, and Forrest City, and there are roads between these cities. Three of them are all connected to each other directly with roads. Lakeside is connected only to Forrest City, and the only other road from Forrest City connects it to Hillsview. Well, whenever you have a bunch of entities—cities, in this case—that have connections to each other, you have a data structure that's called a graph. Graphs, in this sense, which are studied in a field called graph theory, are used for everything from airplane connections, to ecological webs among species, to social networks.

Let me give you a little terminology. In a graph, we call the things that we're representing a vertex or a node. These are the cities in our example, the points that are on the graph. The connection between nodes are edges; in our example, these are roads. Edges let us know that there's a relation between the two nodes—for example, that they're connected by a road. In terms of writing code, graphs can have more than one representation. I'll show you two ways of representing a graph, one that's more global, and one that focuses on adjacent neighbors. The more global option is to represent a graph as two lists: one, a list of nodes; and one, a list of edges.

Now, each node will contain information about itself. So, each of our city nodes might contain just the name of the city, or it could also contain other information, such as city population, or coordinates for the city, and so on. An edge would have the names of the two nodes, in this case the two cities that it connects. If it's a weighted graph, the edge would also store a weight, which in this case might be the length of the road in miles or kilometers.

Let's try to write code to support this. We'll want two classes—one for the nodes, and one for the edges. Remember that a class helps us encapsulate the stuff that goes together, so the node class should incorporate all the stuff in a node, and the edge class should incorporate all the stuff in an edge. So, what would our classes look like?

OK, we'll have two classes: a node class, and an edge class. The node class will have a name for the city, and I also stored a population. We'll set these with our initialization routine, which sets the instance attributes: _name, and _pop. This is why we have the "self" reference—each node can have a different name and population. We make sure that we can access the name and population variables through two accessor functions, getName and getPopulation. Now, likewise, our edge class would have the names of two cities, along with the distance along the road, and these are set with the init initialization routine, which sets local instance attributes for city1, city2, and distance. Then, we have a set of accessor functions to get each city name, or the pair of city names, and the distance.

Now, here's how we might set up our node list and the edge list for the city example. We'll create our five cities, each with some population, and we'll add those to the city list. For example, we create a node for Rivertown with a population of 100 and we append it to the cities list. We'll also create our roads, five of them in this case, and we'll add them to the roads list. For example, we form an edge between Rivertown and Brookside of length 100, and then we append that edge to the roads list. It'd be a simple matter to add another road between two cities, or another city—just create a new edge or a new node and append it on.

Now, think about how you might use an edge. Say you wanted to find the total population that lives along a road. You'd need to find the population of the cities at each end. Population is stored in the city nodes; the road only knows the name of the cities. So, think about this: how could you write a function to find the combined population along an edge, such as edge 0?

Here's the basic process. You'd first get the road you cared about. I said we wanted edge 0, so I've just pulled out the first edge from the roads list and called it road. Then, we've got to loop through the list of cities. For each city in the city list, we check whether the name of that city matches the first name or the second name from the road. If so, we store that population. And, finally, we add up the population. If you had a large list of cities, this might be pretty annoying, because it's an order n operation just to get the population.

Instead of using the names of the two cities, we could use the index of the two cities in the list of nodes. The index is just the position where they are in that list according to whatever order they were put into the list. Using the index makes it easier to find the cities—we can jump right to the city. We don't even need to change our node or edge classes; they'll still work exactly the same. The only difference is that the parameters to the edge class now have a bad name for the parameter. Instead of name1 and name2, we probably want to use a different name so that it's clear what the edge is expected to store. So, let's call them index1 and index2.

We change each parameter from a city name to an index, and we change some of the return functions to match this. To create our edges, we're now going to pass in the indices for the cities. So, for the road between Rivertown and Brookside, we'll use 0 and 1 instead of the city names, and the same will hold for the other cities.

Let's say that we want to get the population on a road now. What would the code look like in this case? This code is a whole lot simpler. We have the indices of the two cities, so we can go directly to that city in the list—there's no more loop that makes us search through each element of the list. This is a constant-time operation; it doesn't matter how many things there are, it always takes the same time. That's instead of the linear one that we had earlier, where the more things we had, the longer it would take. And our code to find this information is a whole lot shorter to write.

Of course, there's a downside to using the index instead of the name: the list of cities must remain unchanged. We can't have the city list being re-sorted or something—that would change which city a particular index was referring to. We need to know the index of each city in the list when we set up our edge, and if we can't live with these restrictions, we can't use this approach, even if it's a lot faster for some operations.

Using an index instead of the name is a common trick in programming. Because it's less direct than storing the name, it's called indirection. Instead of storing the actual value—the name—we store an index to the thing containing the name. A dictionary is another way of getting a similar effect. Indirection also works well for the second way we could store graphs, called an adjacency list.

Let's say that we want to be able to take a given city and find all the roads from that city. That's a painful operation in the approach we've just described. We'd have to go through the list of edges trying to find the ones that have our city as the first or second city in the edge.

Instead of keeping a single list of all edges in the graph, let's instead keep just a local list of the edges for each node. Each node will keep track of the edges connected to it. In this case, we'll have just one list: a list of nodes. Each node will have the name of the city, other information about the node, like population, and then a list of edges. The edges in this case just need to keep track of the city at the opposite end of the road, and then the weight, such as the length of the road or the time it would take to travel that road.

Let's see what the code for this might look like. Now, you might want to try creating some code yourself, first. Here's one way to do it. We've defined an edge by just giving a single city and a weight value, rather than two cities like we had previously. Like before, we could have used an index instead of a name if we wanted. Our nodes will have a city name, a population, and then a list of roads. Each element of that list of roads will be an edge. We'll also have addNeighbor and addNeighborRoad defined. AddNeighborRoad takes an existing road as input, and it adds it onto the list of roads connected to this city, stored in the _roads list in the class. AddNeighbor will take in a city name and a weight for the edge as input parameters. It first creates a road to that city, with that weight, and then it appends that road onto the roads list.

We can create a set of cities, just like before—nothing changes in this part of the code for us. However, creating an edge in the graph, that's a connection between two cities, is more complicated. To make things easier, we can define a function, addRoad, that lets us add a road between two cities, and this function will take in the city names and the distance, and will create a road link for each city. It does this by creating new edge objects, one to each city. Then, it'll search through the list of cities to find the matching city name, and when it does so, it'll add the edge it created earlier to that city, by calling addNeighborRoad. So, in this way, both cities along a road get a local edge saying that they're connected to a neighbor. As an alternative, which is also shown here, we could call the addNeighbor routine for each city. Either way will work, and it will create a road in each city that links to the city on the other side.

Now, adding our connections is just a matter of calling the addRoad function that we just defined. Going back to our cities and roads example, the calls to add the five roads we defined would be just like you see here. This allows us to find neighbors much more easily. For instance, we can print out a list of all the neighbors, by city, with just a couple of loops. We first will loop through all of the cities, and then, for each one, we'll print out a line saying that we're printing out the list of neighbors, and then we get that list of neighbors and loop through the list. For each neighbor, we print out the name of the city and the distance away. So, in the end, we can find out all the neighbors of all our cities.

Notice that going through to find neighbors of any particular node was a whole lot easier this way. However, it did require a somewhat more complex set of routines to set things up. And, if we wanted to do something like find every edge, this data structure isn't as well suited as the previous one.

OK, so that was two ways of storing graphs: first, by keeping a global list of all edges; and second, by keeping a list of edges in each node. This second type is called an adjacency list. The global list of all the edges is probably most useful—no surprise—if you find yourself regularly needing to look at all the edges. That's the approach commonly used to represent geometric models, like you would have in 3-D graphics.

The second approach, the adjacency list, where you keep a list of the edges within each node, is useful in most of our typical graph operations, such as airline connections, social networks, and so on. The adjacency list works well because most graph algorithms are already designed to work just by looking at one node at a time and its neighbors.

There's also a third method to store graphs, and I won't dwell on it here, but it's called an adjacency matrix. In that one, instead of a list, there are matrix entries that note which nodes are connected. This can be useful for operations where you need to quickly run over lots of different values, or perform certain computations that can be expressed using linear algebra. It can be the most compact form of a graph, especially if there are a lot of edges, and this is a key factor when graphs are huge. It's also the fastest of the representations if you need to check whether a particular pair of cities is connected.

Now, for any given graph, we can define a variety of graph algorithms. Some of these algorithms are simple. For example, returning a list of all the cities adjacent to one city, similar to that algorithm that we just saw—well, that's a very basic algorithm. The representation used to store the graph will determine exactly how the algorithm will perform. Graph algorithms let us analyze all sorts of stuff about the structure of graphs. For example, the breadth-first search algorithm lets us analyze how many degrees of separation there really are between two people in a social network. We'll see the details of implementing breadth-first search in the next lecture.

Now, with roads, we can usually travel the road in either direction—we just say those nodes are connected. Graphs like this are called undirected graphs. A graph where people are friends is undirected: if personA is friends with personB, then personB is also friends with personA.

However, we can also have cases where two things are linked, but it's not an equal connection between the two sides. For instance, imagine cities connected by airline routes. Not all airline routes fly round trips; sometimes, a plane will fly from city 1 then to 2, then to 3, and then back to 1. In this case, the edges go from one city to another, but not necessarily the other way around. So, there should be an edge from city 1's node to city 2's node, and from 2 to 3, and one from 3 back to 1. These are called directed edges, and the resulting graph, made up of directed edges, is called a directed graph, or sometimes a digraph. Web pages and the links between them form a directed graph. If web page A has a link to web page B, there's not necessarily one from B back to A.

Storing a directed graph is not much different than storing an undirected graph. If we have a big list of edges, then we just need to make sure that each edge has a start and an end—our earlier code doesn't even need to change at all. Each edge already had city1 and city2 attributes, so we don't need to change it.

For an adjacency list, we also don't need any fundamental change to the node or edge classes. Each edge is essentially already a directed edge—it's stored with the starting point. We already had to create two roads—one from A to B, and the other from B to A—for each road. So, for a directed graph, we just have edges stored on the one side where the edge starts.

Now, we say that a graph is connected if there's some sequence of edges that connects every pair of nodes, and a graph has a cycle if there's some way to follow a set of edges and end up right back where you started. In our city example, there's a cycle, since you could go from Rivertown, to Hillsview, to Brookside, and then back to Rivertown.

OK, let's see a directed graph in an application involving money. Now, different currencies can be traded from one currency to another, at some exchange rate. For any pair of currencies, there's some rate at which you can trade one into the other, and we can form a directed graph of these exchanges. It will be a really dense graph, because every currency can be exchanged for a different one. It's a weighted graph, also—each edge can give the rate of exchange for the first one into the second one.

Now, currency arbitrage refers to taking advantage of an imbalance in the currency exchange rates, so that you can make money through changing currencies. Here's how this would work. Let's say that you can change U.S. dollars to euros, getting 0.95 euros per dollar. Then, you can change euros into British pounds, getting 0.75 pounds per euro. Then, you can exchange 1 pound for 175 yen. And, finally, you can exchange 1 yen for .0085 U.S. dollars.

So, if you started with $1000, you could convert that to 950 euros, and then to 712.5 pounds, and then to 124,687 yen, and then to $1059.84, and that's more than you started with. Wow, it's like getting free money. And, believe it or not, imbalances like this do come up from time to time, and there are some people who've become very wealthy exploiting these imbalances. Now, if we store currency exchange rate as a directed graph, what we want to do is we want to find a cycle in which the product of all the edges is greater than one. And that would mean that we could use arbitrage to generate money.

OK, let's see how we would write code to do this. We first create classes to hold the currencies and the exchange rates between them. So, we'll have a currency class like you see here. The init function will set up a name and an empty list of exchange rates, both as instance attributes. We'll also have accessor functions to return the name of the currency and the list of exchange rates. Plus, there'll be two functions allowing us to set exchange rates: one, addRateEdge, will assume we've already created an edge that describes the exchange rate, and are passing it in; and the other one, addRate, will just take in the currency name and the exchange rate for that currency and it'll create the edge. In both cases, the edge simply gets appended onto the list of exchange rates.

We'll also have some functions designed to let us specify pairs of currencies, and then set up the appropriate edges for those currencies. This is very similar to how we set up roads between cities. Finally, we'll set up a group of currencies—in this case dollars, pounds, euros, and yen—and then will set up exchange rates between all pairs. Now comes the fun part—we want to find out if there is some conversion path that'll let us convert between these to make money. I'll quickly walk you through some of this code, but you'll probably want to study it a while to really understand it.

First, I'll create a member function of the currency class called findArbitrage. We'll call this for a particular currency. It'll have a "for" loop for all the exchange rates in that currency. For each currency, it'll have another loop to find the particular currency in the overall list—that's the purpose of the inner "for" loop and "if" statement. We then call findRates for that currency.

FindRates is going to be our main routine; it'll make recursive calls to itself to find whether some chain exists. It takes in the main currency that we're trying to find a cycle for as one parameter, and then the current combined exchange rate, and then how many conversions have already occurred. First, it handles two base cases for recursion. The first checks to see if we're back at the main currency that we care about. If we are, we see that we have a cycle, and we check to see if it made us money by checking whether the current_value is greater than one. If so, we print out that we've found a way, and we show what that combined exchange rate is, and we return true. We also have a second base case where we've had too many exchanges. If we get to this point, we just quit and return false. In this case, I've said that we can't have more than three exchanges, so this checks whether the depth is greater than three.

The other part of the routine goes through all the conversion rates possible from this currency, using a "for" loop. It computes the overall conversion for that rate, then it finds the currency that this corresponds to, and that's the purpose of the inner "for" loop and the "if" statement. Once it finds that, it recursively calls itself within the "if" statement. The call to itself passes in the main currency, the new combined exchange rate, and it increments the number of exchanges so far by one. Now, if that returns true, it means that there was a cycle to this point, so it prints out the combined exchange rate, and its currency name, and then it returns true itself. But, if we got through all the rates and we didn't already return true, it means that we didn't find a cycle through this exchange, so nothing printed and we just return false.

Now, finally, if we run this code with a simple call to findArbitrage on the first currency, we do indeed find a cycle. For the exchange rates that I put in, we can convert 1 dollar to 0.7 pounds, then to .9333 euros, then to 217.7 yen, and then finally to $1.85. Wow, that's a big improvement. Now, obviously, these are not real exchange rates. If they were, we could use this information to make ourselves very, very wealthy.

All right, what if we have a graph that's connected but doesn't have a cycle? A connected, undirected graph that does not contain a cycle is called a tree. Trees are such a useful structure that a whole set of algorithms have been developed just for trees.

So, here's an example of a tree. All the nodes are connected to each other, and there's no cycle in the graph. Now, usually, when we talk about trees, we'll designate one node as the root. The root of a tree can be thought of as the starting point, or the central point—it's the top level of a hierarchy. And the rest of the tree can then be arranged in terms of levels from the root, where the root is at level zero, and each subsequent level is formed based on how many edges must be followed to get to the root. All the nodes connected to the root are considered its children, and they form the first level; the nodes that they're connected to form the second level, and so on. For any node, the node it's connected to at the previous level is called its parent, and the nodes below it are called its children.

Now, looking back at our tree graph, say that the highlighted node was our root—our zero. Then, the other nodes would be at level 1, 2, or 3. In a typical drawing of a tree, we'll put the root at the top, and the children in levels below. Now, because trees have this particular structure, they often have a particular way that they're stored in code. Trees almost always use an adjacency list, where the edges are stored inside each node, and they usually store the parent and the children separately. So, any one node will store its own information, along with an index or some other notation—like a name for the parent node—along with a list of its children. In code, we'll keep a variable to give the parent, and we'll keep a list of variables that are the children. We can add additional children whenever we need to.

A very common type of tree is called a binary tree. In this case, every node has no more than two children. We'll usually call them a left child and a right child. So, a node will hold a parent, a left child, and a right child. Binary trees have lots of uses, but a common one is to store objects in sorted order. We call these binary search trees. Unlike arrays or lists that we might have to sort every time we add a new value, a binary tree can keep the items always in sorted order. As you might guess, it's usually faster to add an item to a binary tree than to add it to an array or a list that you have to keep sorted. As you can see in this example of a binary search tree, at any node in the tree, all the descendants on the left-hand side are less than the node, and all those on the right-hand side are greater than the node. Notice, for instance, that 21 is greater than the root, 15, so it's on the right-hand side of the root. It's greater than the next node, 18, so it's also on the right-hand side of it. But, it's less than the next node, 23, so it's on the left-hand side of that one.

Let's see how this works in code if we want to add a new item to the binary search tree. As with many tree and graph algorithms, we're going to use a recursive definition. The basic idea is to call insert on the root of the tree, and recursively work our way down through the tree, until we add the node at the right point. So, we start by comparing it to the value at the root. If our new node is less, we want to go to the left, and if it's greater, we want to go to the right. Whenever there's not another node to go to, then we can make this new node at that position. So, each time, we'll either set this node as the left or right node, or else we'll call insert recursively.

Let's see a quick example of how this works before we look at code. Say we have our tree from before, and we want to insert the number 7. Seven is less than 15, so we go to the left. It's less than 8, so we go left again. And it's greater than 3, so we go right. And, there's nothing already to the right, so we insert 7 there—that is, we set 7's parent to be 3, and we set 3's right child to be 7.

So, let's try writing the code for this insert routine. Here's the node class that we start with. It's the same as the binary tree node that I showed before, but I've changed the name to a value. We can also define a set of nodes, like you see here, and our goal will be to take that set of nodes and turn it into a binary search tree by inserting one node at a time. So, how would we insert one node at a time? Remember, you'll want to write a recursive function called insert that takes in one node index and adds it to the tree.

Our code for the insert routine will be like this. We have "insert," and it takes in the index of the node to insert. The first thing it does is compare the value of the node being inserted to the current node's value. That is, it gets the node by taking nodelist sub insert_node, and it calls getValue on that node to get that node's value. It gets compared to the val part of the current node. If it's less, we'll work on the left-hand side; otherwise, we'll work on the right-hand side. If we're on the left, we check to see if there's anything on the left. If the index of the left node is minus 1, that means there's no node there. So, we set the left node to be this one, and we're done. Otherwise, there is a node on the left already. So, we find that node by going to nodelist sub self_left, and we call insert on it, passing in the insert node. Now, this recursive call will insert the node somewhere on that left side. The right side of the tree works the exact same way.

Now, if we have a bunch of nodes that we want to insert into a tree, here's how that'll look. We set the first node as the root. Then we go through the remaining nodes, inserting them one by one at the root. Each of these will add the node into the tree; for the values that we had earlier, inserting them in this order will form the tree that we saw previously.

Having this binary search tree is nice, and there are various things that we can do with it. One simple thing we can do is print out the entire tree in sorted order. To print the tree in sorted order, think of how to handle the root node. First, we would want to print the left branch; then, we'd print the current value; and then, we would print the right branch. And this is true for any node, not just for the root—we always want to print the left side, then the current value, then the right side. So, let's try writing code to do this.

To code for an "in order" printing, I called the routine printInOrder. We'll first check to see if there's a left node; if so, we recursively call printInOrder on that side. Then, we print the current value. And, finally, we check to see if there's a right node, and if so, we recursively call printInOrder on that side. Notice that what we've got here is basically another sorting routine. We're putting elements into the binary search tree in order, and then, when we print them out, we get a sorted list. Sure enough, if we take our set of nodes, insert them all into the tree, and print it back out, we get a sorted output list. Now, compared to the sorting routines that we saw previously, this one is, on average, as fast as that $n \log n$ mergeSort algorithm that we saw, plus it works really fast, on average, if you have to update the sorted list.

Graphs offer a structure for capturing an incredibly wide diversity of relationships, and the connections that are formed all over. They represent connections between locations, such as airline routes between cities; connections between people, such as friends in a social network; connections among species, like in a food web; and connections among data, like the hyperlinks in web pages. These and many other relations are well represented on a graph. Once relationships are captured in a graph, it's algorithms that let us use the graph effectively in our programs.

In the next lecture, we're going to look at a famous graph algorithm called breadth-first search, and we'll use that to create a fun word game. I'll see you then.

Graph Search and a Word Game

The fundamental graph algorithm you will learn about in this lecture is called the "breadth-first search." Searching through a graph to connect a starting node with another node can take one of two approaches: either follow edges as far as you can until you can go no farther, or gradually spread out from the starting point. The breadth-first search, as the name suggests, takes the latter approach, which is more balanced.

[BREADTH-FIRST SEARCH ALGORITHMS]

› Let's imagine that we have a social network, where people form the nodes, and we have an edge connecting people if they're friends with each other. If we want to know the shortest way to connect two people through a sequence of friends, we can find that out through a breadth-first search.

› In **Figure 23.a** on the following page, the node marked "0" is the node we're starting at, and the striped node is the one we're trying to find. In our social network, node 0 is the first person and the striped node is the person we want to connect to. People who are "friends" in the social network are represented as "neighbor" nodes in the graph.

› We'll number the nodes as we find them, and we'll keep a list of nodes, visiting them in order. The first thing we do is look at all of the neighbors of node 0. It has 3 neighbors, so we number them 1, 2, and 3. We didn't find the goal among them, so we are done with node 0.

› Now we move on to the next node, node 1. We will check its neighbors, numbering them. It has 4 neighbors, but one of those, node 0, already has been seen, so we don't number it. We check nodes 4, 5, and 6, giving them numbers. Then, we're done with node 1.

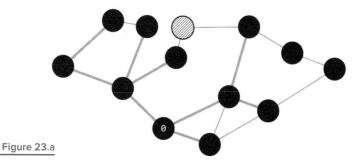

Figure 23.a

> We move on to node 2, which also has 4 neighbors, but two of them, nodes 0 and 3, have already been seen. So, we look at the two remaining neighbors, giving them numbers.

> Next is node 3. All of node 3's neighbors have been seen, so we have nothing else to do there.

> The process continues with node 4, and then with node 5. Finally, when we get to node 6, we have found our result. It turns out that there is a path from node 0 to 1 to 6 to our goal node. In other words, the person represented by node 0 has a friend who is friends with the friend of the person represented by the striped node.

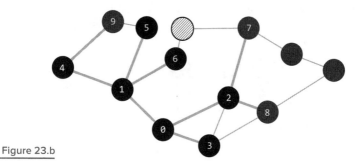

Figure 23.b

> With breadth-first searches, the general idea is that we visit a node, check all of its neighbors, and put them in a list to visit next if they haven't been visited. If we want to get that path out at the end, we need to keep track of each node along the way.

> Let's see how we would implement that algorithm in code. First, we'll write some pseudocode for the algorithm.

> To run a breadth-first search, we will need some additional information at each node. We'll want to classify each node as either "unseen" or "seen." It will start as "unseen," and when we first discover it, we'll mark it "seen." Also, we'll want to keep track of the previous node that was used to "see" this node for the first time so that we can get a list of edges out at the end.

> Next, we'll keep a queue of which nodes to visit. A queue is "first in, first out." We can implement a queue with just a list, and we have an "enqueue" to add something to the end of the queue and "dequeue" to take the next one from the front. Initially, the only node in our queue will be the starting node.

> Then, we'll go through and visit the nodes. Each time, we'll take whichever one is next in the queue. We can then check its neighbors. For each neighbor, we'll ignore it if it's already seen or visited—that means we've already discovered that node and don't need to worry about it again.

> However, if it's unseen, we will mark that neighbor as "seen" to make sure it knows that it was discovered from whatever node we are on now. We need to check to see if we've found the goal node, and if so, we can stop our loop. Otherwise, we need to add this node to the queue.

> At the very end, we will need to go back over the path that we found, by following the list of which node discovered the goal, then which one discovered that one, and so on until we're back at the start.

```
Input: A graph, a starting node, S, and a goal node, G
Output: A path of edges between G and S

1.  Add information to each node:
    a.  Unseen/seen - initialize to "unseen"
    b.  Previous node in BFS - initialize to none
2.  Initialize queue of nodes to visit with S, and initialize S
    to "seen"
3.  While goal is not found and queue is not empty:
    a.  Get next node in queue
    b.  Check all neighbors. If neighbors are "unseen":
        1.  Mark neighbor as "seen"
        2.  Set neighbor's previous node to current node
        3.  See if the neighbor is the goal, if so, exit the loop
        4.  Add this node to queue
4.  If goal was found:
    a.  Create list of edges by following "previous node."
```

› Given this pseudocode, let's see how we would implement it in actual code. Let's assume that we still are working with the social network. We'll have nodes for people, and each person will have a list of friends—that is, its neighboring nodes. We'll assume an unweighted graph, so our "edge" is just going to be a number of another node. This means that we don't even need an edge class—each node can just keep a list of neighbors, which are the indices for the neighbors.

› And we can have our "makeFriends" routine that lets us link two people together as friends. It will go through the "people" list to find the index of each of the names of the two people, and then add the corresponding index to the friend list of each.

```
class node:
    def __init__(self, name):
        self._name = name
        self._friends = []
```

```
        def getName(self):
            return self._name
        def getFriends(self):
            return self._friends
        def addFriend(self, friend_index):
            self._friends.append(friend_index)
    def makeFriends(name1, name2):
        for i in range(len(people)):
            if people[i].getName() == name1:
                n1 = i
            if people[i].getName() == name2:
                n2 = i
        people[n1].addFriend(n2)
        people[n2].addFriend(n1)
```

> In order to run the breadth-first search, we'll need to augment our node structure, to have the additional features of being able to mark a node as "seen" or "unseen" and note the previous node on the breadth-first search path.

> We'll use a number to designate "unseen" and "seen"—0 and 1, respectively. We'll keep this in a local variable, "status," that we set to 0 on initialization. We'll also provide routines that let us set the status to "Unseen" or "Seen," and we'll provide routines that give us a "True" or "False" as to whether it's seen or not.

```
class node:
    def __init__(self, name):
        self._name = name
        self._friends = []
        self._status = 0
...
    def isUnseen(self):
        if self._status == 0:
            return True
        else:
            return False
```

```
        def isSeen(self):
            if self._status == 1:
                return True
            else:
                return False
        def setUnseen(self):
            self._status = 0
        def setSeen(self):
            self._status = 1
```

> We also need to augment the node so that it has some information about which node discovered it during the search. We'll add a routine that lets us set that node. Later, we'll need to do some more with this when we print out our result, but that's enough to be able to write our basic breadth-first search routine.

```
class node:
    def __init__(self, name):
        self._name = name
        self._friends = []
        self._status = 0
        self._discoveredby = 0
    def getName(self):
        return self._name
    def getFriends(self):
        return self._friends
    def addFriend(self, friend_index):
        self._friends.append(friend_index)
    def isUnseen(self):
        if self._status == 0:
            return True
        else:
            return False
    def isSeen(self):
        if self._status == 1:
            return True
```

```
        else:
            return False
    def setUnseen(self):
        self._status = 0
    def setSeen(self):
        self._status = 1
    def discover(self, n):
        self._discoveredby = n
    def discovered(self):
        return self._discoveredby
```

> At this point, we've augmented our nodes to hold the required information. We'll now actually write a function to do this search for us. We need to take in the graph, which is going to be our node list, a starting node, and a goal node. The nodes are just the index of the node.

> Let's see how we start our routine. We'll first have our queue routine— exactly the same as the one we developed previously. Then, we have the beginning of our breadth-first search (BFS) routine. The BFS function will take in a "nodelist," a start, and an end.

> The first thing to do was to mark the starting node "seen" and add it to the queue. So, within our routine, we create a new, empty queue, called "to_visit." We then mark the starting node as visited by going to nodelist[start]—the starting node—and calling "setSeen," which will mark it as "seen." We then add the start node to the queue, by calling "enqueue."

```
class queue:
    def __init__(self):
        self._queue = []
    def enqueue(self, x):
        self._queue.append(x)
    def dequeue(self):
        return self._queue.pop(0)
    def isEmpty(self):
        return len(self._queue) == 0
```

```
def BFS(nodelist, start, goal):
    to_visit = queue()
    nodelist[start].setSeen()
    to_visit.enqueue(start)
```

› The next thing to do is create a loop where we pull out the next node and visit its neighbors. At the beginning, we need a variable to keep track of whether we've found the goal—that'll be "False" at first. We'll then have to have our loop, which will be a while loop with two conditions: the goal was not found, and the queue is not empty.

› Now we have a loop, and the first thing we need to do is get an item out of our queue, and then get its neighbors. We'll call "dequeue" to get the next node out of the queue—the index of the next node. We'll call the index that we pulled out "current." For that node, we need to pull out the neighbors, which we can do with a single function call. We just call "nodelist[current]" and then call the "getNeighbors" method on that, which returns a list of neighbors to visit.

```
def BFS(nodelist, start, goal):
    to_visit = queue()
    nodelist[start].setSeen()
    to_visit.enqueue(start)
    found = False
    while (not found) and (not to_visit.isEmpty()):
        current = to_visit.dequeue()
        neighbors = nodelist[current].getNeighbors()
```

› First, we have a for loop, which will go through all of the neighbors, so we write "for neighbor in neighbors." We next check to see if the node is an unseen one. If it's not, we don't need to think about it. If it is unseen, we change that. Using the "setSeen" command and the "discover" command, we mark the node as "seen" and with a prior node of the current one.

> Finally, we check to see if we have found the goal by directly comparing the neighbor with the goal. If so, we mark "found" as "True," which will stop this loop the next time around. If not, we add this neighbor onto our queue of nodes to check.

```python
def BFS(nodelist, start, goal):
    to_visit = queue()
    nodelist[start].setSeen()
    to_visit.enqueue(start)
    found = False
    while (not found) and (not to_visit.isEmpty()):
        current = to_visit.dequeue()
        neighbors = nodelist[current].getNeighbors()
        for neighbor in neighbors:
            if nodelist[neighbor].isUnseen():
                nodelist[neighbor].setSeen()
                nodelist[neighbor].discover(current)
                if neighbor == goal:
                    found = True
                else:
                    to_visit.enqueue(neighbor)
```

> If the goal was found, we need to find the list of nodes that got us to the goal. Because each node along the way from the start to the goal has a reference of who discovered the node, we can just read this list backward to get our result.

> Let's assume that we do this through a function call—to a function named "retrievePath." There are several ways to write this.

```python
def retrievePath(nodelist, start, goal):
    #Return the path from start to goal
def BFS(nodelist, start, goal):
    to_visit = queue()
    nodelist[start].setSeen()
    to_visit.enqueue(start)
    found = False
```

```
while (not found) and (not to_visit.isEmpty()):
    current = to_visit.dequeue()
    neighbors = nodelist[current].getNeighbors()
    for neighbor in neighbors:
        if nodelist[neighbor].isUnseen():
            nodelist[neighbor].setSeen()
            nodelist[neighbor].discover(current)
            if neighbor == goal:
                found = True
            else:
                to_visit.enqueue(neighbor)
return retrievePath(noswliar, start, goal)
```

> One way to implement this is to use a recursive approach. We start out seeing if we need a path for just one node—that is, if the start and the goal are the same. In that case, we create a list containing just the start. We set up an empty list, called "path," append the start value on, and return it. Otherwise, we will find the previous node that comes right before the goal.

> We recursively get the path from the start node to that previous node— that is, we call our retreivePath function using that previous node as the goal. Then, we just append the goal onto the end of that, and return.

```
def retrievePath(nodelist, start, goal):
    #Return the path from start to goal
    if start == goal:
        path = []
        path.append(start)
        return path
    else:
        previous = nodelist[goal].discovered()
        previous_path = retrievePath(nodelist, start, previous)
        previous_path.append(goal)
        return previous_path
```

> Once we've finished our breadth-first search algorithm, we can test it, using a small graph for five people who have several friend relationships. When we run this, we get a list—John, Sue, Fred, Kathy—which is indeed a path connecting the two friends.

```
people = []
person = node('John')
people.append(person)
person = node('Joe')
people.append(person)
person = node('Sue')
people.append(person)
person = node('Fred')
people.append(person)
person = node('Kathy')
people.append(person)
makeFriends('John', 'Joe')
makeFriends('John', 'Sue')
makeFriends('Joe', 'Sue')
makeFriends('Sue', 'Fred')
makeFriends('Fred', 'Kathy')
pathlist = BFS(people, 0, 4)
for index in pathlist:
    print(people[index].getName())

OUTPUT:
John
Sue
Fred
Kathy
```

> If you've ever heard of a "Bacon number," in which you try to connect actors who have acted in movies together, all the way to a connection to Kevin Bacon, this is the algorithm used to determine that. If we could form a graph of everyone in the world, with a link between people who know each other, we could use this algorithm to check the claim that any two people are separated by only six degrees of separation.

Reading

Lambert, *Fundamentals of Python*, chap. 12.

Exercise

There are many other graph algorithms besides breadth-first search (BFS). One of these is depth-first search (DFS), which aims to explore as far as possible.

Imagine that the queue used to keep track of nodes to visit in the BFS algorithm is instead replaced by a stack. Assume that you had the following graph and were starting at node E, trying to find node G. Assume that neighbors are listed in alphabetical order in each node. What is the order in which the nodes are visited?

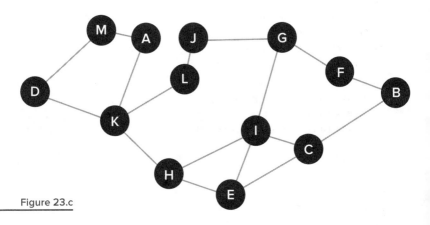

Figure 23.c

Graph Search and a Word Game

et's learn an algorithm and build a game. Pulling together several of the topics that we've discussed previously, we're going to build a word game based on a graph. The fundamental graph algorithm we're going to use is called the breadth-first search.

Searching through a graph to connect a starting node with another node can take one of two approaches. You can either follow edges as far as you can go until you can go no farther, or gradually spread out from the starting point. Breadth-first search, as the name suggests, takes the latter approach, which is more balanced. Let's imagine we have a social network, where people form the nodes, and we have an edge connecting people if they're friends with each other. If I want to know what's the shortest way to connect two people through a sequence of friends, I can find that out through a breadth-first search.

Look at this graph, since it will illustrate the process. Let's say that the green node is the node that we're starting at, and the yellow node is the one that we're trying to find. In our social network, the green node is the first person, and the yellow is the person we want to connect to. People who are friends in the social network are represented as neighbor nodes in the graph.

We'll number the nodes as we find them, and we'll keep a list of nodes, visiting them in order. Once we've finished a node, we'll color it black. It'll be a whole lot easier to understand if you see it, so let's do that now. We start with node 0, our starting node. The first thing we do is we look at all of its neighbors. It has three neighbors, so we number them 1, 2, and 3. We didn't find the goal among them, so we are done with node 0.

Now we go on to the next node, node 1. We will check its neighbors. It has 4 neighbors, but one of those, node 0, already has been seen, so we don't number it. We check nodes 4, 5, and 6, giving them numbers. Then, we're done with node 1.

On to node 2. Node 2 also has four neighbors, but two of them, nodes 0 and 3, have already been seen. So, we look at the 2 remaining neighbors and give them numbers. Next is node 3. All of node 3's neighbors have been seen, so we have nothing else to do there. The process will continue with node 4 and with node 5, and finally, when we get to node 6, we have found our result. It turns out that there is a path from 0 to 1 to 6 to our goal node. In other words, the green person has a friend who is friends with yellow's friend.

So, that's the general idea. We visit a node, check all of its neighbors, and we put them into a list to visit next if they haven't been visited already. If we want to get that path out at the end, we'd need to keep track of each node along the way. Let's see how we would implement that algorithm in code. First, we'll write some pseudocode for the algorithm.

To run a breadth-first search, we will need some additional information at each node. We'll want to classify each node as either unseen or seen. It will start as unseen, and when we first discover it, we'll mark it as seen. Also, we'll want to keep track of the previous node that was used to see this node for the first time, so that we can get a list of edges back out at the end.

Next, we'll keep a queue of which nodes to visit. A queue is first in, first out. We can implement a queue with just a list, and we have an enqueue to add something on to the end of the queue and a dequeue to take the next one from the front. Initially, the only node in our queue will be the starting node.

Then, we'll go through, and we'll visit the nodes. Each time, we'll take whichever one is next in the queue. We can then check its neighbors. For each neighbor, we'll ignore it if we've already seen it—that means we've already discovered that node, and we don't need to worry about it again. However, if it's unseen, we will mark that neighbor as seen, and then we'll make sure it knows that it was discovered from whichever node we are on right now. We need to check to see if we've found the goal node and if so, we can stop our loop. Otherwise, we need to add this node to the queue. At the very end, we will need to go back over the path that we found, by following the list of which node discovered the goal, then which one discovered that one, and so on until we're all the way back at the start.

OK, given that pseudocode, let's see how we would implement that in actual code. Let's assume that we're working with the social network. We're going to start out with pretty much the same operations that we had in the adjacency list way of storing graphs that I showed you earlier when we were using cities and roads. That is, we'll have nodes for people, and each person will have a list of friends, that is, its neighboring nodes. We'll assume an unweighted graph, so our edge is just going to be a number of another node. That means that we don't even need an edge class—each node can just keep a list of neighbors, which are just the indices for its neighbors. And, we can have our makeFriends routine that lets us link two people together as friends. It will go through the people list to find the index of each of the names of the two people, and then it'll add the corresponding index to the friend list of each.

In order to run breadth-first search we'll need to augment our node structure, to have the additional features I mentioned earlier—being able to mark a node as seen or unseen, and noting the previous node on the BFS path. We'll use a number to designate unseen and seen— just 0 or 1. We'll keep this in a local variable, status, that we set to 0 on initialization. We'll also provide routines that let us set the status to Unseen or Seen, and we'll provide routines that give us a true or false as to whether it's seen or not. We also need to augment the node so that it has some information about which node discovered it during the search. We'll add a routine that lets us set that node. Later, we'll need to do some more with this when we print out our result, but that's enough to be able to write our basic breadth-first search routine.

So, at this point, we've augmented our nodes to hold the required information. We'll now actually write a function to do this search for us. We need to take in the graph, which is going to be our node list, a starting node, and a goal node. The nodes are just the index of the node. So, let's see how we start our routine off. We'll first have our queue routine—exactly the same as the one we developed a while back. Then, we have the beginning of our breadth-first search routine or BFS. The BFS function will take in a nodelist, a start, and an end.

Now, the first thing to do was to mark the starting node seen and add it to the queue. So, within our routine, we created a new, empty queue, called to_visit. We then marked the starting node as visited by going to nodelist[start]—that's the starting node, and calling setSeen, which will mark it as seen. We then add the start node to the queue, by calling enqueue.

The next thing to do is to create a loop where we will pull out the next node, and we'll visit its neighbors. For this part, see how much of this you can write, before watching, then again after watching. I'll go through this slowly so you can stop and see a little bit, for when you get stuck.

OK, at the beginning, we need a variable to keep track of whether we've found the goal—that'll be False at first. We'll then have to have our loop, which will be a while loop with two conditions. One is that the goal was not found, and one is that the queue is not empty. So, now we have a loop, and the first thing we need to do is get an item out of our queue, and then get its neighbors. See if you can continue writing from here.

OK, we have our loop, and we need to get the next node out of the queue. So, we'll call dequeue to get the next node, and by that I mean the index of the next node. We'll call that index that we pulled out current. Now, for that node, we need to pull out the neighbors, which we can do with a single function call. We just call nodelist[current], and then call the getNeighbors method on that. That method returns a list of neighbors to visit. Remember the steps to do with the neighbors? Let's try coding what needs to be done at this point.

OK, first, we have a for loop, The for loop will go through all of the neighbors, so we write: for neighbor in neighbors. We next check to see if the node is an unseen one - if it's not, we don't even need to think about it. If it is unseen, we change that—using the setSeen command and the discovered command, to mark the node as seen and with a prior node of the current one. Finally, we check to see if we have found the goal, by directly comparing the neighbor with the goal. If so, we mark found as true, which will stop this loop the next time around. If not, we add this neighbor onto our queue of nodes to check.

OK, there's one more part to code. If the goal was found, we need to go ahead and find the list of nodes that got us to the goal. Since each node along the way from the start to the goal has a reference of who discovered the node, we can just read this list backward from the goal back to the start to get our result. Let's assume we do this through a function called retrievePath. We need to write retrievePath. There are several ways we could write it—see what you can come up with.

OK, one way to implement that is to use a recursive approach. We start out seeing if we need a path for just one node—that is, if the start and the goal are the same. In that case, we create a list containing just the start. We set up an empty list, called path, and we append the start value on, and we return it. Otherwise, we will find the previous node that comes right before the goal. We recursively get the path from the start node to that previous node. That is, we call our retreivePath function using that previous node as the goal. Then, we just append the goal onto the end of that, and we return.

So, we've finished our breadth-first search algorithm. We can test this out, using a small graph that I created for five people who have friend relationships. In this case, we call BFS with a start of 0 and a goal of 4. That's the first person, John, and the last person, Kathy. We'll take that result, and we'll print the names of the friends in order. So, when we run this, we get a list, John, Sue, Fred, Kathy—which is indeed a path connecting the friends.

If you've ever heard of a Bacon Number in which you try to connect actors who have acted in movies together, all the way to a connection to Kevin Bacon—this is the algorithm used to determine that. If we could form a graph of everyone on earth, with a link between people who know each other, we could use this algorithm to check the claim that any two people are separated by only six degrees of separation.

So, given this graph algorithm, let's see how we can use it for a completely different type of application, now for something completely different. There are lots of fun brain teaser puzzles out there, and I bet you've played with many of them. Let me tell you about one of these puzzles that's always been fun for me, even though I haven't always been that good at it. One of the things that I think is so interesting is that this is a problem that can be quite challenging for people, but it's a very straightforward puzzle for a computer to solve.

The game is a word game where we try to transform one word into another one. The key is that you can change only one letter at a time, and with every change, you still need to have a valid word. For example, say that you wanted to change the word car to the word let. Can you come up with a sequence of words, each one different from the previous by only one letter, that gets you from car to let?

Well, here's one option. We could change the *r* in car to a *t*, ending up with cat. Then, we can change the *c* in cat to a *b*, ending up with bat. From there, we can change the *a* to an *e*, ending up with bet. And finally, we change the *b* to an *l*, and we have gotten to our goal, let. Now, there were other ways to get there, but this was one way. What we're going to develop is a way for the computer to play this game. We'll give the computer a starting word and an ending word, and the challenge will be to let it come up with a chain of words to get from one to the other. This is also going to help us see ways to tie together lots of the things that we've encountered so far. Let's start with the overall design.

We can assume that we'll be given a starting word and an ending word, and we'll produce a chain of words. This should sound a whole lot like the social network example that we just had. We have a graph, with a starting node, and an ending node, and a chain between them. That's what we have here, also, so we should think about how this problem could be modeled as a graph. And then, all we'll need to do is run our breadth-first search algorithm on that graph.

Obviously, the nodes of the graph need to be words. For there to be an edge between two words, there should be exactly one letter different between them. If the words differ by more than one letter, then there's no edge. The graph will be unweighted, and undirected.

So, we have a rough outline of the program. We'll need to set up the graph itself. Then, we can ask the user for a starting and ending word, run our breadth-first-search to find a chain, and output the results.

To set up the graph, we'll first need to read in a set of words that are valid words. We'll then need to form a graph from those words. To form a graph, we'll compare words, and if they differ by exactly one letter, we'll add an edge between them.

Now, we need to stop and think for a minute before we write any code. We're going to read in a long list of words, and then we're going to need to compare every pair of words to see if they differ by exactly one letter. Let's think about what the running time for that will be. If we read in n words, we compare the first one to n-1 other words. Then we compare the next one to n-2 other words. The net result of all of this is going to be something that's order n-squared.

So, if we have about 1000 words, which is actually pretty small, then we'll have on the order of a million, well actually half a million, comparisons. That's a lot of comparisons. And, to make it worse, 1000 is not a lot of words. The English language has hundreds of thousands of words. If we were to have a word list containing a regular dictionary, we might never finish building the graph.

So, we need to limit the number of pairwise comparisons by limiting the set of words, staying within a number that our n-squared process can find in a reasonable amount of time. Computers these days are fast, and doing a million comparisons, or even a few million, is not unreasonable. But, to do tens of millions can start becoming noticeably slower. So, let's limit our word list to no more than a few thousand words. If we have too many words to compare, we could spend our whole day just waiting for the graph to build.

The first thing that we need to do is define the data structures and functions needed for our graph. A node in the graph should represent a word, so we'll store a word in each node. Since we're going to run a breadth-first search, we'll need to keep track of a discovered by link, and a seen/unseen value, as well. The code will look a whole lot like the code we had in our earlier breadth-first search on the social network. So, we're going to start with that code, and just modify it as necessary.

Here's our class. It's identical to the node class that we were just using in the breadth-first search example, with one difference. We're storing the value for each node using the term Word instead of Name since each node is a word rather than a person. Again, everything else—getting and adding neighbors, marking things as seen and unseen is identical.

Our addLink routine will be similar to the previous one, but will have some differences. Remember that when we joined friends before we would form an edge an edge between a pair of nodes. We'll create two versions. One, much like the previous one, will take in two words we want to connect. We'll call this addWordLink. AddWordLink will take in the list of words and the two words that we want to link. We'll go through the list of words to find the index for each of the ones that we're looking for. An alternative will be a routine that we just call addLink that we assume takes in the index of the two things we are linking. The parameters passed in will be the word list, as well as the indices of the two that we need to form the edge between. In this case, we don't need to search for the words to find the indices, so the code is significantly shorter.

The remainder of our breadth-first search is unchanged. Our queue structure is no different than when we first introduced it. Retrievepath is exactly the same. And, BFS, the breadth-first search algorithm, is also exactly the same. None of those rely on the actual values in the nodes, just their connectivity. So, there's not a single thing that needs to change for our graph of words versus our social network graph. That's great.

So, let's go through the process of setting up the game. We'll first need to read in a set of words, and we'll be reading this in from a file. As we mentioned before, we need to be careful about the size of the file—that is, the number of words—in this list. We could limit ourselves to only certain categories of words, for example, words with 3 letters, or 4 letters or something like that. We could limit ourselves to the most common English words, or any of a variety of choices. You can do a quick search on the web and find many different lists of words. I'd recommend finding one that's of reasonable size—say no more than about 3000 words, and saving it in a file.

I've found a list of common English words, about 2000 of them, in order of frequency, and saved it into a file, called dictionary.txt. There's one word per line in the file. So, our first task is to read in the file and create our word list in memory. We'll create one node per word, and store it in a list of nodes. What would the code for this look like?

Well, first, we'll have our list of nodes that we initialize to an empty list. In this code, we'll call that node list words. Next, we open up our file that contains all the words in it for reading. I'll call that dict, short for dictionary, and open the file dictionary.txt for reading. Next, I'll go through every line of dict using a for loop. Remember that there's one word per line of the file, so for each line, I want to get that word, create a node, and add that node to the list of nodes. The way we do this here is to create a new node, called word, where we take the line, we strip away any whitespace—that's the strip() command. Once we've created that node, we append it onto words list—that's our list of nodes.

So, at this point, we've read in a bunch of words and we've turned them into nodes. Now, we'll need to actually form the graph. Remember, we'll want to check every pair of words, and form a link if there is just one letter different between them. To do this, we probably need a function that will let us compare two words, and return true if, and only if, they are different by just one letter.

Let's write our code for that function. The function needs to take in two strings, that is, the two words, and return true if they're different by only one letter. What do you think this code should look like? Here, we've written a function called compareWords. It first checks to see if the words are the same length, and if not, it returns False, since they can't be different by only one letter. Otherwise, it will go through a for loop, letting the index go from 0 to the length of one of the two words. It keeps track all along the way of how many letters are different through a numdifferent variable. For each index, it compares the letters at that index and then it increments numdifferent if they're different by one. After doing this, if the number of different letters is exactly one, we return True; otherwise, we return False.

Now, given that code, how would we form the graph itself? Remember, we need to compare every word to every other word, and add a link if they're different by just a single letter.

OK, what we're going to do is loop through all of the words in the list, and compare to each of the other words in the list. So, we will have nested for loops. The outer for loop will use an index, i, to go through each word in the list. The inner for loop will then go from i plus one to the end of the list. Notice that the inner loop doesn't go over every item, just the following ones, since the earlier items would have already been compared. For each of those pairs, we will compare the two words, calling compareWords that we just wrote. If the comparison is True, that is, if they differ by just one letter, then we add an edge to the graph by calling addLink, with the i and j indices passed in.

At this stage, we've built our entire graph. Yay. The next thing in our program is to get the words that we want to find a chain between—the starting and the ending words. This can be done with just a couple of lines of code. So, now comes the main event—actually finding a chain between these two words. This is where our breadth-first search comes in.

First, remember how our BFS routine was defined. The BFS takes in the list of nodes, the index of the starting node, and the index of the ending node. It's the index of each node that we pass in as a parameter. We don't have that right now—we just have the word itself. So, we need to find the index of each of those words in the list of all words.

So, given that we have two strings, word1 and word2, how would we find the indices in the list of nodes, that is the list of nodes, that is the list words? We'll loop through all of the nodes in our nodelist and find indices that matches our starting and ending words. So, we loop with an index, *i* that goes from 0 to the length of the list, words, and for each element, it checks to see whether that node matches the starting or ending word. If it does, we save that index. Notice that we also keep track of the index, and if it turns out that one word or the other is not in the list, we will give the user a message that the word was not in the dictionary and exit. There are other ways we could deal with this if we wanted to, like as throwing an exception, or looping until the user gives us a valid word. But, in this case, we're just exiting the program, and the user can run it again to try a new combination.

So, now we have the index of the starting word and the index of the ending word. We can call the breadth-first search. We just call the function BFS, passing in the list words, and the starting and ending indices. BFS will return the path, which is a series of indices showing the path from the start to the goal. We store this in the variable path. It might seem weird that this main part of the code comes down to a single function call, but this is an advantage that we get from using the data structures and algorithms that we know of—the actual tasks we want can sometimes be very simple.

There's one more thing to be done, and that's to output the path. Remember, we have a list of node indices, giving the path from the starting word to the ending word. How would we print out this list to the screen? Well, this is pretty straightforward. We will loop through the elements of the path. Then, we just use that index to get the node from the words list and call getWord on that node to get the word. This is printed out to the screen and voila. we have printed out a chain of words from the start to the goal.

Let's run this one time to see how it works. Let's go back to our example, and enter car and let as our start and goal words. When we do this, we do indeed find a chain from car to bar to bat to bet to let. That's slightly different from the one I came up with in my head, where instead of bar I had the word cat. Now, realize that if you try this yourself, you might get a different list—it'll depend on the dictionary you use, and on the order that the words appear in that dictionary.

So, we can say we've achieved success. But, there's one big problem with our program. If you've got this whole thing typed in and working, try testing it out for a while, and I bet you'll pretty quickly come across the error. Try testing it now.

Well, if you tested it out, you probably found out that the program will sometimes crash. And, if you did enough investigating, you'd figure out that the problem is occurring when there's not actually a chain between the two words. What's happened is that we've run BFS, and instead of finding a chain, it runs out of edges, and there's no path.

To fix this, we're going to need to modify the BFS routine. First, remember the BFS routine? We have a loop that keeps pulling off nodes from the queue until we've either found the goal or we run out of nodes. We then return the results of retrievePath. If you ran the code in the debugger or looked closely at the error messages when your program crashed, you'd find that BFS was crashing in retrievePath. See if you can figure out a simple fix to the BFS routine, so that it won't crash if there's not a path. Here's one simple fix. Instead of just returning retrievePath, we first check to see if a path was found. If so, we call retrievePath, just like before, and return it. If not, we return an empty list. That's a really simple fix.

Now we probably want to put a check into our output, also. We can check to see if we have an empty path and if so, we print that no chain was found. Otherwise, we print the chain like before. There are a lot more variations that you could add on to this routine, and if you find this program fun, I'd encourage you to try. For example, try using a much bigger dictionary, or try turning the program around—where the computer finds a chain of at least length 3 and then challenges the user to come up with a chain.

This word game has helped to demonstrate the power of data structures and algorithms. We took what was a challenging problem, and because we could represent it as a graph, and use a basic graph algorithm to solve it, a relatively complicated program became easier to write. Whenever we can find data structures and algorithms to fit our problem, the whole task of programming becomes much simpler.

The program we developed in this lecture would perform poorly if there's a really large word list provided at the beginning, due to the order n-squared number of checks between pairs of words. And that means that it could benefit from the techniques that we'll explore in our next, and final, lecture, where we will take up the subject of parallel computing.

I'll see you then.

24

Parallel Computing Is Here

Parallel computing is both the future and present of computer programming. One of the biggest challenges that programmers will face in the long term is how to make effective use of the increasing parallelism that is being provided. To the extent that this can be solved, we will be able to see actual performance benefits that keep pace with processor improvements. In this lecture, you will learn about parallel computing.

[PARALLEL COMPUTING]

> In the 1960s, Gordon Moore, one of the founders of Intel, made a famous prediction: that the number of transistors on an integrated circuit would follow an exponential growth rate, doubling every so many years. This idea came to be known as "Moore's law," and it has driven the computer chip design industry for many years. And though the rate of growth may have slowed, we're still seeing big improvements as our computers become smaller and faster.

> But there's a big difference between simply having more transistors and being able to use them effectively. As chip designers have had more and more to work with, it's been increasingly difficult to figure out how to use those additional transistors to get bigger and more powerful processors.

> Instead, designers have increasingly turned to parallelism to make use of the resources available. Instead of one bigger processor, they've used the transistors to make two processors—or four processors—on the same chip. This has led to dual-core, quad-core, and multicore home computers.

> Parallel computing is not a new idea. IBM researchers began exploring it in detail in the 1950s, and the first supercomputers in the 1970s were parallel machines. All of the supercomputers you've heard about are massively parallel machines. But parallelism is becoming increasingly widespread, as individual processors become multicore processors, a feature that has even migrated to smartphones.

> When a single processor becomes faster, we could expect everything running on it to run faster. But putting in a dual-core processor—in other words, using parallelism—doesn't necessarily cause our programs to run faster. The particular computation we're doing will determine whether we can actually make use of the parallelism provided.

[PARALLELISM IN PRACTICE]

> In the following code, there are four computations getting assigned to variables *a* through *d*. The order we execute these statements doesn't really matter. In any order, we end up with the exact same variables having the exact same values. We would say that this code is easily parallelizable. We could do all four of these statements at the exact same time, and we would come out with the exact same answer.

```
a = 3*8
b = 7/12
c = 3.14159*4.0*4.0
d = (12+3)*(5-8)
```

> On the other hand, in the following lines of code, we have to compute *a* before we can compute *b*, because *b* needs to know the value of *a* to do its computation. Likewise, we need to compute *b* before *c* and *c* before *d*. There's no way we could compute these statements in a different order; they have to go in a particular sequence. This code could not be parallelized—there's no way to execute two or more of these statements at the same time.

```
a = 3.3+8.5
b = a*4.0*4.0
c = 16 - b
d = c/4.0
```

› Different applications will have different levels of parallelism, and a typical computation will have some pieces that can be parallelized and some that can't.

› Parallel computers are arranged in many different ways, and the ways you can use parallelism can change depending on how the processors are set up and how they can communicate with each other. Some parallel processing is done automatically and is hidden from you. The graphics processor, for example, automatically processes all the graphical elements that need to be drawn in parallel.

› But to make full use of parallel processing, we need to do it explicitly. We'll focus just on Python on a standard home computer. And, for this case, the main way we take advantage of parallelism is through **threading**, or **multiprocessing**.

› With threading, we'll be creating functions that can run in a different **process**, or "thread," than the main program. The main program will **spawn** these other processes, each of which will be running their respective functions. Those spawned processes will execute separately from the main program, and if there are multiple processors available (such as on a multicore computer), they'll run on these different cores at the same time—that is, in parallel. If there's just a single core central processing unit, these processes will still run just fine; there just won't be any overall improvement in the performance.

› The following is a very simple example of a multiprocess "Hello, World" program.

```
from multiprocessing import Process
def print_function():
    print("Hello, World!")
```

```
if __name__ == '__main__':
    p = Process(target=print_function)
    p.start()
```

> First, we'll be using the multiprocessing module. It's part of the Python standard library, so we just import it to get it. The main thing we're going to want from this module is a class definition called "Process." We will be creating instances of Processes.

> Next, we'll define a function that is the thing we're going to run in parallel. This function is going to be the thing spawned by the main program. In our case, our function is just called "print_function," and all it does is print "Hello, World!"

> In the main part of the program, there's a particular line of code we need to include that checks the name of the process: It's an if statement, and your code should all be indented from there. This line is where the Python multiprocessing module separates which code is part of the main, "primary" program as opposed to all the other spawned processes. Remember to include this line so that your code can work correctly.

> Next, you'll actually create an instance of the Process object. When we initialize the Process object, we have to pass in the function that we want the process to run, as the "target" parameter. In this case, our function is print_function, so we pass in "target=print_function" as our parameter.

> Finally, we spawn the process by calling the "start" method on the process.

> If we run this code, the interpreter comes along, creates the Process object, and then spawns it. That's all that happens in the main program, in this case. In the separate process that was spawned off, we have "Hello, World!" printed out, and that's what we see as the output.

```
from multiprocessing import Process
def print_function():
    print("Hello, World!")
```

```
if __name__ == '__main__':
    p = Process(target=print_function)
    p.start()

OUTPUT:
Hello, World!
```

> What if the function that will form our process takes in some parameters? In the following code, we've modified the print function to take in a name so that we can print "Hello" to that name. We can set up the arguments to be passed into the function through the use of an "args" (short for "arguments") parameter when we create the process.

```
from multiprocessing import Process
def print_function(name):
    print("Hello,", name)
if __name__ == '__main__':
    p = Process(target=print_function, args=("John",))
    p.start()
```

> The term "arguments" is another way of referring to the parameters being passed in to a function. In this case, we set the args to be "John," followed by a comma. The comma is used because the arguments list is expecting at least two args—two arguments—and that's because the arguments list gets turned into a tuple, which makes it non-mutable. A tuple of one is not possible, but simply adding a comma gives the tuple the appearance of two arguments to work with. If you don't put in the comma, you can get assignment errors. But set up with two arguments, this will print out "Hello, John."

> Now let's look at how we could spawn multiple processes in practice. The following is a variation on our earlier program. Notice that our function just takes in a number and prints a message "Printing from process" and then the number that was passed in.

```
from multiprocessing import Process
def print_process(number):
    print("Printing from process", number)
if __name__ == '__main__':
    process_list = []
    for i in range(20):
        p = Process(target=print_process, args=(i,))
        process_list.append(p)
    for p in process_list:
        p.start()
```

> In our main routine, we'll create a list of 20 processes. We'll have a loop, with *i* ranging up to 20, and for each one, we'll create a process in which "print_process" is the function and *i* is used as the parameter. After that, we'll go through and actually start each process, in a separate loop.

> When we run this, the following is the output. Notice that every process number, 0 through 19, gets printed once. But the order that these are printed seems pretty random; the earlier numbers seem to be getting printed before the later ones, but they're certainly not in the same order.

```
Printing from process 1
Printing from process 0
Printing from process 2
Printing from process 4
Printing from process 3
Printing from process 12
Printing from process 7
Printing from process 13
Printing from process 5
Printing from process 11
Printing from process 9
Printing from process 8
Printing from process 17
Printing from process 14
Printing from process 6
```

```
Printing from process 15
Printing from process 19
Printing from process 10
Printing from process 16
Printing from process 18
```

> Remember that each of those print statements was getting printed from a totally separate process. You can think of it as though it's a totally separate program that's running completely independently of the others, possibly on a different processor. And those different processors might have other things running on them—for example, some operating system commands or other applications running in the background. If you run this code a few times, you should see a different result every time—there are 20 factorial possible orderings.

[PARALLEL PROCESSORS]

> The effectiveness of parallelism is measured by how effectively parallel processors can be applied to a particular problem. If you had two processors, the best situation would be if you could use both of them all the time with no time wasted. In this case, your overall running time would be cut in half. Four processors could cut running time in a quarter.

> However, in reality, we can't fully utilize the processors we have. Most problems are only partly parallelizable. In fact, there's a law called **Amdahl's law** that helps us calculate a limit for how much any given level of parallelism could speed up a computation.

> According to this law, a problem that's only 50% parallelizable cannot attain better than double the speedup time, no matter how many processors we throw at it. For a problem where 75% could be parallel, the maximum speedup is 4 times. For 90%, it's as large as 10 times, and if 95% can be parallel, speedup can be at most 20 times. However, these are theoretical upper limits; in practice, there can be other constraints, too.

> A follow-up to Amdahl's law, called **Gustafson's law**, helps us determine how much larger of a problem we can handle given more processors. Both these laws relate how much of the program needs to be done sequentially versus how much could be done in parallel.

> For example, graphics applications tend to be highly parallelizable. In a three-dimensional game, there are often hundreds of thousands of triangles being drawn, but the order they're drawn is not so important. Many scientific computations are also very parallelizable, with calculations taking place over a large grid, each piece of which can be handled separately from the others.

> Addressing these types of problems has contributed to the rise of another form of parallelism called grid computing—or, more generally, **distributed computing**—in which physically distinct, often dispersed, computers are loosely coupled with one another to handle distinct pieces of a single problem. Distributed computing can be thought of as a type of parallelism, because computation is being done on various computers at remote locations at the same time.

[PITFALLS AND ALTERNATIVE WAYS TO USE PARALLELISM]

> There are many pitfalls along the way to becoming a good parallel programmer. For example, having to pass information only via things like queues can take some getting used to. Also, you basically can't use the "input" command as part of a parallel program—all the processes will stop while waiting for input. But you now know what's needed to write some simple parallel programs and how to parallelize existing slow code to get a speedup.

> In addition to creating parallel applications directly, there are some less direct ways that we can make use of parallelism in our code.

> If you've run multiple programs on your computer at one time, you're probably taking advantage of parallelism. Each program is running as a separate process, so if there are multiple programs running, they can potentially be running on separate processors. More commonly, when there are multiple processes running on one processor, the operating system takes care of "time sharing" the processor—basically, making sure that each process gets some fraction of time so that they all make progress together.

> In any case, we can initiate parallel computation by simply spawning new applications on our computer. And, fortunately, it's really easy to do this. If we use the "subprocess" module, we can spawn a new process in the operating system. Unlike the processes that we were using earlier, these don't remain tied to the Python program, so once they're spawned, they will continue to run on the computer, even if the Python program ends.

Reading

Lubanovic, *Introducing Python*, chaps. 10–11.

Exercise

What code would you write to spawn a new process, running a program named "myProgram.exe"?

Parallel Computing Is Here

Back in the 1960s, Gordon Moore, one of the founders of Intel, made a famous prediction. He said that the number of transistors on an integrated circuit would follow an exponential growth rate, doubling every so many years. This idea came to be known as Moore's Law, and it's driven the computer chip design industry for many years. And although the rate of growth may have slowed, we're still seeing big improvements as our computers become smaller and faster.

But, there's a big difference between simply having more transistors, and being able to use them effectively. As chip designers have had more and more to work with, it's been increasingly tough to figure out how to use those additional transistors to get bigger and more powerful processors. Instead, designers have increasingly turned to parallelism to make use of the resources available. Instead of just one bigger processor, they've used the transistors to make two processors on the same chip. Or four processors. This has led to home computers that are dual-core, quad-core, and multi-core.

Parallel computing is not a new idea. IBM researchers began exploring it in detail in the 1950s, and the first Cray supercomputers in the 1970s were parallel machines. All of the supercomputers you've heard about are massively parallel machines. But, parallelism is becoming increasingly widespread, as individual processors become multicore processors, a feature that has even migrated to smartphones.

Now, when a single processor gets faster, we could expect everything running on it to run faster. But, putting in a dual-core processor, in other words, using parallelism, doesn't necessarily cause our programs to run faster. The particular computation that we're doing will determine whether we can actually make use of the parallelism that's provided.

Let's get look at some code just to illustrate. In this code, we have four computations getting assigned to variables $a–d$. Notice that the order we execute these statements doesn't really matter. We could compute c first, then b, then d, then a. In any order, we end up with the exact same variables having the exact same values. We would say that this code is easily parallelizable. We could actually do all four of these statements at the exact same time, and we come out with the exact same answer.

On the other hand, look at these lines of code. Notice that we have to compute a before we can compute b since b needs to know the value of a to do its computation. Likewise, we need to compute b before c, and c before d. There's no way we could compute these statements in a different order—they have to go in a particular sequence. This code could not be parallelized—there's no way to execute two or more of those statements at the same time.

Now, different applications will have different levels of parallelism. And, a typical computation will have some pieces that can be parallelized, and some that can't. You can think of this same thing in non-computing terms. If you're making a meal, you can imagine that it's easy to parallelize the making of two different dishes. But, it's not possible to parallelize everything. For example, you can't put the frosting on a cake until you've first baked the cake and mixed the frosting. You can also see why you might get a benefit from having 2 or 4 people to cook dinner, but that doesn't improve indefinitely.

So, how can we actually make use of parallel computing? Parallel computers are arranged in lots of different ways, and the ways you can use parallelism can change depending on how the processors are set up and how they can communicate with each other. Some parallel processing is done automatically and is hidden from you. The graphics processor does this, for instance—it automatically processes all the graphical elements that need to be drawn in parallel. But, to make full use of parallel processing, we need to do it explicitly. We'll focus just on Python on a standard home computer. And, for this case, the main way we take advantage of parallelism is through threading or multiprocessing.

I need to first explain the idea of threading. We're going to be creating functions that can run in a different process or thread than the main program. The main program will spawn these other processes, each of which will be running their respective functions. Those spawned processes will execute separately from the main program, and if there are multiple processors available like on a multicore computer, they'll run on these different cores at the same time—that is, in parallel. Now, if there's just a single core CPU, these processes will still run just fine. There just won't be any overall improvement in the performance.

Let's see what some multiprocessor code will look like. This a super-simple example, of a multi-process Hello, World style program. Let's look at the different parts of this. First, we'll be using the multiprocessing module. It's part of the Python standard library, so we just import it to get it. The main thing that we're going to want from this module is a class definition called Process. We will be creating instances of Process. Next, we'll define a function that is the thing we're going to run in parallel. This function is going to be the thing spawned by the main program. In our case here, our function is just called print_function, and all it does is print Hello World.

In the main part of the program, there's a particular line of code we need to include that checks that the name of the process. It's an if statement, and your code should go indented in from there. This line is where the Python multiprocessing module separates which code is part of the main or primary program as opposed to all the other spawned processes. Just remember to include this line so your code can work correctly.

Next, you'll actually create an instance of the Process object. When we initialize the Process object, we have to pass in the function that we want the process to run, as the target parameter. In this case, our function is print_function, so we pass in target = print_function as our parameter. And finally, we spawn the process by calling the start method on the process.

Now, if we run this code, what happens is that the interpreter comes along, creates the Process object, and then spawns it. That's all that happens in the main program. Now, in the separate process that was spawned off, we have Hello, World printed out, and that's what we see as the output.

Let's look at a variation. What if the function that will form our process takes in some parameters? Here, we've modified the print function to take in a name, so that we can print hello to that name. We can set the arguments to be passed into the function through the use of an args parameter when we create the process. args is short for arguments, which is another way of referring to the parameters being passed in to a function. In this case, we set the args to be John comma. Why the comma? Well, the arguments list is expecting at least two args, two arguments, and that's because the arguments list gets turned into a tuple, which makes it non-mutable. A tuple of one is not possible, but simply adding a comma gives the tuple the appearance of 2 arguments to work with. If you don't put in the comma, you can get amusing assignment errors—for instance, the string John will get turned into a tuple of four individual letters. And then, the print statement will give an output error for getting called with four arguments. But set up with two arguments, this will print out Hello, John.

OK, now let's look at how we could spawn multiple processes in practice. Here's a variation on our earlier program. Notice that our function just takes in a number, and prints a message Printing from process and then the number that was passed in.

Now, in our main routine, we'll create a list of 20 processes. We'll have a loop, with *i* ranging up to 20, and for each one, we'll create a process in which print_process is the function, and *i* is used as the parameter. After that, we'll go through and actually start each process, in a separate loop. Now, I wonder if you can guess what will happen here?

Well, here's the output I got when running it. Notice that every process number, 0 through 19, gets printed once. But, the order that these are printed seems pretty random. Not totally random—the earlier numbers come before the later ones, but they're certainly not in the same order. What's going on?

Well, remember that each of those print statements was getting printed from a totally separate process. You can think of it as though it's a totally separate program that's running completely independently of all the others, possibly on a different processor. And, those different processors might have other things running on them, like the operating system commands or applications just running in the background. Try running this code yourself a few times and you should see a different result every time—there are 20 factorial possible orderings. Now, there are some other details to parallel programming, but that's enough to get us started.

The effectiveness of parallelism is measured by how effectively parallel processors can be applied to a particular problem. If I gave you two processors, the absolute best possible situation would be that if you could use both of them all the time with no time wasted. In this case, your overall running time would be cut in half. Four processors could cut running time in a quarter. But, in reality, we can't fully utilize the processors we have. Most problems are only partly parallelizable. In fact, there's a law called Amdahl's law that helps us calculate a limit for how much any given level of parallelism could speed up a computation.

According to this law, a problem that's only 50% parallelizable cannot attain better than a double speed up time, no matter how many processors we throw at it. For a problem where 75% could be parallel, the maximum speed up is four times. For 90%, it's as large as 10 times, and if 95% can be parallel, speed up can be at most 20 times. However, these are still theoretical upper limits—in practice, there can be other constraints, also.

A follow-up to Amdahl called Gustafson's law helps us determine how much larger of a problem we can handle given more processors. Both of these laws relate how much of the program needs to be done sequentially versus how much could be done in parallel. For example, graphics applications tend to be highly parallelizable. In a 3D game, there are often hundreds of thousands of triangles being drawn, but the order they're drawn isn't so important. A lot of scientific computations are also very parallelizable, with calculations taking place over a large grid, each piece of which can be handled separately from the others.

Addressing these types of problems has contributed to the rise of another form of parallelism called grid computing, or more generally, distributed computing, in which physically distinct, often dispersed, computers are loosely coupled with one another to tackle distinct pieces of a single problem. Distributed computing can be thought of as a type of parallelism, since computation is being done on various computers at remote locations, all at the same time. Let me discuss it for just a minute.

The most basic type of distributed application is the remote procedure call or RPC. A procedure is just a function, and the basic idea is that you're making a typical function call in your program. But, instead of the function executing on your computer, it executes on a remote computer. Often, that remote computer is a server set up to respond to the RPCs. The remote computer might just have more computing power available, or it might have access to data that you don't on your own machine. The Pyro module—that's P-Y-R-O—is one way to write programs that communicate with each other remotely, through these remote function calls.

Also, since people don't often have the ability to set up their own servers at remote locations, several companies will host servers for you. Amazon Web Services is one of the most well-known, and there's a module for that called PiCloud—spelled P-I-Cloud.

Let's reconsider a few of the programs we've developed in this course. See which of these you think could be made parallel: Remember the program where we looked at weather data to predict temperature and rain for a specific date? We went through a large list of data to find days that matched the date we cared about. Could that be parallel, or not? Yes. That could've been parallelized—although dates do come one after one another in the calendar, here, it was ok to check the dates in any order.

How about our financial simulation? There were actually two parts to this simulation. First, how about where we were computing account balances over many years? Parallel or not? Well, no. Here, each year is dependent on the previous year, so this can not be parallelized. The years are so chained to each other that we're forced to process earlier years before we can go on to later years.

In our financial simulation, we also ran multiple scenarios to get a Monte Carlo simulation of that financial program. So how about multiple scenarios? Parallel or not? Yes. The multiple scenarios part of the code could be parallelized—each run has its own set of random data, and it's independent of every other run. Simulations where we run the same thing many times, just with different random data each time, are some of the best cases for massively parallel processing.

How about our word game, where we were doing paired comparisons between words to form a graph in the word game? Parallel or not? Yes. Each word pair can be compared apart from all the others. This has a big potential of being parallelized. So, let's try this, let's modify our game. After all, the code was rather slow at the beginning, as we tried to set up the graph. We were comparing every word to every other word. Wouldn't it be nice if we could speed that up?

Now, to do this, we need to understand how information can be passed back and forth in a multiprocessor program. When we're running multiple processes, these processes are effectively operating as separate programs. Any changes they make to data within their own process won't be shared with other processes running in parallel or with the main program. Information from one process to another needs to be passed back and forth through special data structures that are designed to work in a multiprocessor environment.

The main tool for passing information like this is the multiprocessor queue. It's part of the multiprocessor module and it's not the same as a standard queue that can be found in other modules or that we would write ourselves. This queue can be passed as a parameter, and any process can add on to it safely, with the information remaining for all of the processes to use.

Let me remind you of the previous version of our code for building up the graph structure words. We have two nested loops to compare all the words in the list of words with all the other words in the list. For each pair, we would call the compareWords function, and if they differ by exactly one letter, we call addLink to connect them.

To parallelize this, we'll break the comparisons into smaller groups. Basically, we can divide up that outer loop, where i goes over the whole range, into smaller chunks, where, say, one process will handle about 100 of those i values. That's kind of an arbitrary choice, but we want to balance the number of processes with the amount of work each one does. We don't want too many processes or the overhead of starting each of them will take away any gains. But, if we have too few, we won't actually be able to get the benefits of parallelism. We want at least as many processes as we have cores to process them.

Now, I mentioned that separate processes can't actually affect the common data, but they have to pass information back and forth. So, it's not feasible to have each process actually modify our graph and call addLink. Instead, we'll have each process return a list of pairs of words that it finds that should be linked, and then we'll actually do the linking back in the main program. We can get this list of words via that multiprocessor Queue that we just discussed. Each process will add word pairs into the queue, and then the main program will take them out of the queue and form links.

So, first, let's look at the function that we'll want to use in our parallel processes. We'll call this function findlinks. As input, it will take the wordlist, the Queue where it should store any pairs that it finds, and the starting and ending values of i to use in the loop.

The body of the function is very similar to the code we had previously for finding and forming links. We have an outer loop indexed by i. We loop here only from the starting i value to the ending i value that were passed in as parameters. The inner loop will be indexed by j, and is identical to the one before, as is the if statement comparing two words by calling compareWords. Finally, where we used to have a command to add a link, we instead will add an *i, j* tuple to the queue that was passed in as a parameter.

And, that's it for the function that each process will run: each process will perform these checks between pairs of words and stick any that need to be linked into the queue.

Now, let's look at the code to actually set up the processes, which is a little more complicated. Let's take a look. We begin with the special if statement that's needed for multiprocessing. All of our main program will be indented under this. After reading in our word list, we set up a queue, and we create an empty list of processes. We then create a for loop. The For loop will take groups of 100 words, which is why the index ranges from 0 to the length of the wordlist minus 100, in steps of 100. We'll create a process object, using the findlinks function we defined earlier as our target. We then pass in arguments of the word list, the queue, and then the starting and ending values for the outer loop. These are given by our current loop value, *i*, as well as *i* plus 100 for the ending. After that loop, we create one final process to handle any words remaining that didn't fill up a full 100 words from the list. There will be a small number of words, under 100, left over that weren't caught in the for loop. With these processes created, we then start all of them. This spawns completely separate processes that will run on their own on any processors available. Remember that these processes will be putting pairs of indices into the multiprocessor queue.

Now, while this is going on, the main program can start processing the pairs on the queue. As long as the queue is not empty, it can pull off an element using the get command, and assign the tuple to *i* and *j*. Then, an add link between nodes i and j. Remember, we couldn't add the links to the nodes in the process itself since the changes would not have affected the main program. Finally, we take all the processes and join them. The join command is used to make sure that other processes have finished before we move forward. By calling join, we make sure that we don't go too far before the existing processes are finished. Finally, we go through the queue one last time in case any straggler process put words on the queue before we're finished.

So, that's the set of changes needed to turn this code into a parallel version. What do you think will happen if we run the code? To give you an idea, the original code took my laptop about 35 seconds to set up a graph for a set of about 5500 words. I have a dual-core laptop. So, how fast do you think it will be able to set up the graph with the parallel version?

In my case, it took about 25 seconds. Notice that in an ideal world, the two cores would have halved my running time, to about 18 seconds. It didn't do quite that well, since there was some extra time needed to start, and join the processes, and to do the extra work of keeping things in a queue. But, a drop from 35 seconds to 25 seconds is still more than a 25% reduction. So, when we care about time, it's clearly going to be a benefit to use parallelism.

There are more commands available in the multiprocessing module that you might find interesting. For instance, Managers will let you share data between processes, and process Pools will let you set up sets of processes that can be used as needed later on. I'll mention that there's also a Threading module available. Threading works a whole lot like multiprocessing, but it has the additional benefit that memory is shared among all the processes, called threads, so they can affect each other. However, Python does not really let code run in multiple CPU threads, so if we have a process that's CPU-intensive, like our word matching was, threading doesn't actually give a performance increase for many classes of problems. So, if you're really interested in increasing speed, it's better to stick to the multiprocessing module.

Now, there are a lot of pitfalls along the way to becoming a good parallel programmer. For instance, having to pass information only via things like queues can really take some getting used to. Also, you basically can't use the input command as part of a parallel program—all the processes will stop while waiting for input.

But, you now know what's needed to write some simple parallel programs on your own and how we can parallelize existing slow code to get a speedup. You should also have a much better idea of how the whole threading process is working when you encounter threaded programs, and you can form judgments for yourself about how your parallel computer will or won't perform better on some application.

In addition to creating parallel applications directly, there are some less direct ways that we can make use of parallelism in our code. I'll show you one example. It'll be our final program in this course, and it's one that you might find useful for optimizing the way you open applications on your desktop.

If you've run multiple programs on your computer at one time, you're probably taking advantage of parallelism right there. Each program is running as a separate process, and so if there are multiple programs running, they can potentially be running on separate processors. More commonly, when there are multiple processes running on one processor, the operating system takes care of time sharing the processor—basically making sure that each process gets some fraction of time, so they all make progress together.

In any case, we can initiate parallel computation by simply spawning new applications on our computer. And, fortunately, it's really easy to do this. We saw an example midway through the course when we demonstrated code to open a browser window. With just a few lines of code, you could pop open a browser window to some website. Starting a different application isn't that much tougher.

If we use the subprocess module, we can spawn a new process in the operating system. Unlike the processes that we were using earlier, these don't remain tied to the Python program, so once they're spawned, they will continue to run on the computer, even if the Python program ends.

Let's look at a quick example. Say we wanted to open up the notepad program on a Windows machine. The program is located in the Windows directory on the C drive. We could import the subprocess module. Then, we call subprocess.run and give a string with the application to run. In this case, that would be C:\Windows\notepad.exe. Remember that for a backslash in a string, we need to use a double backslash. If you have an older installation of Python, you might need to use the Popen command instead of run, but the effect is the same. Running this will launch the notepad program.

You can do the same thing for any executable file on your computer. Just spawn a process for that file by using the subprocess.run command, and put in the exact location of the file on your computer. Even if you leave the Python program, those processes will stick around. You can specify command-line arguments to files, by including that within the string. A command-line argument is when you pass a parameter to a routine by specifying it on the command line when you start the function. For example, notepad will take a command line argument of the name of the file to open.

So, the code you see here will spawn two processes. The first will open notepad with a file dictionary.txt located one directory up from where the Python file that we're running is. The second will open Microsoft Excel, using a spreadsheet in my Documents folder. Obviously, you would need to modify the file names and locations to match your own machine, but the basic format is the same.

So, try implementing a file like this yourself. Do you ever find yourself opening more than one application at the same time? Maybe you open a file explorer and a photo editor together, so you can drag and drop files from the explorer into the window? Or, maybe you open a spreadsheet for trip information at the same time you open up a web browser to a travel site? Whatever the case, you can easily create a small Python script—in other words, a Python program, that'll do this. Then, save it to your desktop or some other location where it'll be easy to find, and you can spawn those programs by running that single file.

While these might seem like really simple operations and programs, they are spawning additional processes, the same way that the Process spawning that we saw earlier was working. And we're potentially taking advantage of parallel computing power on the processor itself.

Parallel computing is the both the future and the present of computer programming. One of the biggest challenges that we'll face as programmers in the long term is how to make effective use of the increasing parallelism that's being provided. To the extent we can solve this, we'll be able to see actual performance benefits that keep pace with processor improvements.

Well, we've reached the end of our course. And, there was much rejoicing. Congratulations.

Looking back over the course, we've really come quite a ways. If you've made it this far, you've covered not only the topics commonly covered in a first programming course, but with the data structures and algorithms topics, you've seen material often found in a second course. And, our discussion here about parallelism brings you to the frontiers of current-day practice.

Following this course actively, means that you now have the skills to do a good amount of programming on your own. Just remember that programming is a skill like any other, and it can be developed through practice.

One great way to develop your Python skills further would be to take any of the programs from the course and try to add your own improvements. Another would be to pick a topic that's interesting to you, and select a module that deals with that topic. For graphics, you might start with the turtle and pyglet modules. For simulations and data visualization, there's random and matplotlib. For working with files and applications on your own computer, you might start with os and shutil. There are thousands of modules out there, so find one that does something you find interesting. Then, using that module just try writing some programs for fun.

You never need to understand everything about a module to start trying to work with it—that 's the beauty of abstraction. And, everyone needs to look up syntax sometimes, there's nothing wrong with getting help from a book, an online source, or another person.

Programming can be an almost uniquely fun and satisfying endeavor—there's really nothing quite like it. Now that you've seen programming, from lots of different angles, let me tell you why programming has held my interest for decades now. I think that now you can appreciate each of these points for yourself.

First, programming is a problem-solving exercise. When we have a larger goal in mind, we have to figure out how to turn that idea into code. Figuring out just how to apply all the different tools available to solve a problem can be both challenging and fun. Even debugging, as painful as it can be at the time, repeatedly offers a mystery to solve. And, when everything finally comes together and works, it's an incredible feeling that you overcame all the obstacles and turned some mental model into real working software.

Second, programming lets you express your creativity. You can dream up all sorts of ideas and use programming to actually see them come to life. If you noticed, most of our methods for software development were more about design than they were about actual specific code. Programming gives you a different way to exercise your design skills.

And third, programming affects the way you think. Programming teaches you to approach problems in a logical, orderly fashion, to develop plans that can be followed sequentially, and to recognize how to break a complex problem into more manageable pieces. Abstraction can be a useful approach in the real world, just like it is in the computer.

So, as you go out from here, I'll be happy if you've been able to experience and take with you the spark of enjoyment I get from programming. Even if programming is just a side hobby in your life, it can be a source of satisfying challenges and fun activity. It can become a life-long passion.

Thanks for spending this course with me. Always look on the bright side of life, and Happy Programming.

LECTURE 13

Note: If you use a different board definition, your other functions would change, too.

```
1    board = [[0, 0, 0], [0, 0, 0], [0, 0, 0]]

2    def make_move (board, position, value):
         position -= 1           # change position to be 0-8
         pos1 = position // 3    # integer division gets the row
           number
         pos2 = position % 3     # modulus gives the column number
         board[pos1][pos2] = value

3    def first_row(board):
         if board[0][0] == 'X' and board[0][1] == 'X' and board[0]
           [2] == 'X':
             return 'X'
         elif board[0][0] == 'O' and board[0][1] == 'O' and
           board[0][2] == 'O':
             return 'O'
         else:
             return '.'
```

LECTURE 14

```
import turtle
def drawA():
    # Draw the left side of the A
    turtle.left(60)
```

```
turtle.forward(20)
# Draw half the right side of the A
turtle.right(120)
turtle.forward(10)
# Draw the cross-part of the A
turtle.left(60)
turtle.backward(10)
turtle.forward(10)
# Draw remainder of the right side
turtle.right(60)
turtle.forward(10)
# Return the turtle to original orientation
turtle.left(60)
# Move turtle over a small amount
turtle.up()
turtle.forward(5)
turtle.down()
```

LECTURE 15

```
1   import pyglet
    window = pyglet.window.Window(width=400, height=300,
      caption="ExerciseWindow")
    Im1 = pyglet.image.load('BlueTri.jpg')
    @window.event
    def on_mouse_press(x, y, button, modifiers):
        window.clear()
        Im1.blit(x,y)
    pyglet.app.run()
```

```
2    import tkinter
     class Application(tkinter.Frame):
         def __init__(self, master=None):
             tkinter.Frame.__init__(self, master)
             self.pack()
             self.hello_button = tkinter.Button(self)
             self.hello_button["text"] = "Print repeatedly"
             self.hello_button["command"] = self.printtimes
             self.hello_button.pack(side="bottom")
         def printtimes(self):
             global times
             for i in range(times):
                 print("Hello!")
             times += 1
     times = 1
     root = tkinter.Tk()
     app = Application(master=root)
     app.mainloop()
```

LECTURE 16

```
import random
from matplotlib.pyplot import show, hist
rolls = []
for i in range(10000):
    roll = (random.randrange(6)+1) + (random.randrange(6)+1) +
      (random.randrange(6)+1)
    rolls.append(roll)
hist(rolls, bins=16)
show()
```

LECTURE 17

1   20
     100.0
     10
     300.0

2   40
     1800.0
     50
     750.0

3   ```
     def print(self):
         print(self.item+"   barcode: "+str(self.barcode))
         print("Price:",self.price)
         print("Current Inventory:", self.quantity)
         print("Sold so far:", self.sales)
     ```

4    ```
     class Movie:
         title = ""
         genre = ""
         rating = 0.0
     ```

5   ```
         def __init__(self, t, g, r):
             self._title = t
             self._genre = g
             self._rating = r
     ```

6    ```
     movielist = []
     rating = 1.0
     while rating >= 0.0:
         title = input("Enter the movie title:")
         genre = input("What is the genre of this movie?")
         rating = float(input("How do you rate the movie?"))
         if rating >= 0.0:
             movie = Movie(title, genre, rating)
             movielist.append(movie)
     ```

LECTURE 18

1   a)
```python
class Videogame(Game):
    platform = ""
```

    b)
```python
class Boardgame(Game):
    numpieces = 0
    board = [0,0]
```

2 In "Videogame" class:

```python
def print(self):
    print(self.name)
    print("Up to ", self.numplayers, "players")
    print("Can be played on", self.platform)
```

  In "Boardgame" class:

```python
def print(self):
    print(self.name)
    print("Up to ", self.numplayers, "players")
    print("Has", self.numpieces, "pieces, and a board of
      size ", self.board[0], "by",self.board[1])
```

3
```python
tetris = Videogame()
tetris.name = "Tetris"
tetris.numplayers = 1
tetris.platform = "Windows"
tetris.print()
```

4
```python
import pickle
outfile = open("Game.dat", 'wb')
pickle.dump(tetris,outfile)
outfile.close()
```

5
```python
import pickle
infile = open("Game.dat", 'rb')
savedgame = pickle.load(infile)
infile.close()
```

LECTURE 19

1   Joseph
     James
     John

2   John
     James
     Joseph

3   Michael Palin
     Michael Palin
     Terry Gilliam

4   {2, 3, 37, 5, 7, 11, 23, 29, 31}   (Note: The order
    {17, 19, 13}   of elements in a set
    {2, 3, 37, 5, 7, 11, 13, 14, 15,   does not matter.)
      16, 17, 18, 19, 23, 29, 31}
    {2, 3, 5, 7, 11, 14, 15, 16, 18, 23, 29, 31, 37}

LECTURE 20

1
```python
def swap(lst, i):
    temp = lst[i]
    lst[i] = lst[i+1]
    lst[i+1] = temp
```

2
```python
def one_bubble_pass(lst):
    returnval = False
    for i in range(len(lst)-1):
        if lst[i] > lst[i+1]:
            swap(lst,i)
            returnval = True
    return returnval
```

```
3    def bubblesort(lst):
         keepgoing = True
         while keepgoing:
             keepgoing = one_bubble_pass(lst)
```

LECTURE 21

1   It computes the product of all the elements in a list. Notice that the recursive call gives 1 for an empty list. For a larger list, it multiplies the first element by the result of the call on the rest of the list.

2   a)   "swap" is a constant time function. The time taken to perform a single swap function is independent of the length of the list.

      b)   "one_bubble_pass" is a linear time function. Each element of the list is visited once, on a single pass through the list.

      c)   "bubblesort" is a quadratic function. In the worst case, there are a linear number of passes through the while loop, each of which calls "one_bubble_pass," which is again linear.

LECTURE 22

1

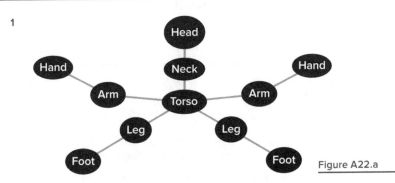

Figure A22.a

2   4. This happens when traveling from one foot, hand, or head to another.

3   Yes. It is connected and does not have any cycles.

4

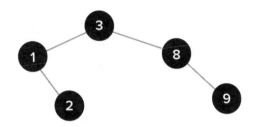

Figure A22.b

5
```
cities = {}
cities['Rivertown'] = 1000
cities['Brookside'] = 1500
cities['Hillsview'] = 500
cities['Forrest City'] = 800
cities['Lakeside'] = 1100
...
road = roads[0]
pop1 = 0
pop2 = 0
pop1 = cities[road.getName1()]
pop2 = cities[road.getName2()]
```

LECTURE 23

E, H, K, M, L, J, G.

We start with node E as our first node.

If we assume that we put items on the stack in the order they appear in each node, then it will put nodes C, I, and H on the stack in that order.

We will next visit the top node on the stack, which is H. It will put K on the stack (I has already been seen).

We will next visit K. It will put M on the stack.

M will be visited next, and there we will put L on the stack.

When visiting L, we will put J on the stack.

When visiting J, we will find G, our goal.

Notice that nodes I and C are placed on the stack but never are popped off.

The route to G will be E–H–K–M–L–J–G.

Clearly, a stack does not produce the shortest path, unlike the queue.

Alternative answer: E, C, A, B, D, F, G.

If we instead assume that items are put on the stack in the reverse order they appear in each node, then at node E, we will first put H, then I, and then C on the stack.

We would then visit node C. It would put F, then D, and then A on the stack.

A would be visited next. There, we would put B on the stack.

We would next visit B. All of its neighbors would have been seen, so we will return.

Next, we would visit the next node on the stack, D. Again, its neighbors have already been seen.

The next node on the stack is F. When we visit F, we will find G as its neighbor and be done.

Notice that nodes I and H are placed on the stack but never are popped off.

The route to G will be E–C–F–G.

In this case, the stack managed to find the shortest route to G, but this is not guaranteed.

The depth-first search approach will still find some path to the goal, if one exists, but it might not be the shortest path. But a depth-first search is used as a substep in other graph algorithms.

LECTURE 24

```
import subprocess
subprocess.Popen("myProgram.exe")
```

This mirrors the subprocess spawning as shown in the lecture. We will have the program "myProgram.exe" running in a separate process at the same time as our Python program is running.

Glossary

abstract interface: When a class defines a function that cannot be called. The function must be defined by a child class that inherits from that class. [Lecture 18]

abstraction: To simplify the details of something complex and present a simpler view that provides the essence of the complex idea. Abstraction provides much of the power of computer science, where complex functionality is presented as something simpler. In programming, functions provide abstraction, allowing several operations to be described with one function call. [Lecture 9]

adjacency list: A list of nodes connected by an edge from a given node. [Lecture 22]

adjacency matrix: A matrix describing the edges connecting all pairs of nodes. [Lecture 22]

algorithm: An ordered sequence of steps to accomplish some task. [Lecture 20]

Amdahl's law: A rule that determines the theoretical limit for how much speedup can be obtained through parallelism. [Lecture 24]

append: To add on to the end of a list. [Lecture 7]

assignment: A statement that gives a value to a variable, metaphorically like putting a value into a box. In Python (and many other languages, including C, Java, and Fortran), assignment is indicated with an equal sign (=); this is different from a check for equality. In Python, assigning to a variable that has not previously been used will create a new variable with that name. [Lecture 2]

asymptotic analysis: Technique for assessing the efficiency of an algorithm. Asymptotic analysis describes the growth in running time as a function of growth of input. [Lecture 21]

attribute (also called **field** (Java) and **member variable** (C++)): A variable defined for a particular object. This is usually defined in a class, so that all objects in that class have that attribute. [Lecture 17]

base case: A special case in a recursive function that returns without making a recursive call. The base case is what causes a recursive routine to eventually stop. [Lecture 21]

big-O notation: A way of describing asymptotic running times. Written as $O(x)$, where x gives the "order" of the running time. From fastest to slowest, running times include $O(1)$: constant; $O(\log_2 n)$: logarithmic; $O(n)$: linear; $O(n \log_2 n)$: linearithmic; $O(n^2)$: quadratic; and $O(2^n)$: exponential. [Lecture 21]

binary file: A file stored in binary format, which is typically more efficient but is not able to be read by humans. [Lecture 6]

binary search: A process for searching in a sorted list in which you repeatedly check the midpoint of the list and then search in either the upper or lower half of the remaining list. [Lecture 20]

binary search tree: A binary tree in which the nodes contain items ordered such that for any node, the left descendants are all smaller items and right descendants are all larger items. [Lecture 22]

binary tree: A tree in which each node will have at most two children. [Lecture 22]

blit (block-level image transfer): A method of combining two images by copying one image onto the other at a particular location. [Lecture 15]

Boolean: A type of value that can be true or false. [Lecture 3]

Boolean operator: An operator that is applied to Boolean variables. The common operators are "and," "or," and "not." [Lecture 3]

bottom-up design: Creating a complex function by tying together existing basic functions. [Lecture 14]

branching: The result of having conditionals within code. The code is said to have branching, because any one execution can follow only certain "branches" of the program. [Lecture 3]

breadth-first search: Algorithm that searches a graph from a starting node to find a path to another node by examining all nearby nodes before nodes farther away. Can be used to find the shortest path from one node to another in an unweighted graph. [Lecture 23]

breakpoint: In a debugger, a point at which the execution of a program will be stopped so that the current values of variables can be examined. [Lecture 11]

buffer: Queue of data or events to be handled. For example, user input, such as mouse movements or keyboard key presses, are often stored in an event buffer. [Lecture 19]

bug (also called **error**, **fault**, or **defect**): An error created in the process of programming. [Lecture 11]

call: To cause a function to execute. A function will be "called" by the main program or by another function, and this will cause the function itself to be executed. [Lecture 9]

callback function: In event-driven programming, the function that is called by the event monitor to respond to a particular event. [Lecture 15]

call stack (also called **control stack**, **runtime stack**, or **frame stack**): Function activation records that keep track of all the variables and data defined in that part of the program. [Lecture 19]

central processing unit (**CPU**): The processor for the computer. This executes the commands and performs operations. [Lecture 2]

chaining: In hash tables, refers to making a list of all items that map to the same hash value. [Lecture 19]

child class (also called **derived class** or **subclass**): A class that inherits attributes and methods from a parent class. [Lecture 18]

child node: A node that is reachable by an edge from a given node and that is one level farther away from the root node. [Lecture 22]

class: A way to group both data (defined in attributes) and functions (defined in methods). Can be thought of as a type of variable. Classes form the heart of object-oriented programming. [Lecture 17]. *See also* **object**.

closing: To complete work with a file from within a program. Closing the file ensures that it will not be corrupted by the program. [Lecture 6]

command: An instruction given to the computer. [Lecture 1]

comparison operator: An operator that can compare two values, giving a Boolean result. Common examples are equality and inequality, greater than, and less than. [Lecture 3]

compiler: A program to convert code from a programming language into machine instructions. Compilers will take all code in a program together and process it into a set of machine instructions. [Lecture 1]

concatenation: Combining two strings to form a new string. [Lecture 2]

conditional: A programming construct that checks some condition to determine whether it is true or false and then executes different code depending on the result of that check. [Lecture 3]

connected graph: A graph in which there is some sequence of edges connecting every pair of nodes. [Lecture 22]

constructor: A function called when an object is instantiated. In Python, this is the "__init__" function. [Lecture 17]

cycle: A sequence of edges that, when followed, returns to the starting node. [Lecture 22]

data structure: A way of organizing data systematically so that certain operations on that data can be performed easily. Usually used as a way to organize large amounts of similar data. [Lecture 19]

debugger: A program that can be used to examine the state of a program at any time. Debuggers are often part of an integrated development environment and can be used to step through a program line by line. [Lecture 11]

default parameter: A value to be assigned to a parameter in a function if that parameter is not specified by the user. [Lecture 10]

dictionary: A data structure for storing key-value pairs. Implemented using a hash table. [Lecture 19]

directed edge: An edge that connects from a source node to a destination node. [Lecture 22]

distributed computing (also called **grid computing**): Using physically distinct computers that are loosely coupled with each other (such as over a network) to perform a computation. [Lecture 24]

divide and conquer: Taking a large problem and dividing it into several smaller problems that are easier to solve. Typically, this involves dividing a large data set into two or more smaller data sets that can be processed more easily. [Lecture 21]

docstring: A (sometimes multiline) string description of a function's behavior; docstrings can be printed when we ask for help about a function. [Lecture 9]

edge: A connection between two nodes. Edges can be weighted or unweighted. [Lecture 22]

edge cases (also called **corner cases**): Situations that are at the "boundaries" of a range of inputs. These should be a part of any test suite. [Lecture 11]

encapsulation: The concept of grouping data and functions to operate on that data together in a package. Encapsulation is provided by classes and objects and is a primary benefit of object-oriented programming. [Lecture 17]

equality/inequality operator: An operator to check whether two values are (or are not) equal. In Python, the equality operator is the double equal sign, ==, which is distinct from the single equal sign assignment operator. The inequality operator in Pytyon is !=. [Lecture 3]

escape character: In a string, a character used to help specify special non-alphanumeric information, such as line breaks and tabs. In Python, this is the forward slash: \.

event: An occurrence, typically coming as input from an external source, that we want the computer to respond to. Common examples are keyboard button presses, mouse motion, and mouse clicks. [Lecture 15]

event-driven programming: A programming approach where functions are written to respond to events. Commonly used in interactive graphical programs. [Lecture 15]

event monitor: A software control function that takes in events, such as keyboard presses or mouse movements, and makes sure that the appropriate function gets called in response. [Lecture 15]

exception: A way of identifying that a runtime error has occurred. Exceptions are raised when a runtime error occurs and are handled later. In Python, the "try...except" commands are used to handle exceptions that occur. [Lecture 11]

execute (also called **run**): To have a computer process a set of instructions given in a program. [Lecture 1]

expression: A portion of code that, when executed, produces a value from some combination of values, variables, and operations. [Lecture 2]

file: A set of data stored in secondary or tertiary memory. Programs must read a file into main memory to use it or can write from main memory to a file. [Lecture 6]

floating-point number (also called **float**): A number containing a decimal point, typically with some values specified before and after the decimal. For example, 3.14159 is a floating-point number. [Lecture 2]

flowchart: A method for defining an algorithm by creating a graphical layout of the instructions. Shapes are used to describe operations, and arrows are used to indicate the sequence of steps. [Lecture 20]

for loop: A loop that repeats a certain number of times, with the number of times controlled by an iterator. [Lecture 5]

function (also called **procedure**, **routine**, **subroutine**, or **method**): In programming, a command that (possibly) takes some input, performs some action, and then (possibly) returns a result. [Lecture 9]

function activation record: A region of memory set aside for a function to work in, including the function's parameters and any variables defined in the function. The function activation record is destroyed when the function returns. [Lecture 10]

function body: The part of the function definition besides the header, describing the actions the function will take, along with when and what to return. [Lecture 9]

function header: The initial line of a function definition, giving its name and describing its parameters. [Lecture 9]

global variable: A variable that is in scope both outside and within a function. Declaring variables as global is a way to initialize certain types of data without using objects. [Lecture 10]

graph: A data structure used to store items and their relationships to each other. Items are stored at nodes, and the relationships between items are stored by edges connecting nodes. [Lecture 22]

graphical user interface (GUI): An interface for a program in which a user interacts with graphical elements such as buttons or locations on the screen. It is implemented using event-driven programming. [Lecture 15]

Gustafson's law: A rule that determines how large of a problem can be handled, given more processors. [Lecture 24]

hardcoding: When a specific value is set within the code, rather than being read in from a user. Hardcoding tends to be easier to code in the short term but is less flexible in the long term. [Lecture 12]

hash function: A function that can take a key phrase and convert it to a number that can be used to index into a list being used for a hash table. [Lecture 19]

hash table: Data structure that maps data with indices in a very large range into a smaller set of indices that can be stored more compactly. The index for a data element is called the key. [Lecture 19]

index: A number assigned to the position for each variable in a list. By convention, the first index number is usually zero. [Lecture 7]

indirection: When an intermediate structure is used to describe a connection between two entities. For example, rather than storing a list of entities, instead there might be a list of indices stored, with the entities stored in a separate structure found by examining each index. [Lecture 22]

infinite loop: A loop that repeats without ever ending. [Lecture 5]

inheritance: When one class (the child class) is defined to have all the attributes and methods of another class (the parent class). [Lecture 18]

in-place sort: A sort in which the original list is modified to put the elements in sorted order. [Lecture 20]

input/output (I/O): The interface between a computer and the outside world. Input can come from many possible sources, including keyboard or mouse input, network connections, sensors, etc. Output can be text or a graphical display that is output to the screen, a printed document, data sent over the network, commands to an attached device, etc. [Lecture 2]

insertion sort: A sort in which one new element is repeatedly inserted into an already sorted list. [Lecture 20]

instantiation: Creating a new object. This happens when the object is first encountered in a program. [Lecture 17]

integer: A number with no fractional component. Integers include -2, -1, 0, 1, 2, etc. [Lecture 1]

integrated development environment (IDE): A software program used to program code. An IDE will include an editor in which code can be written and easily used methods for compiling and executing code. There are typically many more tools that are also included, such as a debugger and hint systems. [Lecture 1]

interpreter: Like a compiler, an interpreter is a program to convert code from a programming language into machine instructions. Unlike a compiler, interpreters will convert code one line at a time as it is needed for execution. [Lecture 1]

iteration: One pass through a loop. [Lecture 5]

iterative development: Developing software by starting with a simple, basic implementation, then adding small amounts to the software, making sure that the software is working before going further. [Lecture 4]

iterator: A variable that gets initialized to a starting value and is incremented for each iteration of a loop, until it reaches a maximum value. [Lecture 5]

key: In a hash table, the value that is used as an "index" into the table. Keys can be any immutable data type. [Lecture 19]

keyword: In a programming language, any of a several special words reserved for exclusive use in commands and not permitted as identifiers for variables, functions, objects, and so on. Python keywords include "print," "import," "class," "global," "finally," "True," and "False." [Lecture 2]

keyword argument: When a parameter value is specified by giving the name of the parameter. While other parameters are processed from left to right, keyword parameters can be specified in a different order. [Lecture 10]

library: A collection of functions, classes, and variable definitions that can be imported into another program to extend its capabilities. [Lecture 12]

list (also called **array**): Data stored sequentially so that it can be referred to by its index. Typically, the data in a list will be of the same type. [Lecture 7]

logic error: An error that causes the program to produce incorrect results, due to incorrect design of the program. [Lecture 11]

loop: A programming construct that repeats a set of commands over and over. [Lecture 5]

loop invariant: A condition that is true at the beginning of every iteration of a loop. Helpful in algorithm design. [Lecture 20]

main memory: Short-term working memory that holds the data currently being used by the computer. This is separate from the CPU but is connected directly. Main memory holds the variables that programs use. [Lecture 2]

main program: Part of the computer program that is executed first, apart from any function definitions. [Lecture 10]

memory: Part of the computer that can store data. Memory is arranged in a memory hierarchy. [Lecture 2]

memory hierarchy: Arrangement of memory in the computer. Higher levels of the hierarchy are much faster and easily accessible to the processor but are more expensive and limited in size. The hierarchy includes registers within the CPU at the highest level, then cache memory (sometimes divided into multiple levels itself) that is near the CPU, then main memory that is connected directly to the CPU on the motherboard, then secondary memory (stored on a hard disk or similar drive), and then tertiary memory (stored remotely). [Lecture 2]

mergesort: A recursive sorting routine in which a list is split into two halves, each of which is then sorted recursively. The sorted lists are then merged together. [Lecture 21]

method (also called **member function** (C++)): A function defined for a particular object or class. Parallel to how attributes define data. [Lecture 17]. *See also* **attribute**.

model: The laws and rules that are assumed to govern a particular process. [Lecture 16]

module: A Python library, ending with a ".py" extension, just like other Python programs. [Lecture 12]

Monte Carlo simulation: A simulation in which multiple random values are used to simulate a range of possible outcomes. [Lecture 16]

motherboard: A circuit board in the computer that is used to connect various components, including the processor, main memory, secondary and tertiary storage connections, input/output devices, networks, etc. [Lecture 2]

multiprocessing: Using multiple processors simultaneously to execute different computing processes in parallel. [Lecture 24]

mutable: Data that can change when it is passed as a parameter to a function. Lists and objects are mutable data types. Mutable data is actually a reference; when passed as a parameter, the reference value will not change, but the values in memory at that reference can change. [Lecture 10]

nesting: When one programming construct occurs within another of the same type. For example, if a conditional contains another conditional, or a loop contains another loop, these are said to be nested. [Lecture 3]

node: A vertex in a graph that is used to store information about the items or entities. Nodes are connected by edges. [Lecture 22]

object: A specific instance of a class. An object is a particular variable, with a type given by the class it belongs to. [Lecture 17]

opening: To prepare a file for reading, writing, or appending from within a program. [Lecture 6]

operation: A basic action performed on data, such as addition or other basic arithmetic, from applying an operator or calling a function. Operations are performed by the processor. [Lecture 2]

operator: A programming construct that computes a new value from some basic values. Operators include addition and other arithmetic, comparisons, and indexing. [Lecture 1]

out-of-place sort: A sort in which a new, sorted, list is created while leaving the original list unchanged. [Lecture 20]

package: A collection of modules. [Lecture 12]

parallel computing: Computing more than one value simultaneously. [Lecture 24]

parameter: Values passed into a function. Values for the parameters (sometimes called arguments) are specified when the function is called. Within the function, the parameters are variables that are listed in the header and defined when the function first begins. [Lecture 9]

parameter passing: Copying the value from the function call (sometimes called the argument) into the memory set aside for the parameter variable within the function activation record. [Lecture 10]

parent class (also called **base class** or **superclass**): A class that defines attributes and methods that are inherited by a child class. [Lecture 18]

parent node: A node in a tree that is one edge closer to the root than a given node. [Lecture 22]

path: Designation for the location of a file within a computer's storage system. The path tells where to find a file relative to the computer or relative to the current program being executed. [Lecture 6]

pivot: In the quicksort algorithm, the value used for separating the list into smaller and larger parts. [Lecture 21]

polymorphism: When a single function can take on different implementations. Typically happens when different related classes implement the same function. [Lecture 18]

procedural programming: A long-standing method for programming where functions are created to handle all the various tasks that are needed. Programs are built by calling functions in the appropriate order. [Lecture 13]

process: A program, or part of a program, that can be executed on a computer. [Lecture 24]

processor: The part of the computer that performs computations. The processor has only a limited set of basic operations that it can perform. [Lecture 2]

program: A set of commands given to a computer. [Lecture 1]

programming language: A language developed for people to be able to easily and precisely give commands to a computer. Examples include Python, Java, C, C++, Fortran, BASIC, COBOL, etc. [Lecture 1]

pseudocode: A method for defining an algorithm by writing instructions similar to computer code. The syntax of pseudocode is flexible and generic and does not typically match any particular language. [Lecture 20]

Python Package Index (PyPI): A repository for thousands of Python modules and packages that are not part of the Python standard library. See https://pypi.python.org/pypi. [Lecture 12]

Python standard library: A collection of about 250 modules that is automatically installed as part of Python. See https://docs.python.org/3/library/. [Lecture 12]

queue: A data structure that allows storage and retrieval of data, following a first-in, first-out order. Items are added using an enqueue command and removed using a dequeue command. [Lecture 19]

quicksort: A recursive sorting routine in which a pivot value is chosen, and then all other values are separated into a larger list and a smaller list, which are then sorted recursively. [Lecture 21]

recursion: A process in which a function calls itself, typically with a different set of parameters. [Lecture 21]

reference (also called **pointer**): A location in memory at which some larger amount of data is contained. Data in memory can be changed without changing the value of the reference itself. [Lecture 10]

remote procedure call (RPC): Calling and executing a function on a different computer. [Lecture 24]

root: A node in a tree designated as the one from which all other nodes will be traced. [Lecture 22]

runtime error: An error that occurs when the program is running, causing the program to fail. Runtime errors can be dealt with using exceptions. [Lecture 11]

scope: The region of a program in which a variable or function is defined and usable. [Lecture 10]

search: The process of finding an element within some larger collection, such as a list. [Lecture 20]

selection sort: A sort in which the smallest element is repeatedly selected from the remaining elements. [Lecture 20]

set: A data structure for storing items with no fixed order and no duplicate values. It supports the common mathematical set operations. [Lecture 19]

side effect: Actions that a function takes that are not obviously part of the function's behavior from its definition. For example, a function might change a value of a variable that is not a parameter. [Lecture 9]

simulation: The process of taking a model and set of initial conditions and determining how the process progresses. [Lecture 16]

slicing: Generating a subset of a list. [Lecture 7]

sort: A basic algorithm for taking a list of values and creating a list in which the values are ordered from smallest to largest. [Lecture 20]

spawn: When one process or thread generates another process or thread, to be run in parallel. [Lecture 24]

stack: A data structure that allows storage and retrieval of data, following a last-in, first-out order. Items are added using a push command and removed using a pop command. [Lecture 19]

state: The particular set of values describing a system at a particular point in time. [Lecture 16]

statement: A line of code that gives an instruction to a computer to take some action. [Lecture 1]

storage: Alternate term for secondary and tertiary memory. Refers to memory that is not immediately accessible to programs running on the computer; data in storage must be brought into main memory to be used. [Lecture 2]

string: A sequence of characters. [Lecture 2]

stub: A function inserted during software development that doesn't yet do what it's intended to do, but is just enough that everything around it can run anyway. "Stubbing out" a program means that we are writing stub functions for that program. [Lecture 13]

syntax error: A bug that is due to writing code that is not valid. Programs with syntax errors cannot execute. [Lecture 11]

testing: The way to debug code, by running code using specific input and determining if output is correct. [Lecture 4]

test suite: A set of tests that are run on code to make sure that it is working correctly. As new features are added, the test suite should be continuously verified as working. [Lecture 11]

threading: Allowing multiple computer processes to run in parallel. Each separate process is run in a thread. [Lecture 24]

time step: The amount of time by which a simulation advances in one round of computation. [Lecture 16]

top-down design: Taking a complex task and breaking it into simpler parts, repeatedly, until the basic parts are "obvious." [Lecture 8]

tree: A particular type of connected graph that does not contain a cycle. One of the most widely used data structures; many algorithms have been developed just for trees. [Lecture 22]

tuple: Like a list, but with fixed length and types. Like a list, index values can be used to access elements of a tuple. Tuples are not mutable. Tuples will often combine different types of data in one tuple. [Lecture 7]

turtle graphics: Graphics created by simulating a small robot "turtle" that carries a pen as it moves around, tracing the path it follows. [Lecture 14]

type: The way that data stored in a variable should be interpreted by the computer. Each variable and value will have a type, such as an integer, a floating-point number, a string, etc. [Lecture 2]

undirected edge: An edge that connects two nodes, with no distinction for a source and destination. [Lecture 22]

value: The information stored in a variable. A value can be a number, string, or other type of data. [Lecture 2]

variable: A memory location with a given name that can hold a value. [Lecture 2]

virtual function: A function that is part of an abstract interface. [Lecture 18]

weight: A value stored along an edge, indicating something about the relationship between the nodes it connects. [Lecture 22]

while loop: A loop that repeats as long as some condition is true. [Lecture 5]

widget: In a graphical user interface, individual items such as sliders or buttons that appear in a window and that the user interacts with to generate events. [Lecture 15]

Python Commands

break: Exit a loop or conditional immediately. [Lecture 5]

class: Define a new class. [Lecture 17]

continue: Begin the next iteration of the loop. [Lecture 5]

def: Define a function. [Lecture 9]

dict: Define a dictionary. [Lecture 19]

file.close: Close a file. [Lecture 6]

file.write: Write a string to a file. [Lecture 6]

file.read: Read the whole file as a string. [Lecture 6]

file.readline: Read a line from a file as a string. [Lecture 6]

float: Convert a value to a floating-point number. [Lecture 2]

for... in: For loop with an iterator proceeding through a given set of values. [Lecture 5]

from ... import: Import a module or package. [Lecture 12]

global: Make a variable equivalent to the global variable of the same name. [Lecture 10]

if ... elif ... else: Conditional statement to execute different code depending on Boolean value(s). [Lecture 3]

int: Convert a value to an integer. [Lecture 2]

input: Print text to the screen, and then get input from a user and return. [Lecture 2]

len: Get length of a list. [Lecture 7]

list.append: Add an element onto the end of a list. [Lecture 7]

list.sum: Sum the elements in a list. [Lecture 7]

open: Open a file for reading, writing, or appending. [Lecture 6]

quit: Quit the program. [Lecture 9]

string.split: Split a string into multiple strings based on a character separator. [Lecture 8]

range: Generate values in a range of numbers. [Lecture 5]

return: Return from a function, returning a value if specified. [Lecture 9]

pass: Do nothing. Used when no actual command is wanted. [Lecture 18]

print: Sends output to screen. [Lecture 1]

set: Define a set. [Lecture 19]

str: Convert a value to a string. [Lecture 2]

try ... except ... finally: Try to execute code, and if an exception is raised, handle it in the except section. [Lecture 11]

while: While loop continuing while some condition is true. [Lecture 5]

with ... as: Use to open a file as a given name and close on completion. [Lecture 6]

Python Modules and Packages Used

The Python standard library includes hundreds of modules that are automatically installed with every version of Python. To use these modules, simply import them into your program. See https://docs.python.org/3/library/.

The Python Package Index (PyPI) includes thousands of Python modules and packages of varying degrees of completeness and support. To use these, you must first download and install them on your computer. This can usually be done through the pip interface, by typing "python –m pip install <package name>." You can also visit the PyPI page for the module or the website devoted to the module (if there is one) to find more details and download it directly.

Python Standard Library Modules

math: Math utilities. [Lecture 12]

webbrowser: Open and redirect web browser. [Lecture 12]

shutil: Shell utilities. [Lecture 12]

turtle: Turtle graphics. [Lectures 12, 14]

calendar: Create and display calendars. [Lecture 12]

time: Time utilities. [Lecture 12]

statistics: Statistical evaluation utilities. [Lecture 12]

os: Operating system commands. [Lecture 12]

random: Random numbers and data. [Lectures 13, 16]

tkinter: Graphical user interface setup and handling. [Lecture 15]

json: Converting data to/from JSON format, and then writing and reading JSON strings to files. [Lecture 18]

pickle: Converting Python data to a binary format and writing to or reading from a file. [Lecture 18]

multiprocessing: Create and run multiple processes in parallel. [Lecture 24]

subprocess: Spawn additional processes in the operating system. [Lecture 24]

Python Package Index Modules

numpy: Numerical manipulation (http://www.numpy.org/). [Lecture 12]

pyglet: Graphics, mouse input, and game functionality (http://pyglet.readthedocs.org/). [Lecture 15]

matplotlib: Graphing and plotting charts (http://matplotlib.org/). [Lecture 16]

Bibliography

There are a large number of references for Python programming, including several books and websites. The Python tutorial on the official Python website is probably the most useful standard reference: https://docs.python.org/3/tutorial/.

Most Python books will go into much greater detail in some features or applications of the language than others, so the "best" book will often depend on which topic you wish to learn more about. The following are recommended as good books, overall, for further study.

Gries, Paul, Jennifer Campbell, and Jason Montojo. *Practical Programming*. 2nd ed. Pragmatic Bookshelf, 2013. This book presents a well-organized introduction to Python.

Lambert, Kenneth. *Fundamentals of Python: Data Structures*. Cengage Learning PTR, 2013. This book uses Python to introduce some of the slightly more advanced ideas in computer science: data structures and algorithms.

Lubanovic, Bill. *Introducing Python: Modern Computing in Simple Packages*. O'Reilly Media Inc., 2015. This book provides an overview of Python, including many of the more advanced features of the language.

Matthes, Eric. *Python Crash Course*. No Starch Press, 2015. This book is in two parts: The first provides an introduction to Python, and the second presents three in-depth projects: an arcade-style game, a data visualization, and a web application.

Sweigart, Al. *Automate the Boring Stuff with Python: Practical Programming for Total Beginners*. No Starch Press, 2015. This book—which is available for free online at https://automatetheboringstuff.com—is in two parts: The first presents an overview and introduction to Python, and the second presents several detailed examples of how to use various modules to build interesting and useful applications.

Zelle, John. *Python Programming: An Introduction to Computer Science*. 2nd ed. Franklin, Beedle & Associates, 2010. This provides a thorough and well-organized introduction to Python and computer science basics. It is organized to support a college-level course in Python.

[**NOTES**]

[NOTES]

[NOTES]

[**NOTES**]